D1378689

CENTURY PSYCHOLOGY SERIES

Punishment: Issues and Experiments

ERLING E. BOE
RUSSELL M. CHURCH

PUNISHMENT

edited by

ERLING E. BOE
University of Pennsylvania

RUSSELL M. CHURCH
Brown University

PUNISHMENT
Issues and Experiments

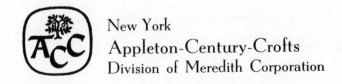

New York
Appleton-Century-Crofts
Division of Meredith Corporation

688-1

Library of Congress Card Number: 68-23894

PRINTED IN THE UNITED STATES OF AMERICA

E 10510

Preface

The punishment procedure is one in which a noxious stimulus is contingent upon a response. Effects of this procedure are both substantial and varied. Twenty-three articles were chosen for this book from the more than 600 articles on punishment that have appeared in the experimental and theoretical literature of psychology since 1900. The experimental reports reprinted here concern four major problems of enduring research interest and activity regarding the effect of punishment on behavior.

The first section of this book, "The Role of Punishment in Discrimination Learning," contains articles that describe conditions under which punishment can facilitate the learning of new responses. The second section, "Theories of Punishment," contains articles relating the role of punishment in suppressing or eliminating a learned response, and various theoretical explanations for the results. The articles in the third section, "Prior Aversive Stimulation," describe the role of one type of previous experience on the effectiveness of punishment. In the fourth section, "Punishment of Learned Aversive Responses," the conditions under which punishment may facilitate the response that it is designed to suppress are examined; this is one of the paradoxical effects of punishment. Within each of the four sections, the selections were arranged according to the systematic development of the problem, and this usually resulted in a chronological sequence of the articles.

Although research related to these major topics was initiated decades ago, it is of more than historical interest. The issues have not been convincingly resolved, nor have they been bypassed or abandoned in favor of more promising avenues of research. Here the older, but still frequently cited, papers are presented in the context of more recent and technically superior research that significantly qualifies the earlier results.

The final section, "Suggested Further Reading," provides specific guides to additional readings on the issues and experiments related to punishment. This section is designed to introduce a variety of topics not adequately covered in the previous selections, and to provide references of primary importance.

This book should be useful as supplementary reading for undergraduate courses in the psychology of learning and motivation. It can serve as an introduction to the major concepts of punishment, and to the major problems involved. The level of difficulty is appropriate for a student who has had an introductory course in psychology that included the basic principles of learning and the rudiments of experimental design and statistical analysis. The book should also be useful to graduate students of psychology as a basic source of material for seminars in which punishment is considered and as a ready source for classic experiments not available in reprint form.

We thank the authors and publishers for their permission to reprint the articles included in this volume. The editors shared equally the responsibility for selection and organization of these articles, for the condensation of several of them, and for the various editorial transitions and footnotes. References have been made in uniform style and placed at the end of the book.

E. E. B.
R. M. C.

Contents

I

The Role of Punishment in
Discrimination Learning

Early research on punishment attempted to compare directly the relative incentive value of reward and punishment. The empirical problem was to determine the number of errors to a criterion of mastery of a two-choice discrimination task as a function of training conditions. The three basic conditions were (1) reward for correct responses, (2) punishment for incorrect responses, and (3) both reward for correct responses and punishment for incorrect responses. The general conclusion from such studies (e.g., Warden & Aylesworth, 1927) was that punishment, either alone or in combination with reward, was more effective for training than reward alone. This is of practical importance because it demonstrates that punishment of an incorrect response increases the rapidity of discrimination learning. Its theoretical importance is that it supports the symmetrical statements that reward tends to strengthen a response (positive law of effect) and that punishment tends to weaken a response (negative law of effect).

Muenzinger (1934) also found that punishment of the incorrect response during discrimination learning helps in the acquisition of a new response, but he challenged the view that punishment necessarily inhibits the response that it follows. In one of the more baffling of the paradoxical effects of punishment on behavior, he found that punishment for the correct response (the one that is rewarded) increased the rapidity of learning as much as punishment for the incorrect response (the one that is not rewarded). This result is of theoretical importance because it demonstrates that punishment has effects on behavior other than weakening the response that it follows.

A restriction on the generality of the principle that punishment of erroneous responses facilitates discrimination learning was suggested by data reported by Yerkes and Dodson (1908). This experiment varied both the intensity of the punishment and the difficulty of the discrimination. The conclusion was that there is an optimal level of punishment intensity for any discrimination task and that this optimal intensity decreases as the difficulty of the discrimination increases. This conclusion (the Yerkes-Dodson Law) has not been adequately tested in recent research on punishment, although both the difficulty of the problem and, more frequently, the intensity of the punishment have been investigated separately.

In a study of the role of the intensity of the punishment on the rapidity of discrimination learning, Wischner, Fowler, and Kushnick (1963) came to the conclusion that increases in the intensity of punishment of the incorrect response lead to improvement in performance, but increases in the intensity of punishment of the correct response lead to a decrement in performance. In a study of the role of problem difficulty, Fowler and Wischner (1965) found that, in the case of relatively difficult problems, punishment of the correct response can increase the rapidity of discrimination learning.

The studies mentioned above demonstrated that punishment can facilitate the original learning of a discrimination task. One of the major practical applications of punishment is to suppress an already-learned response. Whiting and Mowrer (1943) reported a particularly successful procedure for such suppression, a procedure in which punishment of one response is accompanied by reward of a competing alternative response.

1   The relative value of reward and punishment in the formation of a visual discrimination habit in the white rat

Carl J. Warden and Mercy Aylesworth

One of the major problems within the general field of animal motivation is that concerning the relative incentive value of reward and punishment. The terms reward and punishment as here used carry no subjective connotation whatsoever, but are used merely as convenient classificatory terms for stimuli that normally evoke positive and negative reactions respectively when employed as incentives in experimental situations. The chief interest in this topic centers around the relation of this factor to speed or efficiency of habit

Reprinted from the *Journal of Comparative Psychology*, 1927, 7, 117–127. This preliminary report covers one topic in a project on animal drives supported by the Council for Research in the Social Sciences, Columbia University. The problem was suggested and the data gathered by the junior author; the senior author collaborated in technical details and in writing this report.

[Although the purpose of this research is to compare directly the relative incentive value of reward and punishment, its major importance is the demonstration that the rapidity of discrimination learning is increased if, in addition to reward for the correct response, there is punishment of the incorrect response. Others had previously found some evidence that punishment of erroneous responses facilitated discrimination learning, but this was the first study to support this conclusion with statistically reliable results.—Eds.]

formation, and more intensive work has been done on the discrimination type of habit than upon either problem box or maze.

The present study was suggested by the investigation of Hoge and Stocking (1912) who found some evidence that punishment has a higher incentive value, either alone or in combination with reward, than reward alone in the building up of a simple visual discrimination habit in the white rat. Their conclusion to this effect was based upon very slight data, only two animals being tested in each group. In one case correct responses were rewarded by a morsel of food; in a second, correct responses went unrewarded while wrong responses were followed by a shock, while in the third instance a correct response was followed by food and an incorrect response by a shock. They found that both rats in the reward-punishment group perfected the habit—one in 490 trials and the other in 550 trials, while one rat in the punishment group learned in 550 trials and the other failed to learn in 620 trials, and neither of the animals in the reward group had learned after 590 trials. The problem involved a discrimination between a 2 c.p. and a 16 c.p. light, the norm of mastery being 15 correct responses on each of two successive days, and the apparatus a modification of the Yerkes discrimination box. The shock used was furnished by a Porter inductorium and applied in the usual manner.[1]

The purpose of the present investigation was to repeat the work of Hoge and Stocking, using larger groups and modifying the technique in certain details. The main improvement in method, perhaps, consisted in a more standardized shock than that used by Hoge and Stocking, the mechanism for the control of which being identical with that employed in connection with the Obstruction box of this laboratory (Jenkins, Warner, & Warden, 1926). In the present work a current of 0.11 m.a. with a resistance of 1000 ohms was used, and readings were taken daily before beginning the taking of data. The resulting shock was strong enough to cause the animals to lift their feet energetically and sometimes squeal a little in scampering off the grills, without causing them to be too inactive for our purposes after getting off. We used a group of 10 white rats approximately 3 months of age in connection with each of the three incentive conditions previously studied by Hoge and Stocking, i.e., reward, reward-punishment, and punishment.

[1] [See Selection 3 for further details of the Yerkes discrimination box and the Porter inductorium.—Eds.]

The apparatus employed was a modification of the Yerkes-Watson design (see their description, Yerkes & Watson, 1911) and need not be figured in detail. The source of light was a 75 watt Mazda Westinghouse bulb (120 volts) set 10 inches behind the plate at an angle of 45 degrees, in such wise that the center of the bulb coincided with the center of the circular opening (6 cm.) of the plate. The distance from center to center of the openings on either side of the stimulus box was 5¼ inches, and that from the center of the opening to the floor of the control box was 4 inches. A bulb was placed on either side of the box so that a shift from light to dark could be made without disturbing the shutter, by the simple expedient of pressing an electric button conveniently placed on the outside of the stimulus box. The current was supplied to the two bulbs through a common intake. The ground plan of the control section of the apparatus in which the animal was placed for testing is shown in Figure 1.1. The box is 37 inches long, 29 inches wide, and 11½ inches deep (inside dimensions) and the partitions as figured are drawn to scale. The electric grills were equipped with in-

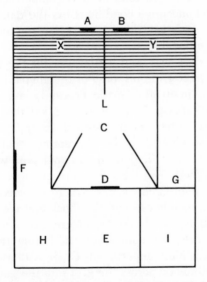

Figure 1.1   Floor plan of control box: *E*, entrance box; *D*, door leading into reaction compartment; *X* and *Y*, electric plates; *L*, central partition separating *X* and *Y*; *A* and *B*, position of lights used as stimuli; *F* and *G*, doors used to restrain animal (*F* open and *G* closed); *H* and *I*, goal compartments; *C*, reaction compartment

dependent switches so that either could be turned off at will by the experimenter, stationed directly in front of the entrance compartment. Since a dark room was not available, the control box was entirely screened in by a hood of black cloth extending 24 inches above the top of the box. Inside the hood and in the exact center above the door, *D*, a 25 watt blue National Mazda lamp was placed and kept burning constantly during the experiment. Small automobile mirrors were fastened to the top of the box above the grills, *X* and *Y*. The animals were visible in the dim light at all times under this arrangement and were observed through a peep hole in the hood above the center of *E*.

The problem was to learn to discriminate between the stimulus patches outlined by the circular opening in the plates, when one was illuminated from behind and the other not. The animals were trained to the dark patch inasmuch as 8 of the 10 in each group showed either a preference for the illuminated patch or no preference at all, the other two in each case showing only a slight preference for the dark patch. The preference series consisted of 10 trials per day for two days with food in both compartments (*I* and *H*), regardless of later incentive conditions. As the data show, the discrimination was much less difficult than that required in the Hoge and Stocking experiment.

The procedure was kept as uniform for the three groups as possible. The characteristic response of the animal under the different conditions of motivation made necessary minor variations in procedure as will appear from the description that follows. When the response was correct, in the reward group, a nibble of milk-soaked bread was allowed in the appropriate goal box; when incorrect the animal was lifted from the goal box, which contained no food, by the experimenter. Food was placed in neither goal compartment in the punishment series; when a correct response was scored the animal merely escaped the shock and was removed from the goal compartment as above. An incorrect response resulted in a shock and, as a rule, the animal retreated from the grill and remained in the reaction compartment, *C*, since there was no incentive for it to continue on across the grill into the goal compartment for that side. Accordingly the animals of this group were removed from the reaction compartment after such retreat from the grill, or from the appropriate goal compartment if they actually crossed the grill instead of retreating. Contact with the grill beneath the light, resulting in a shock, was thus the basis of scoring errors for this group regardless of the nature of the more or less insignificant response that followed this experience. The same procedure was followed likewise when an animal of the reward-punishment group made an error; it was removed from either position, the goal or reaction compartment, depending upon whether it retreated from, or crossed over the grill. In certain instances in both the reward and reward-punishment groups the animal would dash around to the correct goal compartment after making a wrong response before the restraining door (*F* or *G*) could be closed. This occurred in approximately 5 percent of the trials of the former, and 2 percent of the trials of the latter group.

The original plan was to give 15 trials per day and the order of shifting the lights was arranged for such a schedule. This order which was repeated over and over, without regard to the number of trials given per day, was as follows for the dark stimulus patch: left, right, right, left, right, left, right, right, left, left, left, right, right, left, right. Five trials per day were given for the first 7 days, ten trials per day thereafter until the 27th day, after which the 15 trial per day schedule was followed in the case of the reward group, which showed little or no evidence of learning at this stage. The reward-punishment group had completed the problem by the 15th day; the punishment group were so nearly finished on the 27th day that they were continued on the 10 trial per day schedule. The change to the 15 trial schedule on the 27th day for the reward group was made in the hope that they might master the problem within the limit of time available for the study.

During the first day 10 minutes were allowed for each trial provided the animal did not make a "choice" before. From the second day onward this time was reduced to 5 minutes. Animals of the reward group usually reacted within a few seconds. However, the use of the shock in the other two groups induced hesitation and inactivity to such an extent that many of the animals did not react within the 5-minute period. In the reward-punishment group the animals had to be removed without having reacted in 59 out of 760 trials (7.8 percent) while in the punishment group the corresponding value was 425 out of 1500 trials (28.3 percent). The effectiveness of the food in inducing an increased tendency to react promptly in the former group is thus clearly indicated. Failure to react within the 5-minute period was checked as an error, although the data on this point are given separately from the errors, in Table 1.1, under the heading "no reaction."

The positive value of the reward incentive stimulus (food) in bringing about activity, and especially the definite act of going promptly to the goal was also very evident. When reward alone was used the complete reaction of going to one or the other goal compartment occurred in practically every case. Naturally there was little or no incentive for the animals of the punishment group to go to the goal compartments. In 376 trials out of 1500 (25 percent) they were removed without having reached the goal—they reacted to the grill-stimulus patch situation and stopped at that, although they had been fed during the 20 trials of the preference series in whichever goal compartment they happened to enter. This type of response occurred in only 62 out of 760 trials (8 percent) in the case of the reward-punishment group which had, of course, a more definite incentive to keep running till they reached the goal. When both "no reaction" and failures to go on to the goal after reacting are combined, we find that in 53.3 percent of the trials the punishment group did not actually reach the goal while the corresponding value for the punishment-reward group is 15.8 percent.

Bread and milk constituted the main article of diet both before and during the experiment. The animals of each group were allowed to feed for 10 to 15 minutes (or until they were satiated) one hour after the daily schedule of trials for the group had been completed. This interval had the effect of separating the ordinary taking of nourishment from the incentive situation presented in the apparatus. The groups were tested at the same time of day insofar as the conditions of the experiment permitted, the work beginning at 11 a.m. each day. Each trial was timed with a stop watch but these data have not been included in this report since they appear to add nothing of significance.

The results are given in Table 1.1. and the graph of Figure 1.2 in terms of the percent of right, wrong, and "no reaction" responses per day throughout the 41 day training period. At the end of this period the reward group were scoring only about 60 percent right responses and had made little gain in the preceding 300 trials (20th day onward). The punishment group made a perfect record

Table 1.1 Showing the percentage of right, wrong, and "no reaction" responses for each daily series of trials

Days	Reward Right	Reward Wrong	Punishment Right	Punishment Wrong	Punishment "No reaction"	Reward-punishment Right	Reward-punishment Wrong	Reward-punishment "No reaction"
1	30	70	42	44	14	34	62	4
2	28	72	10	10	80	40	26	34
3	36	64	24	14	62	42	26	32
4	32	68	44	18	38	62	18	20
5	38	62	46	18	36	68	20	12
6	32	68	56	14	30	64	30	6
7	44	56	52	8	40	84	14	2
8	42	58	57	11	32	84	15	1
9	45	55	51	7	42	80	20	
10	47	53	55	10	35	95	5	
11	43	57	59	6	35	86	12	2
12	47	53	56	4	40	87	10	3
13	48	52	54	6	40	90		10
14	45	55	71	9	20	100		
15	54	46	67	12	21	100		
16	47	53	80	10	10			
17	48	52	86	6	8			
18	52	48	75	13	12			
19	55	45	60	12	28			
20	57	43	85	12	3			
21	63	37	83	7	10			
22	58	42	80	15	5			
23	52	48	80	10	10			
24	49	51	70	20	10			
25	58	42	100					
26	51	49	70	30				
27	55	45	50	40	10			
28	57	43	50	30	20			
29	57	43	80	20				
30	60	40	90	10				
31	59	41	70	30				
32	55	45	80	10	10			
33	57	43	100					
34	56	44	100					
35	61	39						
36	57	43						
37	62	38						
38	55	45						
39	61	39						
40	65	35						
41	62	38						

The term "no reaction" means that the animal did not make a "choice" within the five-minute test period. Such failure to react did not occur in the case of the reward group.

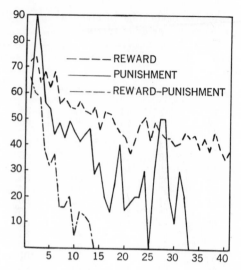

Figure 1.2   Curve showing error elimination for the three groups. Percentage of wrong (including "no reaction") responses are plotted on the ordinate against days of the training period on the abscissa.

on the 33rd day and the reward-punishment group on the 13th day, these differences being so great that no question of interpretation arises. The reward-punishment motivation is by far the best; reward alone is markedly inferior to punishment alone, just how much so we cannot tell since the former group did not perfect the habit at all. The rise in the error curve of the punishment group on the second and third days was due to the large number of "no reaction" responses occurring on those days. The marked rise in this curve on days 26–28 and on several days thereafter was due in large part to the erratic behavior of rat no. 4. This rat after making almost perfect records for several days suddenly took to jumping over the grill on the right hand side, without regard to the stimuli, and this habit had to be broken up before further progress could be made.

The data on number of trials required to form the habit are given in Table 1.2 for each animal of the three groups as well as the averages for the groups. The records were checked against three norms of mastery, i.e., 9 correct out of 10, 18 correct out of 20, and 27 correct out of 30 responses. None of the animals of the reward

Table 1.2   Showing number of trials required to learn under three norms of mastery (A, B, C)

Rat	Reward Norm	Punishment Norm A	Punishment Norm B	Punishment Norm C	Reward-punishment Norm A	Reward-punishment Norm B	Reward-punishment Norm C
1	439	36	89	126	39	64	72
2	242	50	60	68	32	37	47
3	173	47	137	145	46	52	62
4	362	60	125	301	23	99	108
5	145	22	141	174	13	49	57
6	446	32	42	70	24	75	84
7	276	81	134	170	39	56	59
8	255	127	136	147	19	40	45
9	279	35	66	75	49	56	60
10	318	72	114	183	44	69	79
Average	293.5	56.2	104.4	145.9	32.8	59.7	67.3

Norm A, 9 correct out of 10 trials; norm B, 18 correct out of 20 trials; norm C, 27 correct out of 30 trials. None of the rats of the reward group reached norm C and only one (no. 8, after 265 trials) reached norm B. When rat no. 4 of the punishment group is not included (see text) the average for the group is 128.6 instead of 145.9 as above.

group reached the highest norm and only one (no. 8) reached the norm of 18 correct responses out of 30 consecutive trials, doing so only after 265 trials. The data for the lowest norm only, therefore, are included in the table for the reward group. A comparison of the averages for the three groups is thus possible only on the basis of the data of norm A. The average number of trials to learn for the groups, when so checked, is as follows: reward, 293.5, punishment, 56.2, and reward-punishment, 32.8. It is noteworthy that the number of trials is more than doubled in the case of the two latter groups when the norm is raised to 27 correct responses out of 30 trials (norm C).

It is evident that norm A is not high enough to insure dependable results in work of this sort. It does not rule out the possibility of apparent success in discrimination which is, in fact, only apparent and due to chance factors. For, as appears from Table 1.1, the reward group as a whole never averaged on any given day higher than 65 percent correct responses, and yet each of them made a record of 9 correct out of 10 trials at least once during the training period. That this record was due to chance factors mainly is shown by the fact that only one animal of the group (rat number 8) was able to reach norm B and none norm C, although in many cases the requirement of norm A had been met before one-half of the training series (223 trials) was completed. The use of a high norm of mastery appears to be more necessary in discrimination work than in habit formation of the maze type (Warden, 1926). The order of shifting the lights, and the greater likelihood of the setting up of position habits in a simple situation of this sort, probably operate as important factors in this connection.

The general principle suggested by the work of Hoge and Stocking seems to be fully established by the present work, for this type of problem. This conclusion should, however, be limited to simple and easy discrimination, inasmuch as several investigators (Cole, 1911; Dodson, 1915; Yerkes & Dodson, 1908) have shown that in more difficult discrimination too much punishment (shock) must not be employed if the best results would be obtained.[2] Before an unqualified generalization can be made concerning the relative incentive value of reward, punishment, and reward-punishment these must be studied in relation to a series of discriminations ranging between wide extremes of difficultness.

A criticism of the control box used by ourselves and others, insofar as its use in studying the relative value of incentives is concerned, should be made by way of offering a suggestion regarding further work on this topic. The shock is usually administered by means of a grill placed directly in front of the stimulus patches while the food or reward is placed at some distance from the patches and can be reached only by making a turn after crossing the grill. Doubtless the value of the punishment incentive is greatly increased by the fact that it tends to stop the animal directly in front of the discrimination stimuli while the reward incentive (food) does not. In order to obtain strictly comparable data the reward and punishment factors should be administered at points equidistant from the stimulus patches. That is, either the food (or other reward object) should be located in the front end of the control box near the grill, or perhaps better, the grill should be placed in, or near the goal compartments rather than directly in front of the stimulus patches.

[2] [See Selection 3.—Eds.]

So far as we know, this matter of the identity of location of incentive stimuli has not been adequately controlled in any work so far done on the relative value of reward and punishment in this type of habit formation.

2   Motivation in learning

Karl F. Muenzinger

I.   Electric Shock for Correct Response in the Visual Discrimination Habit

It has been known for over twenty years (Hoge & Stocking 1912) that in order to reduce the number of trials and errors for white rats

Reprinted from the *Journal of Comparative Psychology*, 1934, *17*, 267–277.

[In all experiments on the role of punishment in discrimination learning prior to this experiment by Muenzinger, punishment followed the incorrect response. In those experiments punishment increased the rapidity of learning, apparently because the noxious stimulus inhibited the response that it followed. If, however, punishment following the correct response (the one that leads to reward) also increases rapidity of learning, then a reinterpretation of the previous results would be required. In this important experiment, Muenzinger finds that subjects shocked for correct responses are similar to those that are shocked for incorrect responses, and that both groups learn the discrimination habit more quickly than an unpunished control group. He concludes that the major role of punishment is not to weaken or to strengthen a response, but to make the subject respond more readily to the significant cues. Further research by Muenzinger and his colleagues, reviewed by Church (1963) and Fowler and Wischner (1969), replicated the basic experimental results that punishment of the correct response may facilitate discrimination learning. This has been one of the most curious of the paradoxical effects of punishment on behavior, and it has been the basis of considerable research (see, for example, Selections 4 and 5).–Eds.]

learning a visual discrimination habit one has to add to the usual reward for the right response some punishment, such as electric shock, for the wrong response. This fact and similar ones have been the main support for the generalization forming a part of the law of effect, namely, that the function or punishment is to accelerate the dropping out of the punished response, or in other words, punishment tends to inhibit the punished response and to facilitate the acquisition of some alternative response. To be sure, this is the old and orthodox statement of the law of effect; below I shall refer to one of its more recent formulations.

As a matter of methodology it is perhaps relevant to point out that this generalization is based on a set of facts that have not been subjected to that systematic variation which we have demanded in connection with other psychological problems. It is the so-called "wrong" response that has always been punished in situations in which the conditions of placing the reward favored the performance of some alternative, the so-called "right" response. In order to be sure that the function of punishment is really that of the inhibition of the punished response, we ought to punish the response favored by the reward, the "right" response. In such a case we should expect according to the law of effect that a conflicting tendency be set up in a response that is both rewarded and punished, that is, a facilitating and inhibiting tendency which would manifest itself in a slowing down of the course of learning.

Accordingly, the purpose of our experiment was to punish a group of animals for the right response in the visual discrimination habit and to compare its course of learning with that of another group that was punished in the orthodox fashion for the wrong response and also with that of a third group that was not punished at all.

Apparatus and Methods

The apparatus was a T-shaped discrimination box the dimensions of which are indicated in Figure 2.1. The alleys were shielded by ground glass from the 15 watt lamps. In order to close the wrong alley a door was used that slanted in such a way that it could not be seen from the place where the choice had to be made. Reward

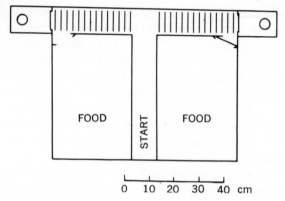

Figure 2.1   Discrimination box

in the form of cheese crumbs was always left in both food compartments.

The shock-producing stimulus was a direct current of 0.15 milliampere, i.e., about twice the threshold value for young rats (Muenzinger & Mize, 1933). Since the strength of the shock was an important factor in the situation, care was taken to control it within narrow limits, a variation of 100,000 ohms producing a change of 0.3 percent in the current.[1] A commutator driven by a synchronous motor produced impulses occurring every 0.375 second and lasting 0.075 second. Since a previous investigation (Muenzinger & Mize, 1933) had shown the rat's skin resistance to vary around an average of 300,000 ohms, a resistance of this size was used in place of the shocking grid whenever the current was adjusted and checked before and after an animal was given its daily series of runs.

Three groups of animals (Wistar strain) were used,[2] 25 in each group. All were trained to go to the lighted alley. Group I, the experimental or shock-right group, was shocked while crossing the correct alley on the way to the open food box. Group II, the first control or shock-wrong group, was shocked while it was in the

[1] The current represented the saturation level of the plate current of a UV-202 vacuum tube (plate voltage 520 volts). This level was controlled by the filament voltage as described elsewhere (Muenzinger & Walz, 1934).

[2] The writer wishes to thank Professor Charles Poe of the Chemistry Department of The University of Colorado for furnishing the animals.

wrong alley. Group III, the second control or no-shock group, received no shock at all. In all cases of wrong choice the animal was left in the apparatus until it had reached the open food box through the right alley.

The sequence of turns for the lighted alley was R(ight) L(eft) LRRLRLLR for the even tens, and LRRLLRLRRL for the odd tens of trials.

The rats were 45 days old when the training began. They were fed a normal balanced diet for 30 minutes per day for the first 6 days, counting the preliminary training, and then 45 minutes per day until the end of the experiment. The preliminary training, lasting for two days, consisted in letting them find some cheese in each of the food boxes. They were then placed twice just outside each food box and permitted to run back and again find some cheese. During the first four days of the regular training series they were given 5 trials per day and thereafter 10 trials per day until they had had 100 trials. Only those that had by this time not reached the criterion of learning, that is, two consecutive daily series of ten perfect trials, were continued until they reached the criterion or until they had had 200 trials.

On the first day the current switch was closed only once or twice for one second while an animal was on the grid in order not to frighten it too badly; thereafter it was closed continuously.

Results

The results can be expressed in terms of the number of errors for the first 100 trials and also in terms of the number of trials required to master the habit.

The errors for the three groups for the first 100 trials are presented in Tables 2.1, 2.2, and 2.3. The cumulative error curves are given in Figure 2.2. The averages, standard deviations and critical ratios of differences are presented in Table 2.4. As far as errors are concerned the third or no-shock group is decidedly inferior to the two shock groups.

All animals in the two shock groups reached the criterion of learning before trial 100. Fourteen of the no-shock group had to be continued beyond this point and two of these were stopped at trial

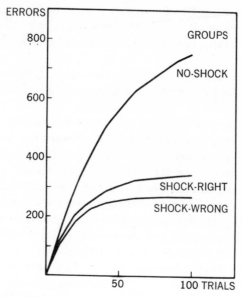

Figure 2.2   Cumulative error curves

200 without having reached the criterion. The frequency distributions of the number of trials immediately preceding the criterion
are given in Table 2.5. The averages for the three groups, standard
deviations and critical ratios of the differences between the averages
are given in Table 2.6. Again, as far as the number of trials to learn
the habit is concerned the third or no-shock group is very much
poorer than the two shock groups, while there is little difference
between the latter.

It should be noted: First, the distributions of errors and trials
of the two shock groups are practically co-extensive, while on the
other hand there is little overlapping between the no-shock group
and the two shock groups.

Second, the differences between the averages of the no-shock
and the two shock groups are significant in every case, while the
differences between the averages of the shock-right and the shock-
wrong groups are comparatively insignificant.

Third, the similarity in learning between the shock-right and
the shock-wrong groups is produced by a moderate shock, slightly

above the threshold value. A severe shock might have produced different effects.

To be sure there is a difference between the two shock groups. Shock for the wrong response was slightly more effective than shock for the right response. Only a further analysis, however, could reveal whether or not this difference has any meaning.

In regard to the differences between the sexes it might be pointed out that the females in the two shock groups, especially those of group I, were more efficient than the males. (Group I: Average number of errors per 100 trials, males 15.5, females 10.8; average number of trials, males 53.1, females 39.0). Using an obstruction box, Warner (1928) found that female rats crossed the electric grid on the way to the food more readily than males in the early stages of hunger. It is probable that there is a connection between his observations and ours, although the scarcity of data does not permit more than idle speculations.

Discussion

If one attempted to summarize the results *in terms of the responses* involved one would have to make some such statement as this: Moderate electric shock in the visual discrimination habit has a weakening or inhibiting effect if it accompanies the wrong response; it has a strengthening or facilitating effect if it accompanies the right response.

Such a paradoxical statement can be avoided or resolved if we state the function of this form of punishment not in relation to the particular response it accompanies but *in relation to the whole performance*. In this case we might say that *moderate electric shock has neither a weakening nor a strengthening effect, but as compared with the use of reward alone its addition makes the animal respond more readily to the significant cues in the learning situation irrespective of whether it accompanies the right or the wrong response.* Strictly speaking, such a conclusion is at present justified only for rats learning a black-white discrimination habit. It may, however, be considered a working hypothesis to be tested in other learning situations and with other animals.

It should also be emphasized that the function of electric

shock in this situation is subordinate to that of food-getting in the motivation of the animal. Any change in conditions whereby the shock becomes the primary factor would naturally alter its function: A considerable increase in current, say to 1.0 or 1.5 milliamperes, will cause the animal to avoid the alley which leads to the food-compartment. Even the same strength of shock given in the same place of the apparatus but with different total situations may exhibit differences in function as recently suggested by Tolman (1933).

To explain the results of our experiment by saying that the shock was an additional cue that helped the animal to learn the habit would imply a disregard of the actual facts. At the time the animal is making a choice between the two alleys its behavior is determined by synchronous visual and possibly other sensory processes. Since shock is not present during the choice but follows it as one of its consequences it cannot possibly have the function of a cue in the orthodox sense.

Our results have a direct bearing on the present controversy over the law of effect. That part of the law which deals with the consequences of what Thorndike calls "annoyers" is flatly contradicted by our results since *the annoyer in the case of the shock-right group actually accelerated the acquisition of the shocked response.* On the other hand this result was possible only because, as pointed out above, a "satisfier" was the superordinate factor in the motivation of the animal. In this connection it is interesting to note that Thorndike has recently stated that "there is no evidence that an annoyer takes away strength from the physiological basis of the connection in any way comparable to the way in which a satisfying after-effect adds strength to it. . . . Annoying after-effects are not dynamically opposites of satisfiers, but are specialized in their action" (Thorndike, 1932a, p. 313). Similar statements have also been made by Lorge (1933b).

While our experiment was in progress Tolman, Hall and Bretnall published the results of a similar experiment (1932). Their subjects were college students learning the "punchboard maze" (a spatial pattern consisting of one each of 30 pairs of holes) under various conditions of reward and punishment. Their results differ radically from ours in that their no-shock group learned best and their shock-wrong group was decidedly the poorest. Their shock-right group was about as efficient as the no-shock group. Since these results definitely contradict not only those of our experiment but also those of practically all animal experiments where shock for wrong responses is used, we immediately repeated and extended Tolman's experiment. We shall reserve specific comments for a separate report and merely state here that by keeping the experimental conditions rigidly the same for all three groups (as Tolman and his co-workers had not done) all significant differences between the three groups disappeared. Evidently, experimental directions given to human subjects are quite likely to mask and obscure the effects of reward and punishment. There can be no doubt that as regards certain aspects of the problem of motivation animal experiments are likely to produce more significant results than human experimentation.

Summary

Three groups of rats were taught a black-white discrimination habit with the usual hunger-food tension. The first group was shocked while it traversed the correct alley, the second was shocked in the orthodox fashion while in the wrong alley, and the third was not shocked at all.

The no-shock group was definitely inferior to the two shock groups, both in regard to the number of errors made during the first 100 trials and the number of trials required to reach the criterion of learning. There was very little overlapping in the distributions of errors and trials between the third and the first two groups. The distributions of trials and errors of the two shock groups were practically co-extensive, although the averages of the shock-wrong group were slightly better than those of the shock-right group.

On the basis of these facts one may say that the function of moderate electric shock in the visual discrimination habit is general rather than specific, that is, it affects the total performance rather than the part-response it accompanies. In other words, its function is to make the animal respond more readily to the significant cues in the learning situation rather than that of inhibiting or facilitating the response which is shocked.

The results flatly contradict that part of the law of effect which deals with the after-effects of annoyers.

This experiment represents the first step in the systematic variation of the factor of punishment. Other steps are in progress and projected.

Table 2.1   Errors of group I, shock-right

Trials	\multicolumn{26}{c}{Animal number and sex}

Trials	1 M	2 M	3 M	4 M	5 M	6 M	7 M	8 M	9 F	10 F	11 M	12 M	13 F	14 F	15 F	16 M	17 F	18 M	19 M	20 M	21 F	22 F	23 F	24 M	25 M	Total
1–10	7	6	5	5	2	7	6	2	6	4	4	7	4	4	4	6	3	7	5	6	7	6	3	5	5	
20	4	3		1	1	3	4	2		5	4	5	5	3	7	6	3	7	4	3	2	1	2	1	3	
30	2	1	2	2			4	2		1	5	1	2	2	2	3	2	4	1	2				2	3	
40	2		1	1	1	1	3	2	1	1	7	2		1	2	3		3		4	1	1				
50	1		2				1	1		1	3	2			2	4		3	1	1		1				
60	1					1	1				1		1		1	1		3						4		
70						1	1			1				2				1		2				2		
80							2				2		1		1	1		2								
90															1					1					1	
Total	17	10	10	9	4	13	22	10	7	13	26	17	13	12	20	24	8	30	11	19	10	9	5	14	12	345

Table 2.? ... group II, shock-wrong

Animal number and sex

%	27 M	28 M	29 M	30 M	31 F	32 F	33 F	34 F	35 F	36 F	37 F	38 M	39 M	40 M	41 F	42 F	43 F	44 F	45 M	46 M	47 M	48 M	49 M	50 M	Total
20	5	7	5	6	8	3	6	6	4	4	7	2	6	1	5	3	5	2	5	4	6	3	7	5	
30	6	5	4	2	6	2	3	6	2	2	6	2	1		1		2			1	2	1	5	4	
40	6	5	4		2	1	2	5			2		1	1	1	1		2	3	2		5		4	
50		2	1		3		1	2		1	1			1	1			1		2			1	2	
60		1	1					2									2			1					
70											2			1										1	
80																								2	
90																								3	
100					1																				
Totals	17	20	15	8	20	6	12	21	6	7	18	4	8	4	8	4	9	5	8	10	8	9	13	21	270

24

Table 2.3 Errors of group III, no-shock

Trials	51 F	52 M	53 F	54 F	55 M	56 F	57 M	58 F	59 F	60 M	61 F	62 F	63 F	64 F	65 F	66 F	67 M	68 M	69 M	70 M	71 M	72 F	73 F	74 M	75 M	Total
1–10	7	8	8	3	4	6	5	9	7	6	5	9	6	9	5	6	4	5	7	10	3	5	6	10	7	
20	8	4	6	3	4	3	5	9	7	5	5	7	6	5	4	6	5	6	5	8	6	3	7	5	6	
30	5	5	5	3	5	2	9	8	2	4	5	5	3	4	3	2	7	2	7	4	3	2	5	4	4	
40	3	3	3	4	5	4	5	4	2	4	7	2	6	1	3	5	6	3	4	2	3	3	2	3	5	
50	7	2	1	2		4	4	2		4	2	4	1	4	1		3		4	5	3	6	3	2	3	
60	4		1	2	1	1	2	3	3	3	1	1	1	2	1	1	4		2	4	3	6	5	3	3	
70	1		1	1	1	1	2	1	1	1	2			2			1	2	3	1	2	4	3	3	4	
80	2		1	1	1	2	1	2	1		3	1		2	1	1	1	1	1		1	1	5	3	4	
90	2		2		1	1		5	2		2			1	2		1	2	1	4			3	4	4	
100	2		1			1	2	6	2		2			2		1	1		1		1	1	3	1	2	
Totals	41	22	28	19	21	25	35	49	27	27	34	29	23	32	20	22	32	21	34	38	24	30	39	38	42	751

25

Table 2.4 Errors for the first 100 trials

	Average number of errors per animal	σ	Diff./σ_D. for group I	Diff./σ_D. for group II
Group I. Shock-right	13.8	6.7		2.14
Group II. Shock-wrong	10.8	5.6	2.14	
Group III. No-shock	30.0	7.9	7.9	10.0

Table 2.5 Frequency table showing the number of animals that reached the criterion of learning at a certain point

Number of trials preceding the criterion	Group I, shock-right	Group II, shock-wrong	Group III, no-shock
10		2	
20	1	6	
30	6	4	
40	4	3	1
50	6	5	1
60	4	2	1
70	2	2	1
80	2	1	4
90			3
100			
110			2
120			1
130			4
140			1
150			2
160			1
170			
180			
190			1
200			2

Table 2.6 Number of trials before criterion is reached

	Average number of trials per animal	σ	Diff./σ_D. for group I	Diff./σ_D. for group II
Group I. Shock-right	48.0	16.25		1.84
Group II. Shock-wrong	38.8	19.2	1.84	
Group III. No-shock	114.4	43.7	7.12	7.93

3   The relation of strength of stimulus to rapidity of habit-formation

Robert M. Yerkes and John D. Dodson

In connection with a study of various aspects of the modifiability of behavior in the dancing mouse a need for definite knowledge concerning the relation of strength of stimulus to rate of learning arose. It was for the purpose of obtaining this knowledge that we planned and executed the experiments which are now to be described. Our work was greatly facilitated by the advice and assistance of Doctor E. G. Martin, Professor G. W. Pierce, and Professor A. E. Kennelly, and we desire to express here both our indebtedness and our thanks for their generous services.

     The habit whose formation we attempted to study quantita-

Reprinted in abbreviated form from the *Journal of Comparative Neurology and Psychology*, 1908, *18*, 459–482 by permission of the Division of Publications, Wistar Institute.
[This study investigates rate of discrimination learning as a joint function of the intensity of the punishment and the difficulty of the discrimination. The authors report that the rate of learning of moderately difficult discriminations is an inverted U-shaped function of the intensity of the punishment, and that the optimal level of punishment decreases as the difficulty of the discrimination increases. Although the results of this study do not clearly support this conclusion, the principle (the Yerkes-Dodson Law) has had an important influence on later theories of motivation. See Brown (1965) for a critical review of relevant experiments.—Eds.]

tively, with respect to the strength of the stimulus which favored its formation, may be described as the white-black discrimination habit. Of the mice which served as subjects in the investigation it was demanded that they choose and enter one of two boxes or passageways. One of the boxes was white; the other black. No matter what their relative positions, the subject was required to choose the white one. Attempts to enter the black box resulted in the receipt of a disagreeable electric shock. It was our task to discover (1) whether the strength of this electric stimulus influences the rapidity with which dancers acquire the habit of avoiding the black passage-way, and if so, (2) what particular strength of stimulus is most favorable to the acquisition of this habit.

As a detailed account of the important features of the white-black visual discrimination habit in the dancer has already been published (Yerkes, 1908), a brief description of our method of experimentation will suffice for the purposes of this paper. A sketch of

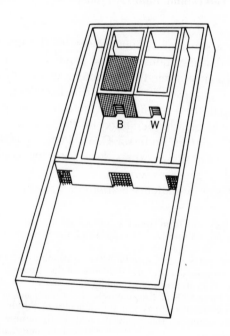

Figure 3.1 Discrimination box: *W*, electric box with white cardboards; *B*, electric box with black cardboards

the experiment box used by us in this investigation appears as Figure 3.1, and a ground plan of the box with its electric attachments, as Figure 3.2.

This apparatus consisted of a wooden box 94 cm. long; 30 cm. wide; and 11.5 cm. deep (inside measurements), which was divided into a nest-box, *A*, (Figure 3.2) an entrance chamber, *B*, and two electric boxes, *W*, *W*, together with alleys which connected these boxes with the nest-box. The doorways between the electric boxes and the alleys were 5 by 5 cm. On the floor of each electric box, as is shown in the figures, were the wires of an interrupted circuit which could be completed by the experimenter, by closing the key, *K*, whenever the feet of a mouse rested upon any two adjacent wires in either of the boxes. In this circuit were an electric battery and a Porter inductorium. One of these electric boxes bore black cards, and the other white cards similarly arranged. Each box bore two

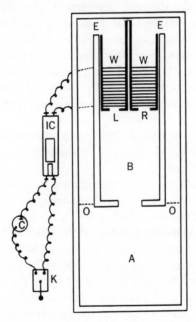

Figure 3.2   Ground plan of discrimination box: *A*, nest-box; *B*, entrance chamber; *W W*, electric boxes; *L*, doorway of left electric box; *R*, doorway of right electric box; *E*, exit from electric box to alley; *O*, swinging door between alley and *A; IC*, induction apparatus; *C*, electric battery; *K*, key in circuit

cards. One was at the entrance on the outside of the box and the other on the inside, as Figure 3.1 indicates. The latter consisted of three sections of which two constituted linings for the sides of the box and the third a cover for a portion of the open top of the box. In no case did these inside cards extend the entire length of the electric boxes. The white and black cards were readily interchangeable [and the order in which they were shifted was determined by prearranged sequences that never left the white and black cards on the same box for more than four consecutive tests].[1]

A dancer was placed in the nest-box by the experimenter, and thence it was permitted to pass into the entrance chamber, *B*. The experimenter then placed a piece of cardboard between it and the doorway between *A* and *B* and gradually narrowed the space in which the animal could move about freely by moving the cardboard toward the electric boxes. This, without in any undesirable way interfering with the dancer's attempts to discriminate and choose correctly, greatly lessened the amount of random activity which preceded choice. When thus brought face to face with the entrances to the boxes the mouse soon attempted to enter one of them. If it happened to select the white box it was permitted to enter, pass through, and return to the nest-box; but if, instead, it started to enter the black box the experimenter by closing the key, upon which his finger constantly rested during the tests, caused it to receive an electric shock which as a rule forced a hasty retreat from the black passageway and the renewal of attempts to discover by comparison which box should be entered.

Each of the forty mice experimented with was given ten tests every morning until it succeeded in choosing the white box correctly on three consecutive days, that is for thirty tests. A choice was recorded as wrong if the mouse started to enter the black box and received a shock; as right if, either directly or after running from one entrance to the other a number of times, it entered the white box. Whether it entered the white electric box or the black one, it was permitted to return to the nest-box by way of the white box before another test was given. Escape to the nest-box by way of the black box was not permitted.

Almost all of the mice used were between six and eight weeks

---

[1] [The bracketed material is editorial transition to maintain continuity where sections have been omitted from the original manuscript.—Eds.]

old at the beginning of their training. [Table 3.1 shows] the general classification of our experiments. They naturally fall into three sets. These are designated by the roman numerals I, II, and III in the table, and will throughout the paper be referred to as the experiments of set I, set II, and set III. These sets of experiments differ from one another first of all as to condition of visual discrimination or, more explicitly stated, in the amount by which the two electric boxes differed from one another in brightness. For set I this difference was medium, in comparison with later conditions, and discrimination was therefore of medium difficultness. For set II the difference was great, and discrimination was easy. For set III the difference was slight, and discrimination was difficult.

Table 3.1   Number of subjects tested under each condition of training

Difficulty of Discrimination	Strength of Stimulus								Total
	125	135	195	255	300	375	420	500	
Easy (Set II)		4	4	4		4	4		20
Medium (Set I)	4				4			4	12
Difficult (Set III)		2	2	2		2			8

For the sake of obtaining results in this investigation which should be directly comparable with those of experiments on the modifiability of behavior in the dancer which have been conducted during the past three years, it was necessary for us to use the same general method of controlling the visual conditions of the experiment that had previously been used. This we decided to do, notwithstanding the fact that we had before us methods which were vastly superior to the old one with respect to the describability of conditions and the accuracy and ease of their control. To any experimenter who wishes to repeat this investigation with other animals we should recommend that, before recourse is had to the use of cardboards for the purpose of rendering the boxes distinguishable, thorough tests be made of the ability of the animal to discriminate when the boxes are rendered different in brightness by the use of a screen which excludes a measurable amount of light from one of them. We have discovered that the simplest and best method of arranging the conditions for such experiments with the dancer as are now to be described is to use two electric boxes which are alike in all respects and to control the amount of light which enters one of them from the top. It is easy to obtain satisfactory screens and to measure their transmitting capacity. We regret that the first use which we wished to make of our results in this investigation forced us to employ conditions which are relatively complicated and difficult to describe. [The details of the conditions of visual discrimination employed in the several sets of experiments were then described.]

To obtain our stimulus we used a storage cell, in connections with gravity batteries, and with the current from this operated a Porter inductorium. The induced current from the secondary coil of this apparatus was carried by the wires which constituted an interrupted circuit on the floor of the electric boxes. For the experiments of set I the strengths of the stimuli used were not accurately determined, for we had not at that time discovered a satisfactory means of measuring the induced current. These experiments therefore served as a preliminary investigation whose chief value lay in the suggestions which it furnished for the planning of later experiments. The experiments of sets II and III were made with a Porter inductorium which we had calibrated, with the help of Dr. E. G. Martin of the Harvard Medical School, by a method which he had recently devised and described (Martin, 1908a, 1908b).

On the basis of the calibration measurements which we made by Martin's method [it was] possible to read directly in "units of stimulation" the value of the induced current which is yielded by a primary current of one ampere for any given position of the secondary coil. With the secondary coil at O, for example, the value of the induced current is 350 units; with the secondary at 5.2 centimeters on the scale of the inductorium, its value is 155 units; and with the secondary at 10, its value is 12 units. The value of the induced current for a primary current greater or less than unity is obtained by multiplying the reading from the calibration curve by the value of the primary current. The primary current used for the experiments of sets II and III measured 1.2 amperes, hence the value of the stimulating current which was obtained when the secondary coil stood at 0 was $350 \times 1.2 = 420$ units of stimulation.

As conditions for the experiments of set I, we chose three strengths of stimuli which we designated as weak, medium, and strong. The weak stimulus was slightly above the threshold of stimulation for the dancers. Comparison of the results which it yielded with those obtained by the use of our calibrated inductorium enable us to state with a fair degree of certainty that its value was 125 ± 10 units of stimulation. The strong stimulus was decidedly disagreeable to the experimenters and the mice reacted to it vigorously. Its value was subsequently ascertained to be 500 ± 50 units. For the medium stimulus we tried to select a value which should be about midway between these extremes. In this we succeeded better than we could have expected to, for comparison indicated that the value was 300 ± 25 units. Fortunately for the interpretation of this set of results, the exact value of the stimuli is not important.

By the use of our calibrated inductorium and the measurement of our primary current, we were able to determine satisfactorily the stimulating values of the several currents which were used in the experiments of sets II and III. The primary current of 1.2 amperes, which was employed, served to actuate the interrupter of the inductorium as well as to provide the stimulating current. The interruptions occurred at the rate of 65 ± 5 per second. We discovered at the outset of the work that it was not worth while to attempt to train the dancers with a stimulus whose value was much less than 135 units. We therefore selected this as our weakest stimulus. At the other extreme a stimulus of 420 units was as strong as we deemed it safe to employ. Between these two, three intermediate strengths were used in the case of set II, and two in the case of set III. Originally it had been our intention to make use of stimuli which varied from one another in value by 60 units of stimulation, beginning with 135 and increasing by steps of 60 through 195, 255, 315, 375 to as nearly 425 as possible. It proved to be needless to make tests with all of these.

We may now turn to the results of the experiments and the interpretation thereof. Before the beginning of its training each mouse was given two series of tests in which the electric shock was not used and return to the nest-box through either the white or the black box was permitted. These twenty tests (ten in series A and ten in series B) have been termed preference tests, for they served to reveal whatever initial tendency a dancer possessed to choose

Table 3.2[a] Number of errors of each subject under each condition of training

Set	Stimulus strength	Subj.[b]	A	B	Series 1	2	3	4	5	6	7	8	9	10	11	12	13	14	15	16	17	18	19	20
I	125	1	6	5	3	6	5	4	3	2	3	2	5	1	0	1	1	1	1	0	0	0	2	2
		2	4	6	4	6	2	6	3	4	4	2	3	4	3	3	2	0	1	1	0	2	1	3
		3	7	5	5	6	4	5	7	5	4	2	5	2	3	1	2	1	3	0	1	0	1	3
		4	5	4	4	7	5	4	5	4	7	3	3	2	5	2	2	3	3	0	0	1		
I	300	1	4	6	4	3	4	3	2	2	2	1	0	0	0	0									
		2	3	4	4	4	5	6	5	2	0	1	0	0	0										
		3	8	6	4	3	5	4	4	0	2	0	2	0	0										
		4	7	6	5	2	6	3	7	2	3	0	0	0											
I	500	1	7	6	3	3	5	3	2	3	3	4	3	2	1	1	1	0	2	0	0	0		
		2	5	4	5	3	3	2	2	2	2	1	2	1	2	0	2	2	0	0	0	2		
		3	6	4	5	1	3	2	2	1	0	0	2	3	1	2	1	0	0	0	1			
		4[c]	1	4	5	3	3	3	4	2	4	3	1	1	0	0	2	2	1	2					
II	135	1	9	8	6	2	2	1	0	0	0	0	0	2	1	1	0	0	1	0	0	0	1	1
		2	8	4	6	2	4	0	2	0	1	0	0	0											
		3	7	6	4	3	4	4	3	2	1	0	0	0											
		4	7	6	4	4	6	1	2	0	1														
II	195	1	6	6	6	5	3	2	1	2	1	1	0	0											
		2	6	8	5	1	1	2	0	1	0	0	0	0											
		3	6	7	7	1	5	2	1	1	1	0	0												
		4	4	3	7	1	4	1	2	0	0	0													
II	255	1	5	7	6	4	1	0	0	0	0	0													
		2	5	5	9	4	3	4	0	0	0														
		3	5	6	7	7	4	2	2	0															
		4	6	6																					

Series

Set	Stimulus strength	Subj.[b]	A	B	1	2	3	4	5	6	7	8	9	10	11	12	13	14	15	16	17	18	19	20
II	375	1	6	5	6	5	5	0	0	0	0	0												
		2	6	5	4	5	8	3	1	0	1	0												
		3	6	3	6	1	3	4	3	0	0	0												
		4	7	6	5	3	2	1	4	0														
II	420	1	5	6	5	4	2	1	0	0	0	0	1	0	0	0									
		2	4	6	5	1	2	0	0	0	0	0													
		3	5	6	5	5	5	3	3	0	0														
		4	6	4	5	0	4	2	1	0															
III	135	1[d]	6	4	4	5	3	4	7	4	7	7	4	4	4	5	3	2	4	3	2	0	1	3
		2[e]	4	7	6	2	6	2	4	4	7	5	4	2	1	3	2	4	3	0	2	2	1	3
III	195	1	4	7	5	3	5	6	6	4	5	2	0	3	2	1	1	0	0	0				
		2	4	8	7	6	6	3	7	4	3	2	0	1	1	0	0	0						
III	255	1	4	4	5	3	2	5	2	2	3	1	1	2	2	3	2	0	3	1	0	0	0	
		2	7	5	6	3	3	5	4	3	2	1	2	1	3	0	0	1	1	0	0	0		
III	375	1	4	3	6	3	4	4	2	3	6	4	1	1	1	3	1	1	1	1	0	0	0	
		2[f]	5	4	6	2	3	2	5	2	5	2	1	2	2	1	1	1	0	1	1	1	1	0

[a] From Tables 3–14 of original article.
[b] Subjects with odd numbers are males; subjects with even numbers are females.
[c] Criterion met on series 21–23.
[d] Criterion not met by series 30.
[e] Criterion met on series 22–24.
[f] Criterion met on series 24–26.

the white or the black box. On the day following preference series
B, the regular daily training series were begun and they were continued without interruption until the dancer had succeeded in
choosing correctly in every test on three consecutive days.

The tests with the weak stimulus of set I were continued for
twenty days, and up to that time only one of the four individuals
in training had acquired a perfect habit. On the twentieth day it
was evident that the stimulus was too weak to furnish an adequate
motive for the avoidance of the black box and the experiments were
discontinued. Four other dancers were trained with a medium stimulus. All of the subjects acquired a habit quickly. We shall take as
a measure of the rapidity of learning in these experiments the number of tests received by a mouse up to the point at which errors
ceased for at least three consecutive series. Comparison of these
results with those obtained with the weak stimulus clearly indicates
that the medium stimulus was much more favorable to the acquirement of the white-black visual discrimination habit. In its results
the strong stimulus proved to be similar to the weak stimulus. All
of the mice in this case learned more slowly than did those which
were trained with the medium strength of stimulus.

The general result of this preliminary set of experiments with
three roughly measured strengths of stimulation was to indicate that
neither a weak nor a strong electrical stimulus is as favorable to the
acquisition of the white-black habit as a medium stimulus. Contrary
to our expectations, this set of experiments did not prove that the
rate of habit-formation increases with increase in the strength of the
electric stimulus up to the point at which the shock becomes positively injurious. Instead an intermediate range of intensity of stimulation proved to be most favorable to the acquisition of a habit
*under the conditions of visual discrimination of this set of experi-
ments.*

In the light of these preliminary results we were able to plan
a more exact and thorough-going examination of the relation of
strength of stimulus to rapidity of learning. Inasmuch as the training under the conditions of set I required a great deal of time, we
decided to shorten the necessary period of training by making the
two electric boxes very different in brightness, and the discrimination correspondingly easy. This we did, as has already been explained, by decreasing the amount of light which entered the black

box, while leaving the white box about the same. The influence of this change on the time of learning was very marked indeed.

With each of the five strengths of stimuli which were used in set II two pairs of mice were trained, as in the case of set I. In general the rapidity of learning in this set of experiments increased as the strength of the stimulus increased. The weakest stimulus (135 units) gave the slowest rate of learning; the strongest stimulus (420 units), the most rapid.

The results of the second set of experiments contradict those of the first set. What does this mean? It occurred to us that the apparent contradiction might be due to the fact that discrimination was much easier in the experiments of set II than in those of set I. To test this matter we planned to use in our third set of experiments a condition of visual discrimination which should be extremely difficult for the mice. The reader will bear in mind that for set II the difference in brightness of the electric boxes was great; that for set III it was slight; and for set I, intermediate or medium.

For the experiments of set III only one pair of dancers was trained with any given strength of stimulus. The results, however, are not less conclusive than those of the other sets of experiments because of the smaller number of individuals used. The varying results of the three sets of experiments are explicable in terms of the conditions of visual discrimination. In set III both the weak and the strong stimuli were less favorable to the acquirement of the habit than the intermediate stimulus of 195 units. It should be noted that our three sets of experiments indicate that the greater the brightness difference of the electric boxes the stronger the stimulus which is most favorable to habit-formation (within limits which have not been determined). Further discussion of the results and attempts to interpret them may be postponed until certain interesting general features of the work have been mentioned.

The behavior of the dancers varied with the strength of the stimulus to which they were subjected. They chose no less quickly in the case of the strong stimuli than in the case of the weak, but they were less careful in the former case and chose with less deliberation and certainty. Figure 3.3 exhibits the characteristic differences in the curves of learning yielded by weak, medium, and strong stimuli. These three curves were plotted on the basis of the average number of errors for the mice which were trained in the experiments

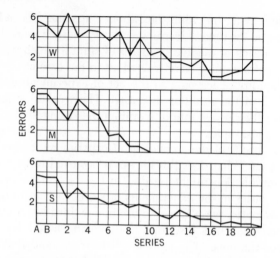

Figure 3.3   Curves of learning. Average number of errors on set I for four mice in each series. *W*, designates the error curve for the individuals which were trained under the condition of *weak* electrical stimulation; *M*, designates the corresponding curve for the *medium* strength of stimulation; and *S*, that for the *strong* stimulus.

of set I. In addition to exhibiting the fact that the medium stimulus yielded a perfect habit much more quickly than did either of the other stimuli, Figure 3.3 shows a noteworthy difference in the forms of the curves for the weak and the strong stimuli. Curve W (weak stimulus) is higher throughout its course than is curve S (strong stimulus). This means that fewer errors are made from the start under the condition of strong stimulation than under the condition of weak stimulation.

Figure 3.4 contains the condensed results of our experiments. It gives, for each visual condition and strength of stimulus, the number of tests required for the acquisition of a perfect habit. This figure very clearly and briefly presents the chiefly significant results of our investigation of relation of strength of electrical stimulus to rate of habit-formation, and it offers perfectly definite answers to the questions which were proposed for solution.

From the data we draw the following conclusions:

1. In the case of the particular habit which we have studied,

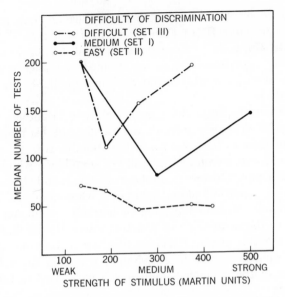

Figure 3.4 A graphic representation of the relation of strength of electrical stimulus to condition of visual discrimination and rapidity of learning

the rapidity of learning increases as the amount of difference in the brightness of the electric boxes between which the mouse is required to discriminate is increased. The limits within which this statement holds have not been determined.

2. The relation of the strength of electrical stimulus to rapidity of learning or habit-formation depends upon the difficultness of the habit, or, in the case of our experiments, upon the conditions of visual discrimination.

3. When the boxes which are to be discriminated between differ very greatly in brightness, and discrimination is easy, the rapidity of learning increases as the strength of the electrical stimulus is increased from the threshold of stimulation to the point of harmful intensity. Our results do not represent, in this instance, the point at which the rapidity of learning begins to decrease, for we did not care to subject our animals to injurious stimulation. We therefore present this conclusion tentatively, subject to correction in the light of future research. Of its correctness we feel confident

because of the results which the other sets of experiments gave. The irregularity of curve II [of Figure 3.4], in that it rises slightly for the strength 375, is due, doubtless, to the small numbers of animals used in the experiments. Had we trained ten mice with each strength of stimulus instead of four the curve probably would have fallen regularly.

4. When the boxes differ only slightly in brightness and discrimination is extremely difficult the rapidity of learning at first rapidly increases as the strength of the stimulus is increased from the threshold, but, beyond an intensity of stimulation which is soon reached, it begins to decrease. Both weak stimuli and strong stimuli result in slow habit-formation. A stimulus whose strength is nearer to the threshold than to the point of harmful stimulation is most favorable to the acquisition of a habit. Curve III [of Figure 3.4] verifies these statements. It shows that when discrimination was extremely difficult a stimulus of 195 units was more favorable than the weaker or the stronger stimuli which were used in this set of experiments.

5. As the difficultness of discrimination is increased the strength of that stimulus which is most favorable to habit-formation approaches the threshold. Curve II, curve I, curve III is the order of increasing difficultness of discrimination for our results, for it will be remembered that the experiments of set III were given under difficult conditions of discrimination; those of set I under medium conditions; and those of set II under easy conditions. As thus arranged the most favorable stimuli so far as we may judge from our results, are 420, 300, and 195. This leads us to infer that an easily acquired habit, that is one which does not demand difficult sense discriminations or complex associations, may readily be formed under strong stimulation, whereas a difficult habit may be acquired readily only under relatively weak stimulation. That this fact is of great importance to students of animal behavior and animal psychology is obvious.

Attention should be called to the fact that since only three strengths of stimulus were used for the experiments of set I, it is possible that the most favorable strength of stimulation was not discovered. We freely admit this possibility, and we furthermore wish to emphasize the fact that our fifth conclusion is weakened slightly by this uncertainty. But it is only fair to add that previous experience with many conditions of discrimination and of stimulation, in connection with which more than two hundred dancers were trained, together with the results of comparison of this set of experiments with the other two sets, convinces us that the dancers would not be likely to learn much more rapidly under any other condition of stimulation than they did with a strength of 300 ± 25 units of stimulation.

Naturally we do not propose to rest the conclusions which have just been formulated upon our study of the mouse alone. We shall now repeat our experiments, in the light of the experience which has been gained, with other animals.

4   Effect of strength of punishment for "correct" or "incorrect" responses on visual discrimination performance

George J. Wischner, Harry Fowler, and Stephen A. Kushnick

The results of studies by Muenzinger and his co-workers (Muenzinger, 1934; Muenzinger, Bernstone, & Richards, 1938; Muenzinger & Newcomb, 1936) have been interpreted as indicating that pairing punishment (electric shock) with the *correct* response does not disrupt, but, in fact, facilitates performance.[1] According to Muenzinger, there is a "general sensitizing" factor in punishment which serves to

Reprinted from the *Journal of Experimental Psychology*, 1963, 65, 131–138 by permission of the senior author and the American Psychological Association. This study was supported in part by Grant No. G-14312 from the National Science Foundation. Grateful acknowledgment is made by the authors to M. Samuels and F. Berlin for their assistance in the conduct of this experiment.

[Further research by Muenzinger and others led to the conclusion that punishment of the incorrect response leads to faster discrimination learning than punishment of the correct response. This experiment compares the two procedures at various levels of punishing shock, and shows that errors decrease with increasing intensity in groups punished for the incorrect response but increase with increasing intensity in groups punished for the correct response. In this study there is no evidence that any of the groups punished for the correct response make fewer errors than the unpunished controls.—Eds.]

[1] [See Selection 2.—Eds.]

slow down the animal and make it more sensitive to the cues to be discriminated at the choice point of a maze.

Muenzinger's original formulation appears to be generally accepted (e.g., Feldman, 1961; Young, 1961), despite more recent findings which question its generality (Muenzinger & Baxter, 1957; Muenzinger, Brown, Crow, & Powloski, 1952; Muenzinger & Powloski, 1951; Wischner, 1947). Wischner has shown that with a non-correction procedure, as contrasted with the correction procedure typically employed by Muenzinger, shock for the correct response retards, rather than facilitates discrimination learning. Wischner states that shock has a specific function with respect to the punished response: the animal very quickly acquires avoidance responses to the cues associated with shock.

The results of the more recent studies comparing correction and noncorrection procedures led Muenzinger to modify his original position to one in which it is maintained that shock serves (a) to produce avoidance and (b) to accelerate learning. Thus, Muenzinger and Powloski (1951) argue that, with a correction procedure, the animal adapts more quickly to the noxious, avoidance-producing quality of shock for the correct response, since selection of the wrong alternative always requires retracing toward the positive cue with which the shock is associated. As a result, the accelerating or "sensitizing" effect of shock takes place sooner with the correction procedure and a facilitation of performance is readily evidenced.

In addition to the recognition of the significance of methodological variables, such as correction vs. noncorrection, there has been some recognition of the import of factors relating to shock per se. For example, Muenzinger has suggested that only relatively mild shock, when paired with the correct response, may be facilitating. Nevertheless, there has been no systematic study of shock parameters. In relation to the general issue of the effect of shock for the correct response, it would appear that factors such as the intensity, duration, locus, frequency, and order of the shocks administered over training, would constitute a significant class of determining variables.

The purpose of this investigation is to assess the effect of different intensities of shock for either the correct or incorrect response on performance in a black-white discrimination entailing a noncorrection procedure. In addition to the shock intensity variable, two training procedures were studied: (a) the more usually employed free-choice procedure and (b) a forced-choice procedure. The latter procedure was included in order to determine the effect, if any, resulting from equating, among groups, the number and order of shock and food experiences received over training.

Method

Subjects

Fifty-six male albino rats of the Sprague-Dawley strain served as Ss. These Ss, which had been selected on the basis of their performance in pretraining tests described below, were approximately 100 days old at the beginning of training. The Ss were caged individually in a colony room in which the temperature was controlled and the normal day-night cycle reversed through artificial illumination.

Apparatus

The apparatus was a simple T maze with walls and floor of galvanized sheet metal and an exterior supporting shell of wood. The stem of the apparatus was 26 in. long, and each arm, as measured from the center of the choice point area, 36 in. long. The height of each section of the maze was uniformly 4½ in. and the width, 3¾ in. The first 8 in. of the stem served as a start compartment, being separated from the remaining portion by a guillotine door. The last 12 in. of each arm were also separated from the remaining portion by a guillotine door and served as a goal compartment. Guillotine doors were also positioned in each arm at a distance of 3 in. from the center of the choice point.

The internal sheet metal composition of the maze was provided by two L shaped strips of sheet metal; one L served as one wall and half of the floor of each maze section and the other L as the other wall and half of the floor. The L shaped strips of sheet metal provided two 1½-in. floor surfaces which were separated by a 1-in. gap. Hinged and weighted transparent Plexiglas tops covered the stem and each arm.

A plate of frosted Plexiglas served as the end wall of each goal compartment. A strip of clear Plexiglas (1 in. wide, ½ in. thick, and 3¾ in. long) with a carved food well (¾ in. in diameter and ½ in. deep) was permanently positioned within each goal compartment, directly in front of the frosted plate. A single 10-w. frosted bulb (120-v. source) was positioned outside of each goal compartment, directly behind the frosted plate. These goalbox bulbs, which served as the discriminative visual stimuli, were enclosed by the frosted plate of each goal compartment and an exterior wooden shell painted a flat black. Exterior maze illumination was provided by two 10-w., 120-v. frosted bulbs, one located near the end of each arm on the stem side of the T maze.

A matched-impedence 60-cps ac shock system was used to deliver shock to the S in either maze arm. In this system the two L shaped strips of sheet metal forming the sides and floor of the maze were connected across the output of a variable transformer. An additional resistance of .30 megohms was placed in series with S which could receive shock when it made contact with both halves of the sheet-metal floor. The narrowness of the maze alley prevented S from avoiding shock by running along only one half of the floor surface.

Additional characteristics of this shock circuit were such that it had to be set by E before each training trial. Shock was delivered to S when it interrupted, in either arm, an infrared photoelectric beam crossing the arm at a point midway between its two guillotine doors. The manual priming feature of the circuit prevented S from receiving more than one shock in any one trial, even though it was possible for S to interrupt a photoelectric beam several times during a trial. When the shock was delivered, its duration was held constant at .2 sec., as metered through a Hunter timing relay, and its intensity was set at either 45, 60, or 75 v. as measured across the output of the transformer. Preliminary testing for threshold of response to the shock indicated that, with the circuit employed, animals manifested a reaction to shock at approximately 40 v.

Procedure

The experimental procedure entailed both a pretraining and a training phase. One week prior to the pretraining phase, the Ss were started, and maintained for the duration of the experiment, on a daily diet of 12 gm. of Purina lab checkers per day, with water available ad libitum. Taming of the Ss also took place during this week and consisted of a daily handling of each S for several minutes.

For both pretraining and training, the Ss were transported to the experimental room in a wood and hardware cloth carrying cage. The Ss were kept in individual compartments of the carrying cage throughout the course of the daily training session. Prior to their daily run in the maze, which took place during the dark phase of the S's day-night cycle, all Ss received approximately 5 min. adaptation to the illumination conditions of the room as provided by the two exterior 10-w. apparatus bulbs, this time being that required by E to prepare for the day's trials.

Pretraining was administered to reduce possible position and brightness preferences and to habituate S to the apparatus, especially the guillotine doors which were used to prevent retracing. No shock was administered during this phase. Over pretraining, each S received a total of 16 forced, reinforced trials, 4 per day, randomly distributed with the restriction that half of the trials were to the left and half to the right with half of each of these sets being to an illuminated goal and half to a dark goal. Forcing was accomplished by lowering one of the guillotine doors at the choice point. The reinforcement provided on each trial was in the form of P. J. Noyes sugar pellets (4 mm., 45 mg.). On the first of the 4 pretraining days, the food pellets were liberally spread throughout the goal box and on subsequent days, the number and locus of pellets were systematically reduced until, on the last day, only two pellets were given and these were in the goal-box food cup. With each forced trial, S was permitted to run to the available goal where it was detained until all pellets were consumed or until 5 min. had elapsed. Upon meeting either of these two criteria, or if the S failed to run to the forced goal within 5 min., it was removed from the maze and replaced in the carrying cage to await its next trial. On the average, the intertrial interval was about 15 min., the interval being determined by the time required to run a block of Ss. Those Ss who consistently traversed the maze and consumed the food pellets within the allotted time were considered for the training phase of the study. This represented about 90 percent of all Ss pretrained. It should be noted that those Ss which were retained showed no reliable brightness or position preferences. Analysis of first training trial choices indicated a 61 percent selection of the illuminated alley.

Training began on the day following termination of pretraining. During training, reinforcement could be obtained only in the illuminated goal box. Since reinforcement was not obtained in the dark goal box during these training trials, Ss were detained in that goal box for 10 sec., the approximate time required by S to consume two food pellets when in the lighted goal. Otherwise, the conditions of reinforcement, schedule of right or left goal-box illumination, intertrial interval, and general handling procedure were the same for both training and pretraining trials.

For the training phase, the 56 Ss were randomly assigned to seven groups of 8 Ss each. There were three shock-right groups (SR), i.e., Ss received both shock and food reward for a correct response but neither for an incorrect response; three shock-wrong groups (SW), i.e., Ss received food reward for a correct response but shock for an incorrect one; and a control, no-shock group (NS), i.e., Ss received only food reward for a correct response. The different shock intensities employed for the three groups within both the SR and SW conditions were 45, 60, and 75 v. The shock-right groups may be designated as SR-45, SR-60, and SR-75; and correspondingly, the shock-wrong groups as SW-45, SW-60, and SW-75.

The six shock groups and the control group were subdivided, with half the Ss within each group being trained on the typically employed free-choice procedure, and half being trained on a forced-choice procedure. The Ss run under the forced-choice procedure were permitted a free choice only on the first trial of successive blocks of four trials. The remaining three trials within each four-trial block were forced-choice trials. Forcing was administered such that, of the four trials within a block, two were to the goal box on the left and two were to the goal box on the right with one trial of each of these sets of two trials being to a lighted goal compartment with reinforcement, and the other being to a dark goal without reinforcement. Thus, after every block of four trials, and at any point in training, occasions of reinforcement and nonreinforcement were equal and balanced over right and left positions for all groups of Ss run under the forced-choice procedure. Similarly, for those shocked Ss run under this procedure, the occasions of shock and no-shock were equal and balanced over right and left positions throughout training.

All Ss received 4 trials per day on the first 6 days of discrimination training and then 8 trials per day thereafter until the end of training. The position of the illuminated, correct goal was varied on these trials in accordance with a predetermined random schedule. Discrimination training was continued until each S met a criterion of 15 correct responses out of a total of 16 free choices with the last 8 being correct, or until a total of 200 training trials had been administered. On every trial, each S was permitted a maximum of 5 min., from the opening of the start-box door, to make a choice. If S did not complete a trial within the allotted time, the trial was recorded as "No-Response" (NR). Actually there were relatively few instances of such trials and these are considered in a subsequent section of the results.

Results

For both the free- and forced-choice groups, only the first trial of every successive block of four was utilized in the major analyses. For the forced-choice groups, this trial was, of course, the only scorable trial. By using only the corresponding first trial of a block of four for the free-choice animals, it was possible to compare performances obtained with the two training procedures. It should be noted, however, that the first-trial data for the free-choice groups are highly representative of their performance over all trials. The results of an analysis of variance involving Trial 1 and averaged total-trial data showed that group mean error differences based on these two measures are insignificant ($F < 1$). Expressed in terms of the correlation between individual error scores based on the Trial 1 and Trial 2–4 data, the product-moment r is .79.

Mean errors over 200 trials for the several groups within both the free- and forced-choice procedures are presented as a function of shock intensity in Figure 4.1. The shock intensity functions for both free- and forced-choice procedures appear to be quite similar. In general, mean errors tend to increase with increasing shock intensities for the SR groups, but decrease with increasing intensities for the SW groups. The regularity of this trend is more clearly evident in the heavy, solid line in Figure 4.1 which represents the pooled data for corresponding shock-intensity groups of the free- and forced-choice procedures.

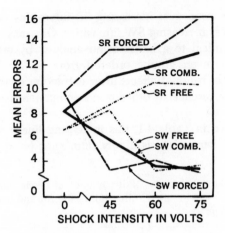

Figure 4.1   Group mean errors over 200 training trials as a function of shock intensity

Since the no-shock or zero intensity condition is part of the intensity dimension of both the SR and SW conditions, its inclusion in an analysis of variance of the data presented in Figure 4.1 precludes the use of a complete factorial analysis of shock conditions (SR vs. SW) and shock intensity. The data were statistically treated in terms of a 2×7 factorial analysis of variance comprising the two training methods and the seven groups employed; i.e., three SR intensity groups, three SW intensity groups, and the NS group. With this analysis, the apparently divergent trends depicted in Figure 4.1 for the SW and SR groups, over increasing shock intensities, can be assessed by orthogonal polynomial comparisons.

The results of the analysis of variance, presented in Table 4.1, show that the between-groups differences are highly reliable ($p <$ .005) and that this effect related primarily to the highly reliable differences among the seven shock intensity groups ($p <$ .001); the difference between the two training procedures, as well as the Procedure $\times$ Shock Condition interaction, is unreliable ($p >$ .20 in both cases).

To assess the significance of the differences among the several shock intensities and between shock conditions (SR vs. SW), an orthogonal polynomial comparison was performed assessing an increasing linear trend over increasing SR intensities vs. a decreasing linear trend over increasing SW intensities. One may view this comparison as identical to a linear trend analysis by orthogonal polynomials of all seven groups ordered from SR-75 through NS to SW-75. As such, residual effects after extraction of this linear component, have reference to other trend components, e.g., quadratic, cubic, etc.

As shown in Table 4.1, this increasing linear SR vs. decreasing linear SW comparison is highly significant ($p < .001$), and in-

Table 4.1   Analysis of variance of group mean errors over all training trials for SR and SW groups

Source	df	MS	F
Between	13	73.22	2.99**
Procedure (P)	1	34.57	1.41
Condition (C)	6	127.68	5.21***
Linear	(1)	743.14	30.32***
Residual	(5)	4.59	<1
P × C	6	25.20	1.03
Linear	(1)	70.88	2.89
Residual	(5)	16.06	<1
Within	42	24.51	

**$p < .01$.
***$p < .001$.

dicates not only a reliable difference between SR and SW conditions, but also, as depicted by the solid line in Figure 4.1, reliable differences among the several shock intensity groups within both SR and SW conditions. With extraction of this significant linear component, residual trend effects are negligible ($F < 1$). This suggests that the best assumption concerning the nature of the shock intensity functions for both the SR and SW conditions is that they are linear.

The differences obtained above between the SR and SW conditions on the basis of all 200 training trials appear to be representative of any portion or phase of training. Figure 4.2 shows the course of acquisition of the discrimination over blocks of 40 training trials. The left panel presents the data for Ss of the free-choice procedure

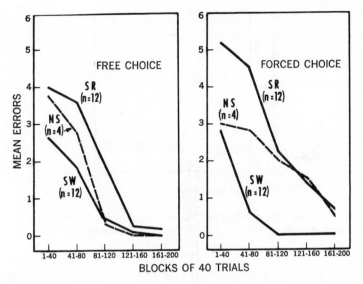

Figure 4.2 Mean errors per 40-trial blocks for groups run under free- and forced-choice procedures

and the right panel for Ss of the forced-choice procedure. The data for the various SR and SW intensity groups within each training procedure have been pooled in order to reduce the cluster of curves. With both procedures, it is evident that, in comparison with the SW groups, the inferior performance of the SR groups is maintained throughout the 200 training trials.

Analysis of nonresponse (NR)

The above analyses do not include NRs made by the Ss throughout the course of training. Figure 4.3 shows group mean NRs over training as a function of shock intensity. The NR scores for the corresponding groups of the two training procedures have been pooled in view of the absence of a significant difference in the frequency of NRs between training procedures and an insignificant Training Procedure $\times$ Shock Condition interaction. Differences in the frequency of NRs among the seven groups shown in Figure 4.3 are highly reliable, $F(6,42) = 2.82$, $p < .025$, and trend analysis of this significant effect shows both reliable linear and quadratic compo-

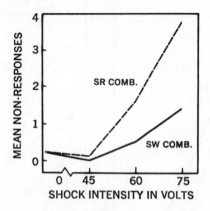

Figure 4.3   Mean NRs as a function of shock intensity for the SR and SW conditions with appropriate free- and forced-choice groups combined

nents, $F(1,42) = 4.70$, $p < .05$ and $F(1,42) = 11.41$, $p < .005$, respectively. The highly significant quadratic component indicates, as shown in Figure 4.3, that the frequency of NRs within both the SR and SW conditions increases with increasing shock intensities; the significant linear component indicates that this effect is somewhat more pronounced for the SR condition.

Although this analysis shows systematic differences in frequency of NRs among the several shock groups and between shock conditions, it should be emphasized that these differences seem to be unrelated to the significant effects noted for the earlier error score analyses. Whereas errors increased with increasing SR intensities and decreased with increasing SW intensities, NRs increased with increasing intensities for both the SR and SW conditions. Moreover, it would appear unlikely that the large error differences obtained between the SR and SW conditions could be accounted for by the relatively small absolute, albeit significant, differences in NR noted between these conditions in Figure 4.3.

Discussion

In relation to the effect of shock for either the correct or incorrect response, the results of the present study clearly demonstrate the importance of the intensity parameter. Significantly, variation in the intensity of shock associated with the correct response served to vary the extent of performance *retardation;* variation in shock intensity associated with the incorrect response served to vary the extent of performance *facilitation.*

With shock intensities lower than those employed in the present study, some facilitation of performance might possibly be obtained for the SR condition. This appears unlikely in view of the fact that threshold for the kind of shock experience provided the Ss is obtained at approximately 30 v. (Campbell & Teghtsoonian, 1958). Thus, any facilitation in performance due to shock for the correct response would have to occur within the relatively narrow range from 30–45 v.

The present results are in striking contrast to those obtained by Muenzinger and his co-workers with both correction and non-correction training procedures. Our findings offer strong support for the view that the primary function of shock is to produce avoidance of the cues associated with it. As Wischner (1947) has indicated, this position does not exclude the possibility that shock may also have the function of slowing down the animal, thus increasing the likelihood of stimulation by and response to the relevant cues, and thereby facilitating performance.

More recently, and primarily on the basis of data obtained in a noncorrection situation, Muenzinger and his co-workers (Muenzinger et al., 1952; Muenzinger & Powloski, 1951) have acknowledged the primary avoidance function of shock. Nevertheless, they (Muenzinger & Powloski, 1951) continue to argue for the accelerating effect of shock for the correct response on the basis of findings, which show that the shock-right condition facilitates performance considerably with a correction procedure but only slightly with a noncorrection procedure. In this connection, the present writers would propose that the "noncorrection" procedure which Muenzinger employed is more comparable to a correction than a noncorrection procedure, as they are typically defined. With Muenzinger's "noncorrection" procedure, S was prevented from retracting following entrance into a choice alley, but the random, left-right positioning of the discriminative stimuli from one trial to the next did not take place until S made a correct response. Thus, as with a correction procedure, S could make several errors or runs to the incorrect goal per "trial," i.e., before the left-right positions of the discriminative stimuli were varied in accordance with their predetermined, random order. It would appear, then, that the inferior performance of the SR groups in the present study, as compared with the relatively better performance of Muenzinger's "noncorrection" shock-right groups, may be related to the degree to which his "noncorrection" method resembles a correction method. This possibility, interestingly enough, has been suggested by Muenzinger and Powloski (1951) in an attempt to reconcile the discrepancy between their results and Wischner's (1947).

Use of either the correction or noncorrection method may underlie the discrepant results obtained with shock for the correct response but this difference does not account for the facilitation of performance which is obtained with one procedure and the retardation obtained with the other. Several explanations of these differences have been offered (e.g., Mowrer, 1950; Prince, 1956; Woodworth & Schlosberg, 1954), but the results of the present study do not contribute to the selection or support of any one of these over another. Rather, the results of this study and those reported more recently by Muenzinger and his associates serve to delimit clearly the generalization, originally proposed by Muenzinger and accepted by many workers in this area, that shock for the correct response facilitates discrimination performance.

Summary

The purpose was to investigate the effect of variation in shock intensity on the acquisition of a black-white discrimination by 56 white rats in a situation involving shock for the correct or incorrect response, a noncorrection procedure, and 2 different training methods (free- vs. forced-choice). Differences in outcome between training methods were negligible. Shock intensity functions showed that errors increased with increasing intensities for shock-right groups, decreased with increasing intensities for shock-wrong groups. All shock-right groups were inferior to no-shock controls, a finding in opposition to the generalization that shock for the correct response facilitates performance.

5   Discrimination performance as affected by problem difficulty and shock for either the correct or incorrect response

Harry Fowler and George J. Wischner

The present study was designed to assess the effect of shock for either the correct or incorrect response on performance in visual-discrimination tasks varying in level of difficulty. The rational for investigating the difficulty-of-discrimination variable stems from one interpretation of the paradoxical facilitating effect of shock for the correct response examined by Freeburne and Taylor (1952). These investigators, suggesting that shock, associated only with the

Reprinted from the *Journal of Experimental Psychology*, 1965, *69*, 413–418 by permission of the senior author and the American Psychological Association. This study was supported in part by Grant No. G-14312 from the National Science Foundation and Grant No. MH-08482 from the National Institute of Mental Health, United States Public Health Service. Grateful acknowledgment is made by the authors to D. Bernstein and N. Ketterle for their assistance in the conduct of this experiment.

[Although most of the research performed by Wischner, Fowler, and their colleagues has served to limit the generality of the principle that punishment of the correct response facilitates discrimination learning, the results of this experiment demonstrate that the phenomenon can occur if (1) the punishment is mild, and (2) the problem is difficult. The most comprehensive review of the experiments relative to this phenomenon, along with theoretical interpretation, is provided by Fowler and Wischner (1969).—Eds.]

correct response, may serve as a differential cue and hence as a secondary reinforcer, trained animals on a task involving shock for
both correct and incorrect responses, a condition precluding any cue
effect of the shock. The finding that this shock-both group performed significantly better than a no-shock group led Freeburne and
Taylor to reject the cue-function interpretation of the facilitating
effect of shock for the correct response and to interpret their data as
supporting a general sensitizing function of shock as originally proposed by Muenzinger (1934).[1] Prince (1956) questioned Freeburne
and Taylor's (1952) results on certain methodological grounds, however, and failed in his experiment to obtain any difference between
shock-both and no-shock groups.

In a very recent study of the effect of various combinations
of food and shock for either the correct or incorrect response, Wischner, Hall, and Fowler (1964), also obtained no difference between
shock-both and no-shock groups. More important was the finding
that a shock-right group, a control absent in both the Prince (1956)
and Freeburne and Taylor (1952) studies, performed significantly
poorer than the no-shock group. This failure to obtain a facilitating
effect of shock for the correct response is in accord with our previous
findings, indicating that shock for the correct response serves only to
retard performance (Wischner, 1947), the extent of this retardation
being greater with increasing intensities of shock (Wischner, Fowler, & Kushnick, 1963).[2]

The present investigation examines further the possibility that
the facilitating effect of shock for the correct response reported by
Muenzinger and his colleagues (Muenzinger, 1934; Muenzinger,
Bernstone, & Richards, 1938) may relate to a possible cue function
of the shock. It is proposed that such an effect might be obtained
with relatively difficult discriminations in which the alternatives, including the discriminative stimuli, are highly similar. Under these
conditions, shock for either the correct or incorrect response may
serve to heighten the discriminability of the alternatives, thereby
delimiting any generalization of secondary reinforcement from the
correct (food-reinforced) goal arm to the incorrect arm, and thus
reducing errors.

[1] [See Selection 2.—Eds.]
[2] [See Selection 4.—Eds.]

Method

Subjects

The Ss for the experiment were 96 naive, male albino rats of the Sprague-Dawley strain, about 100 days old at the start of the experiment. The Ss were caged individually in the experimental room under controlled temperature and an artificially illuminated day-night cycle.

Apparatus

The apparatus was an enclosed T maze with a stem 26 in. long, and each arm, as measured from the center of the choice point, 36 in. long. The height of each section of the maze was uniformly 4½ in. and the width 3¾ in. The initial 8-in. section of the stem was separated from the remaining portion by a guillotine door and served as the start compartment. Guillotine doors were also positioned near the end of each arm, to provide 12-in. goal compartments, and at the entrance to each arm, 3 in. from the center of the choice point, to prevent correction.

Each maze section was constructed of two L-shaped strips of galvanized sheet metal, an exterior supporting shell of wood, painted flat black, and a transparent Plexiglas top. One L-shaped strip of sheet metal served as one wall and half of the floor of the maze section; the other L served as the other half of the floor and the other wall. Together, the two L-shaped strips provided two, 1½-in. floor surfaces which were separated by a ¾-in. gap.

Each goal compartment had a clear Plexiglas food well (¾ in. in diameter × ½ in. deep) and an end plate or wall made of frosted Plexiglas. The frosted, goal-box end plates were visible from the choice point and served as the discriminative stimuli when each was differentially illuminated by a frosted 10-w. bulb located directly behind the end plate in a wooden enclosure painted a flat black.

To effect different levels of problem difficulty, the brightnesses of the two goal-box end plates were varied by operating one of the goal-box bulbs at 120 v. and the other at either 96, 87, 78, or 63 v. These four sets of voltages for the dim and brightly illuminated goal-box end plates provided footcandle ratios of .50, .37, .25, and .12, respectively. Hereafter, reference will be made to these four sets of differential goal-box brightnesses as the Difficult (D), Medium Difficult (MD), Medium (M), and Medium Easy (ME) problem conditions, respectively. Additional illumination, exterior to the maze, was provided by two 10-w. bulbs (120-v. source), one located near the end of each arm on the stem side of the maze.

A matched-impedance shock system consisting of a 60-cps ac source and a series resistance of .3 megohms was used to deliver shock to S in either maze arm. In this shock system, the two L-shaped strips of sheet metal forming the sides and floor of the maze were connected across the output of the transformer; thus, S received shock when it made contact with both halves of the sheet-metal floor. Because of the narrowness of the maze alley, S could not avoid shock by running along only one half of the floor surface.

Shock was delivered to S when it interrupted in either arm, an infrared photoelectric beam crossing the arm at a point midway between its two guillotine doors. A manual priming feature of the shock circuit prevented S from receiving more than one shock in any one trial, even though it was possible for S to interrupt a photoelectric beam several times during a trial. When the shock was delivered, its duration was held constant at .2 sec., as metered through a Hunter timing relay, and its intensity was set at 60 v., as measured across the output of the transformer.

Procedure

The experimental procedure included both pretraining and training phases. One week prior to the pretraining phase, Ss were started, and then maintained for the duration of the experiment, on a daily diet of 12 gm. Purina lab checkers, with water available ad libitum. During this week each S was handled daily for about 3–4 min.

For both the pretraining and training trials, Ss were kept in individual compartments of a hardware cloth detention cage. Prior to their daily run in the maze, which took place during the dark phase of the artificial day-night cycle, all Ss received approximately

5 min. adaptation to the conditions of illumination of the room as provided by the two exterior 10-w. apparatus bulbs.

Pretraining was administered to habituate S to the apparatus and to reduce possible position and brightness preferences. Since the latter would presumably relate to the different brightnesses of the discriminative visual stimuli, the 96 Ss were randomly assigned to four equally numbered groups, each of which was run, during both pretraining and training, under one of the four different problem conditions.

For pretraining, each S received a total of 16 forced, reinforced trials, administered 4 per day and randomly distributed with the restriction that half of the trials were to the left and half to the right, with half of each of these sets being to a bright goal and half to a dim goal. Forcing was accomplished by lowering one of the guillotine doors at the choice point. The reinforcement provided on each trial consisted of P. J. Noyes Formula A rat pellets (4 mm., 45 mg.). On the first of the 4 pretraining days, the food pellets were liberally spread throughout the goal box; on subsequent days, the number and locus of pellets were systematically reduced until, on the last day, two pellets were given only in the goal-box food cup. With each forced trial, S was permitted to run to the available goal where it was detained until all the pellets were consumed or until 5 min. had elapsed. Then, S was removed from the maze and replaced in the carrying cage to await its next trial. On the average, the interval between successive trials within a day was about 15 min., the time required to run a block of Ss.

Training began on the day following termination of pretraining and consisted entirely of free-choice trials. For the training phase, the 24 Ss of each of the four problem-difficulty conditions were randomly assigned to three equally numbered shock subgroups: shock-right (SR), shock-wrong (SW), and no-shock (NS). Shock-right Ss received both shock and food reinforcement for a correct response but neither for an incorrect response; shock-wrong Ss received food reinforcement for a correct response and shock for an incorrect response; the control, no-shock Ss received only food for a correct response.

All Ss received four trials per day for the first 6 days of discrimination training and eight trials per day thereafter. During these trials, food reinforcement, consisting of two pellets, could be obtained only in the bright goal, the right-left position of which was varied throughout training in accordance with a predetermined random schedule. On any training trial, detention time in either the correct or incorrect goal was approximately 10 sec., and the interval between successive trials within a day about 15 min., again the time required to run a block of Ss. Discrimination training was continued until each S met a criterion of 15 correct responses out of a total of 16 free choices with the last 8 being correct, or until a total of 400 training trials had been administered.

Results and Discussion

Group mean errors in blocks of 20 trials are presented in Figure 5.1. The separate panels of this figure provide the mean error scores for the SR, SW, and NS groups within each of the problem-difficulty levels. As shown, mean errors decreased over the course of training

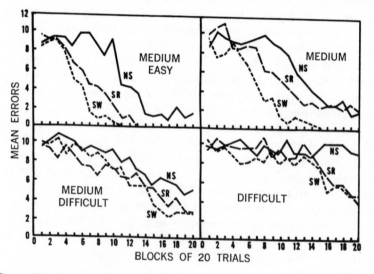

Figure 5.1 Mean errors, per 20 trial blocks, for the shock-right (SR), shock-wrong (SW), and no-shock (NS) groups within each condition of problem difficulty

for all groups except the NS group of the difficult problem. Overall, the rate of error reduction tended to be progressively slower, the more difficult the discrimination task. More important is the fact that, within each difficulty level, both the SR and SW Ss showed more rapid elimination of errors than did the control, NS Ss.

Because of the generally orderly progression of the performance curves for the three shock groups within each difficulty level, only group mean errors for the entire 400 trials were subjected to statistical analysis. These data are presented for the three shock groups in Figure 5.2 as a function of task difficulty. Included in this figure for the "E" or easy problem are data from a previous study (Wischner et al., 1963). The significance of these additional data, presented for comparison purposes, will be considered below.

The results of a 3 × 4 factorial analysis of variance of the data presented in Figure 5.2 for the present study showed that group mean total errors were positively related to level of task difficulty; both the differences among the several difficulty levels and the linear trend in the means for these levels were highly reliable; F (3, 84) = 37.2, $p < .001$ and F (1, 84) = 111.4 $p < .001$, respectively. Residual trends after extraction of the linear component were all non-

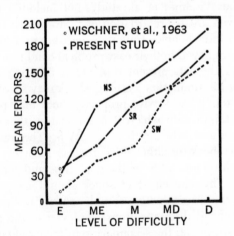

Figure 5.2   Mean errors over the entire 400 training trials for the SR, SW, and NS groups as a function of level of problem difficulty. (The data presented for the "E" or easy problem level are for comparable groups of Ss run in a previous study [Wischner et al., 1963].)

significant, $F < 1$. The overall differences among the three shock conditions were also highly reliable, $F (2, 84) = 16.6$, $p < .001$ and, as indicated by a nonsignificant Shock $\times$ Difficulty Level interaction, $F < 1$, related generally to the range of difficulty levels studied. In addition, separate comparisons, based on the overall error term, showed that the difference between any pair of shock groups was reliable: NS vs. SR, $F (1, 84) = 11.4$, $p < .001$; NS vs. SW, $F (1, 84) = 32.7$, $p < .001$; SR vs. SW, $F (1, 84) = 5.5$, $p < .025$.

In contrast to the data of the present investigation, those presented in Figure 5.2 for the Wischner et al. (1963) study show that the performance of the SR group was retarded relative to that of the NS group. These additional data are for comparable groups of Ss run in the same apparatus under training conditions which, for all purposes, were identical to those employed in the present study, except for the fact that the problem employed was a light-dark discrimination rather than one of the present set of bright-dim discriminations. For this reason, these additional data have been presented in Figure 5.2 as being representative of the effects of shock for either the correct or incorrect response on performance in an "easy" discrimination task. In connection with these data, it should be noted that other data from the Wischner et al. study, not included in Figure 5.2, showed an even greater retardation of performance for SR animals when either a forced-choice training procedure or a higher intensity of shock was employed in their easy problem condition.

In total, the data presented in Figure 5.2 suggest that, within the context of discrimination learning, shock may serve, at least, two functions. Through its aversive property, shock may produce avoidance of the stimuli with which it is associated, thereby increasing errors for SR Ss and reducing them for SW Ss. Through its cue property, however, shock for either the correct or incorrect response may increase the discriminability of the goal arms and thereby facilitate performance. This cue effect of shock should be particularly apparent when the discriminative stimuli are highly similar, as in the case of the difficult discriminations employed in the present study. With this arrangement, the secondary reinforcing effects of the cues present in the correct goal arm may generalize to those in the incorrect arm, to impede formation of the discrimination. But, when shock is consistently administered for one response, both the shock experience, itself, and any fear elicited by it may serve to make the two goal arms more distinctive, thereby reducing the generalization of secondary reinforcement from the correct to the incorrect goal arm and thus reducing errors. In contrast, when the discriminative stimuli are quite dissimilar, as in the simple or easy discrimination, the cue effect of shock should be relatively small, and in the case of the SR condition, possibly be offset or obscured by the shock's aversive or avoidance-producing property.

In view of the present results, and also the fact that Muenzinger and his colleagues consistently obtained facilitation with their SR conditions, certain aspects of Muenzinger's (1934) general procedure are particularly noteworthy. Muenzinger always employed a simple black-white discrimination, but his animals were required, following a correct choice, to run from the positive discriminative stimulus into a gray goal where food reinforcement was obtained. This training procedure would seem to enhance the "difficulty" of the discrimination, in so far as it promotes a temporal dissociation of the positive discriminative stimulus and the food reinforcement, and also affords a greater similarity between the gray goal-box cues associated with food and those present in the incorrect arm. Under these conditions, then, as in the present study, the SR condition could be expected to facilitate performance, since the shock experience, itself, and any fear elicited by it, would serve both to mediate the reinforcing effect of food and to minimize any generalized secondary reinforcing effects of the cues present in the incorrect arm.

Whether the above interpretation may fully account for Muenzinger's results is obviously a matter for additional study of the variables revelant to the problem-difficulty dimension. It should be apparent that, as related to the rate of acquisition of a discrimination, the dimension of problem difficulty may be manipulated by varying the types of factors suggested to be operative in Muenzinger's situation or by varying the similarity of the discriminanda, as in the present study. Aside from these considerations, however, the findings of the present study seem to be of significance for general research in the area. Church (1963) has commented in his recent review of the varied effects of punishment that "an important contribution would be made by the identification of a parameter that would result in facilitation by punishment at some values and inhibition by punishment at other values [p. 388.]" The results of the present study indicate that the dimension of problem difficulty is such a parameter; its isolation now makes possible an assessment of the degree to which other variables may contribute either to the facilitating or disrupting effect of shock for the correct response.

Summary

To assess one interpretation of the paradoxical facilitating effect of shock for the correct response, 12 groups of 8 hungry rats each received visual-discrimination training for food under no-shock, shock-right, and shock-wrong conditions and 4 levels of problem difficulty. Difficulty was manipulated by varying the relative brightness of the discriminanda. Performance was progressively retarded with increasing levels of difficulty. However, with the more difficult discriminations, performance relative to that of the no-shock Ss was facilitated by the shock-right condition and more so by the shock-wrong condition. It is suggested that shock may have both an avoidance and cue function, the latter presumably providing the basis for the finding, obtained for the 1st time in our laboratory, that shock for the correct response facilitates performance.

6   Habit progression and regression — a laboratory study of some factors relevant to human socialization

John W. M. Whiting and O. H. Mowrer

There are many problems in human socialization which involve the principles of learning. One of these concerns the relationship between habits which supplant one another during the life cycle. A number of anthropologists and sociologists (Benedict, 1938; Linton, 1942; Mead, 1930; Parsons, 1942; Whiting, 1941) have pointed out that there are numerous forms of behavior which are considered right and proper during one stage of the life cycle but wrong during

Reprinted in abbreviated form from the *Journal of Comparative Psychology*, 1943, 36, 229–253 by permission of the senior author and The Williams & Wilkins Co., Baltimore, Maryland.

[This study compares three methods of suppression of an instrumental response, (1) extinction, in which the response is no longer followed by reward, (2) blocking, in which the instrumental response can no longer be completed, and (3) punishment, in which a noxious stimulus is contingent upon the response. An alternative response is rewarded under all three conditions. The punishment procedure suppressed the original response more quickly and more permanently than the other procedures. Replications and extensions of this research (Azrin & Holz, 1966; Boe, 1964) support the principle that punishment is particularly successful in suppressing a response if an incompatible alternative response is rewarded.—Eds.]

another stage. For example, in our culture, an infant cries when he is hungry. Later, when he reaches the status of child, this habit is either punished or extinguished; and asking for food supplants it. Still later, when he becomes an adult, he must work for food rather than expect to get it for the asking. Despite the obviously complicated nature of this example, the fact remains that a succession of habits is attached to the hunger drive. A similar series is attached to other drives as well. Infants may eliminate as soon as there is sufficient bladder or colon tension. Children may not do so, but must wait until they have gone to the toilet. Children may physically attack their competitors in the play group; adults, in general, may express only verbal aggression and that only under certain conditions. Thus socialization frequently involves habit progression. It is therefore important to analyze the underlying principles and to determine the way in which they operate.

Habits which have been superimposed upon other habits stand in sharp contrast to those which have been continuously rewarded throughout the life cycle. In the former case, the more recently acquired alternative habit must always compete against an older habit; i.e., there is a constant tendency toward regression. On the other hand, when progression is not involved, there is no such competing tendency and the habit is therefore more stable. Clinical observers in our society have frequently commented on the emotional stress which is engendered by the presence of these regressive tendencies. We have not attempted to study the emotional aspects of such conflicts, but we have explored the habit dynamics involved in situations where there is habit progression and a resulting tendency toward regression.

A number of prior animal studies have dealt with the dynamics of habit progression and regression (Hamilton & Krechevsky, 1933; Kleemeier, 1942; Martin, 1940; Mowrer, 1940; O'Kelly, 1940a, 1940b; Porter & Biel, 1943; Sanders, 1937; and Steckle & O'Kelly, 1940) but none of these has systematically investigated the two problems with which we are here concerned. All workers in this field have recognized that in order to produce habit progression, i.e., in order to induce an organism to give up an originally preferred, or "fixated," adjustment and acquire a new one, it is necessary for the original adjustment to be interfered with in some manner. Various methods of achieving this end have been employed, but these have not been compared in any orderly fashion. Such a comparison is, however, important from two points of view: (1) the ease with which habit progression can be produced, and (2) the likelihood of later regression. In this study one of our two major aims has been, therefore, to compare, both with respect to habit progression and subsequent regression, three methods of interfering with the original habit, *viz.*, the use of non-reward, a physical barrier, and active punishment.

Various incidental observations have suggested that both habit progression and the likelihood of later regression are also influenced by the relative effortfulness of the original and alternate adjustments. If the alternate habit is less effortful than the original one, progression can be easily produced and the chances of regression are relatively slight. On the other hand, if the alternate habit is more effortful than the original habit, progression is comparatively difficult to produce and the chances of regression are proportionately increased. From these facts, it seemed probable that in those situations in which the new adjustment is more arduous than the original one, the difficulty of producing progression and later susceptibility to regression would be positively related to the magnitude of the discrepancy between the degree of effort involved in the two adjustments. With this second problem in mind, we have accordingly employed a dynamic learning situation in which the factor of effort could be controlled and systematically varied, along with the three methods of producing habit progression which have already been mentioned.

Apparatus

The general plan of the elevated maze used in this investigation is shown in Figure 6.1. Placed at the starting point, S, a rat was able to go to the goal, G, by either of two paths. What we shall call the original path, S-O-G, was approximately 5 feet long. Either of three alternate paths could be made available: S-A_S-G, the shortest alternate path, which was 10 feet long; S-A_I-G, the intermediate alternate path, which was 20 feet long; and S-A_L-G, the longest alternate path, which was 40 feet long. All paths were 5 inches wide, with a ½ inch railing on either side. The extent of the elevation above the floor was 3 feet.

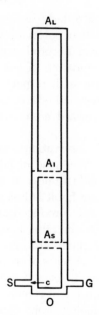

Figure 6.1   Diagram of the elevated maze (viewed from above) which was employed in this investigation. The removable bridges, represented by the dotted lines, were so constructed as to bar entrance to the parts of the maze lying beyond them.

Procedure

In all, 45 young adult albino rats were used in this experiment. At the outset they were randomly divided into 9 groups of 5 animals each. Each group was then randomly assigned to one cell of the diagram shown in Table 6.1. Since all 45 animals could not be run concurrently in this experiment, they were run in sets of 9 animals, each set consisting of one animal randomly selected from each of the 9 cells. However, in the following account of the various steps in the procedure, we shall, for the sake of simplicity, speak as if all 45 animals were run concurrently.

Part I—Fixation on the original path

For a period of one hour on each of the two days preceding the onset of regular training, all animals were allowed to explore that

Table 6.1 Diagram showing the nine different experimental conditions used in this investigation

| Length of alternative path | Method of interfering with original habit | | |
	Non-reward	Barrier	Punishment
Short	SN[a] 5[b]	SB 5	SP 5
Intermediate	IN 5	IB 5	IP 5
Long	LN 5	LB 5	LP 5

[a]SN stands for Short–Non-reward; SB for Short-Barrier; etc.
[b]Five animals were run under each of the nine different conditions.

arrangement of the maze on which they were later to be trained: i.e., for Groups SN, SB, and SP, the alternate path was S-A$_S$-G; for Groups IN, IB, and IP, the alternate path was S-A$_I$-G; and for Groups LN, LB, and LP, the alternate path was S-A$_L$-G. No food was provided at any point in the maze during this preliminary habituation period.

On the first day of regular training each animal was treated as follows: On trial 1, the animal was placed on the maze at G and given a small standardized pellet of moist food (Purina Dog Chow). On trial 2, the animal was placed on path O about one foot from G and then lured to and fed at G. The same procedure was repeated on trials 3, 4, and 5, with the animal being placed approximately one foot further from G and nearer S on each successive trial. On trials 6–15, the animal was placed at S and allowed to go to G, either by the original path or by the alternate path which was open to it, without luring. On the four following days, each animal was likewise given 15 trials, but on these days the animals were always started at S and were never lured. All animals were fed to satiation after each daily training session. They were then deprived of food until the next experimental session, approximately 23 hours later. By the end of the initial 75 trials, all animals had developed a marked (though not perfect) preference for path O and usually ran by this path from S to G in 2 to 5 seconds. On all trials the experimenter recorded the time taken by each animal to go from S to G, the path chosen, and certain incidental observations.

Part II—Progression to alternate path

Following the 5 days of fixation on path O, all animals were given 30 days of training which was designed to make them abandon path O and accept the alternate path which was available to them. Conditions were now such that the animals in Groups SN, IN, and LN received food at G only if they went from S to G via the alternate path. If they went to G via the original path, they received no food and were immediately returned to S by the experimenter. If, on the first day of this new training, an animal had not tried the alternate path after 150 non-rewarded trips to G via the original path, the animal was lured around the alternate path to G, where it now found food. If, after an animal had once been lured to G via the alternate path, it made as many as 10 successive trips to G via the original path, it was again lured to G via the alternate path. On the first day, four animals in Group SN, two in IN, and three in LN had to be lured to G one or more times. On the second day, one animal in Group IN had to be lured to G once, but this procedure was never necessary with any animal after the second day. During this part of the experiment each animal was required to make 15 trips per day to G via the alternate route.

The animals in Groups SB, IB, and LB were physically barred from going to G via the original path during this part of the experiment by means of a square of window glass (which was probably invisible to the rats at a little distance) placed across this path midway between S and G. For the animals in Groups SP, IP, and LP, it was possible to go to G either by the original or by the alternate path, and in both cases they obtained food; but if they selected the original path they received an electric shock from a grill located flush with the surface of the maze midway between S and G. In both the barrier and the punishment groups, if an animal did not reach the goal within five minutes after being released at S, the experimenter attempted to lure it to the goal via the alternate path.[1]

---

[1] The use of luring in this and later parts of the experiment is reminiscent of the use of "instruction" in the socialization of children. By means of symbols we are able to say to a child, "You can solve your problem by doing thus and so." Unable to *tell* our subjects that food would be available to them if they would only go to G via the alternate route, we had to *show* them.

If an animal refused to be lured, it was picked up and carried to G, where it was allowed to eat the available pellet. These special procedures were never necessary, however, after the first few days and were resorted to in the beginning only as a means of preventing an occasional refractory animal from taking a disproportionate amount of time to progress to the alternate path.

During this part of the procedure, an "error" for the non-reward animals consisted of going from S to G via O; for the barrier animals it consisted of touching the glass barrier with any part of the body (including the vibrissae); and for the punishment animals it consisted of receiving a shock from the electrified grill. Running time per trial, route followed, behavior at the choice point, and certain other items were also recorded by the experimenter.

Part III—"Spontaneous" regression

The purpose of this part of the experiment was to determine how the tendency to revert to the original path was related to the length of the alternate path and to the methods which had been employed to produce habit progression. Accordingly, all animals were run 15 trials a day for 5 days under objectively the same conditions as prevailed during Part I, i.e., with all "sanctions" against taking path O withdrawn. This meant that the shock was turned off for the punishment groups, that the glass barrier was removed for the barrier groups, and that food was available at G for the non-reward groups, regardless of whether they reached G by path O or by an alternate path. The data recorded were the same as in Part I.

Theoretical Expectations and Experimental Findings

From the training of infra-human animals both in the laboratory and in everyday life, and from the socialization of children in primitive as well as civilized cultures, a considerable amount of agreement has been reached concerning the basic principles governing the process of learning. These principles generate certain expectations concerning the probable results of the experiment here reported. It is now our purpose to compare these expectations with the results actually obtained.

Part I

As a result of carefully controlled research, as well as common experience, it is known that:

1. Of two or more acts which precede a rewarding state of affairs, that act which is temporally nearest the reward is the most strongly reinforced (gradient of reinforcement); and that

2. Of two or more acts which precede a rewarding state of affairs, that act which involves the least expenditure of effort receives, other things being equal, the greatest amount of *net* reinforcement (law of least effort).

Since the act of turning to the right at the choice point in the maze used in this investigation tended to be more quickly followed by reward than did the act of turning to the left at this point, the first of these principles demands that right-turning at the choice point should be more strongly reinforced than left-turning.[2] And since running from S to G via the original route required less effort than did the running of the alternate routes, the second of these principles demands that the original path should again tend to become dominant, or preferred.[3]

The double expectation thus generated that O would in all cases become the preferred means of going from S to G is confirmed by the findings that in the course of the 75 trials constituting Part I of this experiment, the 15 animals for which the short alternate path was available chose path 0 on 92.0 percent of the trials, the 15 animals for which the intermediate alternate path was available chose path 0 on 95.3 percent of the trials, and the 15 animals for which the long alternate path was available chose path 0 on 97.7 percent of the trials. Since it was possible for the rats, by taking the original path, to reach the goal both more quickly and with less effort, it was obvious that a preference for the original path would develop.[4]

[2] For a more detailed analysis of the role of the gradient of reinforcement in determining preference for one of a number of different routes to the same goal, see Hull (1934a, 1934b).

[3] For discussion of the law of least effort, see Hull (1943), Mowrer and Jones (1943), and Wheeler (1941).

[4] Yoshioka (1929) has shown that in order for rats to develop a reliable preference for one of two paths leading to the same goal, one path must exceed the other in length by at least 10 per cent. In the present experiment, the differential between the original and the alternate paths was in all cases much greater than this.

In the original statement of our reason for using alternate paths of different lengths, we mentioned only the variation in effort which this arrangement would provide. It is clear, however, that with motivation held constant, more *time*, as well as effort, is required by a rat in traversing the alternate paths than in traversing the original path. In other types of experimental situations, the effects of effort and time can be separated, but in the maze here employed this could not be done without unduly complicating the procedure. Henceforth, when we speak of the effects of the greater length of the alternate paths, it will be understood that we include the differential reinforcement introduced by the time factor as well as by the effort factor.

The difference between the short- and the long-path groups is highly reliable, there being less than one chance in 1,000 that such a difference would have been obtained if the "null hypothesis" were valid, i.e., if the length of the alternate paths was of no significance in determining the results. The difference between the long- and intermediate- and the intermediate- and short-path groups are significant at the .04 and .05 levels respectively.

Part II

This part of the experiment involved two major problems: (1) the relation between the ease with which progression from path O to an alternate path could be produced and the amount of effort (and time) required by rats in running the alternate path; and (2) the relation between the ease with which this progression could be produced and the type of "sanction," "tabu," or "discipline" used to interfere with the fixation upon the original path. We shall discuss the former of these problems first.

Let us assume, for the sake of simplicity, that in Part I of this experiment all animals had developed an equally strong and stable fixation upon path O as a means of going from S to G. From the principles which have already been set forth, it follows that if path O were interfered with, the readiness with which an alternate path would be accepted as a substitute would be a function of the amount of net reinforcement provided by the alternate path. In other words, the longer, i.e., the more effortful and the more time-consuming, the alternate path, the less the habit of choosing it would be reinforced each trial and the more slowly would it accumulate strength, or "cathexis." The results shown in Figure 6.2 confirm this expectation. Here it will be seen that the number of "errors" made during this part of the experiment was consistently greatest for the 15 animals for which the alternate path was longest (40 feet), least for the 15 animals for which the alternate path was shortest (10 feet), and intermediate for the 15 animals for which the alternate path was of intermediate length (20 feet). The total number of "errors" made by each of the 45 animals during the 30 days of training constituting Part II of this experiment is shown in Table 6.2.

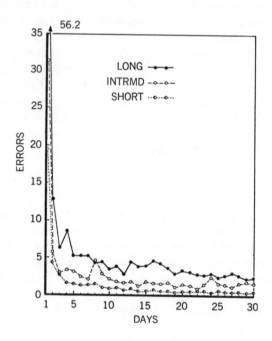

Figure 6.2 Curves showing acquisition of the alternate-path habit as a function of path length. Each point represents the average number of "errors" (see text) made per day by each of three groups of animals, during Part-II training.

The assumption that all animals had had equal practice on the alternate paths at the beginning of the Part-II training is, of course, not strictly accurate. During the Part-I procedure, the animals for which the short alternate path was available took this path an average of 6.0 out of 75 trials (15 trials per day for 5 days), as compared with average scores of 3.5 and 1.7 for the intermediate- and long-path groups, respectively. In other words, at the beginning of Part II, the short-path group had received an average of 2.5 (6.0 − 3.5) more reinforcements per animal on the alternate path than the animals of the intermediate path group, and the intermediate-path group had received an average of 1.8 (3.5 − 1.7) more such reinforcements per animal than those of the long-path group. But a glance at Figure 6.2 shows that the difference between the curves could not be accounted for on the basis of such a small difference in the number of Part-II reinforcements. For example, the animals in the short-path group made fewer errors on the 10th day than the intermediate-path group made on the 30th day, even though the lat-

Table 6.2   Total number of "errors" made by each of 45 animals during the thirty days of training constituting part II of this experiment

Length of alternative path		Method of interfering with original habit		
		Non-reward	Barrier	Punishment
Short		51	28	2
		63	36	2
		67	38	3
		83	56	6
		196	65	8
	Mean	92.0	44.6	4.2
	S.D.	53.0	13.7	2.4
Intermediate		117	41	2
		151	49	3
		180	63	5
		255	85	10
		266	170	21
	Mean	193.8	81.6	8.2
	S.D.	58.1	46.7	7.0
Long		182	60	3
		223	63	4
		402	106	4
		471	162	5
		748	201	13
	Mean	405.2	118.4	5.8
	S.D.	202.4	55.4	3.7

ter had received 300 (15 per day for 20 days) more reinforcements than the former. It is therefore evident that the differences in the three groups, as shown in Figure 6.2, can not be accounted for solely in terms of unequal prior reinforcement but are rather mainly the result of the time and effort factors, as stated above.

It was because of this problem that an attempt, previously described, was made to keep the alternate-path reinforcements received by the three groups during Part-I training as nearly equal as possible. Had it been possible to keep the alternate-path reinforcements strictly constant during Part I, the foregoing discussion would have been unnecessary.

Having thus considered the first major problem involved in this part of the experiment, namely, the relation between the length of the alternate path and the ease with which progression from path O to an alternate path could be produced, we may proceed to the second problem, namely, the relation between the ease with which this progression could be produced and the type of "sanction" used to interfere with the fixation upon the original path. It will be remembered that with the onset of the Part-II training, each of the 45 animals used in this investigation was subjected to one of the nine different experimental conditions described in Table 6.1. We have just examined the results which were obtained when the length of the alternate path was varied and the methods of interfering with the original-path habit were counterbalanced so as not to influence the outcome. We now turn to an examination of the results obtained for the three methods of interference, with length of the alternate path balanced out.

Although there is now good reason for believing that the inhibition of habits through "extinction" involves the same basic principles as inhibition through "punishment" (Mowrer & Jones, 1943), a quantitative difference is involved, i.e., the resulting conflict is more severe in the second case. This fact led to the prediction that the animals in this experiment which were shocked for going to G via the original path would abandon this behavior more quickly than would those which were merely refused reward when they took this path. When an animal went from S to G and failed to find food, the only motivational deterrent to the repetition of this act was the fatigue thus created. But when an animal went from S to G and received shock, a considerably stronger conflict was created, involving *both* fatigue and shock: hence the expectation that the "punishment" animals would abandon path O more quickly than the "non-reward" animals. The curves presented in Figure 6.3 dramatically confirm this expectation.

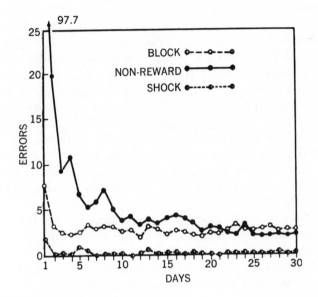

Figure 6.3   Curves showing the acquisition of the alternate-path habit as a function of the method used to inhibit the original-path habit. Each point represents the average number of "errors" made by each of the three groups of animals, during the Part-II training.

The magnitude of the difference between the punishment and the non-reward curves would undoubtedly have been less if the intensity of the shock used with the punishment group had been weaker. Since the intensity of the shock could have been varied downward to zero by any desired series of steps, it should, in fact, have been possible to make the punishment curve approximate the non-reward curve to any specified extent. Why the curve for the barrier group shows better learning during the first 21 days than the non-reward group and then crosses the latter curve is a question which is intriguing theoretically; but since any explanation we might offer here would be largely speculative, we shall postpone dealing with this problem until a later time.

Part III

The results which have just been reported necessarily arouse certain expectations as to what the outcome of the third part of this experiment would be. Any set of conditions under which it is difficult to produce habit progression is likely to be correspondingly conducive to later regression, when the sanctions used in producing the progression are removed. From the previous description of the Part-III procedure, it will be recalled that in this part of the experiment all animals, after completing Part II, were run 15 trials a day for five days under the same conditions as prevailed in Part I. Under the Part-III conditions it was again possible for each animal to go from S to G, without let or hindrance, either by the alternate path which was available or by path O. Food was available at G regardless of the path taken from S to G.

This part of the experiment was designed to test the stability of the alternate-path habit, as a function of the various conditions of the experiment. The analysis consists of a comparison of the effects of differing lengths of the alternate path and of the different types of interference used to inhibit the original path-O habit on the tendency to revert to this habit when all "sanctions" were removed.[5]

The differing lengths of the alternate path should affect the stability of the alternate-path habit. The short-path group should show a more stable alternate habit than the intermediate-path group, and the alternate habit should be more firmly fixed in the interme-

[5] In previous laboratory studies it seems to have been the universal practice to induce regression by means of conflict resulting from the use of electric shock or some other form of "punishment" applied to the subject in connection with the performance of the more recently acquired habit. It will be noted that in the present experiment, we relied entirely upon the factor of effort to produce conflict and the resulting tendency toward regression. The fact that such a tendency is clearly manifested may be taken as further proof that there is a "strain toward inertia" in all behavior, i.e., that there is necessarily present in every act an element of effort, or fatigue, which operates to prevent that act, no matter how satisfying, from becoming perfectly stereotyped, or "fixated." These considerations lead us toward the problem of behavior variability, which has been dealt with in a preliminary way elsewhere (Mowrer & Jones, 1943). They also show that the regression observed in Part III of this study was not, strictly speaking, "spontaneous."

diate group than in the long group. This proposition follows as a corollary from the earlier analysis in which it was shown that, due to the effects of time and effort, the alternate habit was strongest in the short-path group, of medium strength in the intermediate group, and weakest in the long-path group.

The empirical results confirm these expectations. Figure 6.4 shows that the short-path group regressed the least, the long-path group the most, and the intermediate-path group an intermediate amount.

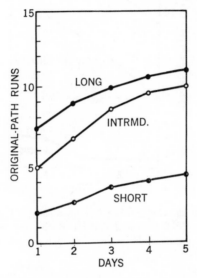

Figure 6.4   Curves showing amount of regression as a function of the length of the alternate-path during the five days of Part-III. Each point represents the average number of regressive (original-path) runs made by the 15 animals in each of these groups.

Similarly, the shock group should regress less than either the non-reward or barrier groups. This follows from the fact that the alternate-path habit was reinforced by food, by escape from shock, and by escape from fear of shock in the former group but only by food in the two others; hence, the alternate habit should be strongest in the shock group and there should be the least amount of regression.

Figure 6.5 shows the differences in the tendency to regress as a function of the method used in producing progression. It can be seen that the shock group regressed markedly less than the other two. That the non-reward group should have shown more resistance

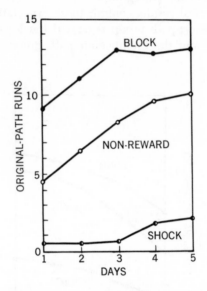

Figure 6.5   Curves showing amount of regression as a function of the type of interference during the five days of Part-III. Each point represents the average number of regressive runs made by the 15 animals in each of these groups.

to regression than the barrier group is presumably related to the crossing of the curves representing these two groups in Figure 6.3. The explanation of this phenomenon is complicated and would take us beyond the scope of this paper.

Discussion

The writers would be the last to maintain that the laboratory investigation which is here reported offers anything like a perfect paradigm of what happens in the socialization of human beings. In fact, one of us has elsewhere (Mowrer & Kluckhohn, 1943) commented at length upon the various ways in which this experiment does *not* parallel the education which both primitive and civilized children receive. However, we believe that in this study we have dealt with certain factors which are inevitably present and operative in the learning dilemmas that human beings have to pass through in order to "grow up" socially and intellectually. And we further believe that the results thus obtained have useful applications and implications if transferred, with due caution, to the human level.

In a sense, the various parts of the experiment parallel the various stages in the human life history. Part I, permitting as it does free access to the goal by the most direct route, parallels the indulgence of infancy—the time when the fewest restrictions are placed by society upon the satisfactions of the infant. Part II, involving interference with previously learned habits, parallels situations which frequently obtain during childhood, when previously learned habits are interfered with by various types of social sanctions and the more indirect habits demanded by society are substituted for them. Part III is more or less comparable to the "age of discretion," i.e., the period during which the individual is "tested" by the withdrawal of many of the external social pressures which were in force in childhood but are supposed to be replaced by good character, or "conscience," in adult life.

Our finding that the ease with which habit progression can be produced is related to the effortfulness of the new adjustment squares well with common experience. This finding suggests the pedagogical maxim that when an original habit, or "fixation," must be interfered with, this end can be most readily accomplished, other things being equal, when a relatively easy alternative adjustment is available.[6] Whether, in circumstances in which there must ultimately be a very considerable discrepancy in the effortfulness of an earlier and a later habit, it is preferable to make the transition abruptly or in small steps is a question which is raised but not answered by our experiment. Our findings also raise certain interesting questions concerning the causes of behavior variability and provide some cues for later research.

[6] Incidental observations made in this study indicate that the longer the alternate path which the animals had to take to their goal, the more "frustrated" they appeared to be. The amount of gnawing on the maze and the number of attempts to "leave the field" (by crawling or jumping off the maze, etc.) were definitely greater in the long-path group than in the other two groups.

The dramatic differences which resulted in this experiment from the use of different methods of interfering with the original habit and thereby producing habit progression again parallel, in a general way, what is known from the training of children. Punishment, such as that provided by the electric shock, is known to be maximally efficient in "breaking" habits, and our results indicate that their inhibitory effects are also most enduring. It is therefore easy to understand the widespread popularity of this method of "discipline." However, if flexibility and capacity to modify behavior with changing circumstances are also regarded as important, the use of punishment appears as a drawback rather than an advantage. As we have seen, those Ss with which shock had been used as a means of interfering with the original habit were slowest to "reality test" (French, 1937; Freud, 1937) and discover that the original habit was again available to them. To the extent that they continued taking a more effortful route to their goal after the original route had become once more available to them, they may be said to have behaved "unrealistically."

As between the use of non-reward and a physical barrier as means of interfering with an original adjustment, it seems clear that, at least under the conditions of this experiment, non-reward is somewhat slower but more permanent in its effects.

Conclusions

1. When rats are free to choose between two routes to the same goal, they develop a preference for the shorter of these routes.

2. This preference is not, however, an all-or-none affair but is a function of the magnitude of the difference in the length of the two routes.

3. Even when this difference is very great (a ratio of 8:1), preference for the shorter path is still not perfect.

4. The tendency for a certain amount of vacillation, or behavior variability, to continue despite very unequal reinforcement raises some fundamental questions which must be further investigated.

5. The ease with which rats can be forced to abandon the shorter of two routes to a goal and accept the longer as a substitute

is inversely related to the discrepancy in the lengths of the two routes.

6. The ease with which rats can be forced to abandon the shorter of two routes to a goal and accept the longer as a substitute is also a function of the method used to interfere with the original habit, punishment (in the form of electric shock) being most effective, a physical barrier next most effective, and non-reward least effective.

7. Although, under the conditions of this experiment, a physical barrier showed an over-all superiority to non-reward as a method of producing habit progression, the non-reward method ultimately surpassed the barrier method.

8. Regardless of the method used to produce habit progression, rats show a tendency in this type of experiment to persist in behavior variability which serves to determine whether the penalty for taking the originally preferred route is "still there."

9. When the "sanctions" used to enforce habit progression are removed, the tendency to revert to the original adjustment is positively related to the degree of difficulty encountered in producing the habit progression.

10. Under the conditions of this experiment, the regression which occurs when "sanctions" are removed is never complete, being inversely related to the level of habit progression which has previously been attained.

11. When regression to the original path is forced, the punishment animals show much greater reluctance to revert to the original adjustment than do the barrier and non-reward animals.

12. The results of this investigation have certain implications for education, mental hygiene, and psychotherapy.

II

Theories of Punishment

Although a number of different mechanisms have been proposed during the past half century or so to explain the behavioral effects of punishment, no theories of punishment have been as fully elaborated as various theories of learning. Instead, admittedly tentative and simple conceptions have been formulated which may constitute the rudiments of more comprehensive and systematic theory. It is perhaps more appropriate to refer to these tentative and simple conceptions as hypotheses rather than theories. For the most part, it has been very difficult to design exeriments which could yield data that support one hypothesis to the exclusion of all others. Major empirical phenomena of punishment can usually be explained equally well by several of these hypotheses. On the more positive side, however, some experimental results are consistent with one group of hypotheses but they cannot be explained by certain alternative hypotheses. The purpose of this section is to trace the historical development of these hypothetical mechanisms of punishment and the concomitant growth of relevant experimental knowledge. The various hypotheses are identified and briefly described below.

The Negative Law of Effect

According to the law of effect formulated by Thorndike in 1913, learning is a reversible process that is strengthened by reward (the positive law of effect) and weakened by punishment (the negative law of effect). Punishment was alleged to produce unlearning (i.e., to undo learned bonds) rather than to produce new bonds or other states that inhibit or interfere with the emission of previously learned responses. In 1932, Thorndike rejected this hypothesis and substituted for it a competing response hypothesis that emphasized competing skeletal responses but also included competing emotional responses. Various types of competing response hypotheses are described below.

The Competing Skeletal Response Hypothesis

A punishing stimulus will elicit unconditioned skeletal responses such as jumping, withdrawal, and freezing that are incompatible with the punished response. Guthrie (1934) proposed that, by the principles of classical conditioning, responses similar to these unconditioned responses may be elicited by external stimuli and by response-produced stimuli that precede the punishment. When these stimuli occur on subsequent occasions, they may elicit the incompatible competing responses which interfere with the originally punished response and thereby reduce its strength. If, however, the reaction to punishment happens to be compatible with the punished response, then the punished response will be strengthened.

The Escape Hypothesis

The escape hypothesis (e.g., Fowler & Miller, 1963) is similar to the competing skeletal response hypothesis in that both emphasize the importance of the reaction to punishment. According to the competing skeletal response hypothesis, reactions to the onset of punishment are learned by the principles of classical conditioning and interfere with the punished response if they are incompatible with it. In contrast, the escape hypothesis states that responses contiguous with the termination of punishment are strengthened by the principles of instrumental learning (i.e., reinforced by escape from the punishing stimulus) and that they interfere with the punished response if they are incompatible with it.

The Fear Hypothesis

As Thorndike observed, punishment can elicit unconditioned emotional reactions as well as skeletal responses. According to the fear hypothesis, as expressed by Skinner (1938) and Estes (1944), punishment results in the conditioning of an emotional response to stimuli present at the time of punishment. Since these conditioned emotional responses are usually incompatible with the punished response, they compete with it and thereby reduce its strength.

The Avoidance Hypothesis

In his 1960 statement of the avoidance hypothesis, Mowrer took the fear hypothesis one step further. Fear becomes conditioned to stimuli present during punishment, particularly to response-produced stimuli. The fear elicited by subsequent tendencies to respond provides an aversive drive which is reduced when alternative instrumental responses, such as withdrawal responses, are emitted. Incompatible responses are thereby reinforced, and the punished response diminishes in strength. The fear hypothesis and the avoidance hypothesis differ in two important ways: (1) the avoidance hypothesis entails a second stage where competing instrumental responses are reinforced by fear reduction, and (2) the avoidance hypothesis attributes considerable importance to the correlation between response-produced stimuli and punishment. Mowrer emphasized the importance of the correlation between response-produced stimuli and punishment in his statement of the avoidance hypothesis, while Estes emphasized the importance of the correlation between environmental stimuli and punishment in his statement of the fear hypothesis. Experimental comparison of the discriminative punishment procedure (wherein a neutral stimulus is presented to signal a period of punishment) and the conditioned emotional response procedure (wherein a neutral stimulus is presented to signal noncontingent aversive stimulation) provides evidence regarding the influence of these two correlations on the magnitude, permanence, and type of response suppression (Hunt & Brady, 1955).

The Discrimination Hypothesis

According to the discrimination hypothesis, punishing stimuli are response-produced cues that change the stimulus complex and tend to alter response rate in the same manner as a nonaversive stimulus. When punishment is introduced for the first time, response rate typically decreases. This might be due, in part at least, to the possibility that punishing stimuli can function as external inhibitors. Furthermore, if punishing stimuli previously have been correlated with nonreinforcement, response rate should likewise decrease. If, however, punishment reinstates conditions of reinforcement, response rate should increase. The research of Holz and Azrin (1961, 1962) demonstrates that punishing stimuli have a cue function, in these respects, as well as an aversive function.

In contrast to the experiments of Part I where erroneous responses were punished during the learning of a correct response, the experiments of Part II concern punishment applied to responses already learned through training with positive reinforcement. This experimental procedure is analogous to the frequent use of punishment as a technique for eliminating undesirable habits in children and pets. It is obvious both from everyday observations and from laboratory experiments that punishment produces an immediate reduction in the strength of punished responses. To be generally useful, however, this immediate suppression of undesirable responses should persist after the punishment conditions have been discontinued. Enduring suppression has been found in a variety of experiments (e.g., Boe & Church, 1967).

7 Two theories of punishment

Edward L. Thorndike

In 1913, Thorndike published the following statement (the law of effect) which set forth his original interpretation of the relationship between reward (the positive law of effect) and punishment (the negative law of effect):

> When a modifiable connection between a situation and a response is made and is accompanied or followed by a satisfying state of affairs, that connection's strength is increased: When made and accompanied or followed by an annoying state of affairs, its strength is decreased. The strengthening effect of satisfyingness (or the weakening effect of annoyingness) upon a bond varies with the closeness of the connection between it and the bond. This closeness or intimacy of association of the satisfying (or annoying) state of affairs with the bond in question may be the result of nearness in time or of attentiveness to the situation, response and satisfying event in question (p. 4). . . . By a satisfying state of affairs is meant one which the animal does nothing to avoid, often doing things which maintain or renew it. By an annoying state of affairs is meant one which the animal does nothing to preserve, often doing things which put an end to it (p. 2).[1]

[This selection was prepared by the editors with the exception of the material quoted from Thorndike.—Eds.]

[1] [Reprinted with the permission of the publisher for Edward L. Thorndike, *Educational Psychology* (New York: Teachers College Press), copyright 1914 by Teachers College, Columbia University. Excerpts from Vol. II, *The psychology of learning.*—Eds.]

This symmetrical and simple conception of learning as a reversible process that is strengthened by reward and weakened by punishment was so compelling and so congruent with evidence from behavioral research that later theorists of punishment usually began by subjecting this hypothesized role of punishment to critical analysis before advancing their own alternative formulations. It is nevertheless interesting that Thorndike was the first to reject the negative law of effect. His experiments (1932a, 1932b) with human subjects that were punished with the word "wrong" for certain responses in a verbal paired-associates task[2] and with chickens that were confined for 30 seconds if they committed an error in a multiple-choice motor task convinced Thorndike that punishment did not weaken learned connections as stated in the negative law of effect. He then revised his interpretation of punishment as follows:

> In the early statements of the Law of Effect, the influence of satisfying consequences of a connection in the way of strengthening it was paralleled by the influence of annoying consequences in the way of weakening it. I now consider that there is no such complete and exact parallelism. In particular, the strengthening of a connection by satisfying consequences seems, in view of our experiments and of certain general considerations, to be more universal, inevitable, and direct than the weakening of a connection by annoying consequences. The latter seems more specialized, contingent upon what the annoyer in question makes the animal do, and indirect (p. 276). . . . An annoyer which is attached to a modifiable connection may cause the animal to feel fear or chagrin, jump back, run away, wince, cry, perform the same act as before but more vigorously, or whatever else is in his repertory as a response to that annoyer in that situation. But there is no evidence that it takes away strength from the physiological basis of the connection in any way comparable to the way in which a satisfying after-effect adds strength to it (pp. 312–313).[3]

In this statement, Thorndike substituted a competing response hypothesis which could include both autonomic and skeletal components for the negative law of effect.

[2] [Reviews of the rather large literature on these conditions of punishment are provided by Hilgard and Bower (1966), Postman (1947, 1962), and Stone (1950).–Eds.]

[3] [Reprinted with the permission of the publisher for Edward L. Thorndike, *Fundamentals of Learning* (New York: Teachers College Press), copyright 1932 by Teachers College, Columbia University.–Eds.]

Even though Thorndike and most subsequent theorists have rejected the negative law of effect, the empirical evidence that is directly against it is not impressive even today. Although relatively weak punishing events like the word "wrong" and confinement for 30 seconds produce little response suppression, stronger stimuli such as painful electric shock produce complete suppression of the punished response if sufficiently intense. It is possible that response suppression when it occurs is wholly or *partly* a function of the mechanism postulated by the negative law of effect.

8   The competing skeletal response hypothesis

E. R. Guthrie

After considering and rejecting the negative law of effect, Guthrie advanced the following truncated version of Thorndike's competing response hypothesis of punishment:

> "The influence upon learning," Thorndike says, "of both satisfiers and annoyers depends upon what they cause the animal to be or do." This is exactly what the writer is suggesting, namely, that the future response to a situation can be best predicted in terms of what an animal has done in that situation in the past. Stimuli acting during a response tend on later occasions to evoke that response (p. 454). . . . It is not the feeling caused by punishment, but the specific action caused by punishment that determines what will be learned. In training a dog to jump through a hoop the effectiveness of punishment depends on where it is applied, front or rear. It is what the punishment makes the dog do that counts or what it makes a man do, not what it makes him feel (pp. 457–458).[1]

Presumably, the punishment-produced responses become conditioned to the cues present at the time of punishment by virtue of their con-

[This selection was prepared by the editors with the exception of the material quoted from Guthrie.—Eds.]

[1] [Excerpts from Guthrie, E. R. Reward and punishment. *Psychological Review*, 1934, *41*, 450–460.—Eds.]

tiguous association, and tend to interfere with the punished response on subsequent occasions. Whereas Thorndike specifically included both autonomic (or emotional) and skeletal responses in his competing response hypothesis, Guthrie specifically denied the relevance of emotional components in his formulation which may be called the competing skeletal response hypothesis. In essence, he asserted that if the reaction to punishment is incompatible with the punished response, that response will be weakened; but if the reaction to punishment is compatible with the punished response, that response will be strengthened.

Other passages in Guthrie's writings (e.g., 1935, p. 165) suggest that the suppressing effect of punishment is not due only to the fact that aversive stimuli may elicit unconditioned responses that are incompatible with the punished response but that the unconditioned response removes the subject from the source of aversive stimulation and is actually rewarded by escape therefrom. On this account, punishment becomes a variety of escape learning, and this interpretation of punishment is called the escape hypothesis. As the next selection by Fowler and Miller indicates, however, it is difficult to distinguish competing skeletal responses from escape responses when punishment of brief duration is used.

9   Facilitation and inhibition of runway performance by hind- and forepaw shock of various intensities

Harry Fowler and Neal E. Miller

A combined facilitating and inhibiting effect of punishment is not typically reported: nevertheless, there are observations along this line. For example, Sheffield (1948) found that, when guinea pigs in an activity wheel received a brief shock while being conditioned to run to a tone, the strength of the conditioned running response on the following trial increased or decreased in relation to whether S had leaped ahead or stopped in response to the shock. Sheffield (1949) also obtained a similar relationship between performance and the manner in which rats initially escaped shock in an obstruction box, i.e., by running forward or backing away.

Reprinted from the *Journal of Comparative and Physiological Psychology*, 1963, 56, 801–805 by permission of the senior author and the American Psychological Association. This study was supported in part by Research Grant M-647 to N. E. Miller from the National Institute of Mental Health, United States Public Health Service. The research was conducted by H. Fowler during his tenure as a United States Public Health Service Predoctoral Research Fellow.
     [This experiment supports Guthrie's view that the effect of punishment depends upon the nature of the response it elicits. Although the authors of the article prefer to interpret their results in terms of the escape hypothesis, they allow for other possibilities such as the competing skeletal response hypothesis.— Eds.]

In a recent study (Fowler, 1963) when hungry rats were trained to run in an alley to food and different strengths of punishment at the goal (0–110 v.) stronger shocks at the goal produced slower running early in training; however, by the end of training, the distribution of speeds for each group of shocked Ss was bimodal, reflecting the acquisition by these Ss of two distinct patterns of performance. Observations of goal-box responses showed that those Ss in the slower half of each shock group tended upon receipt of food to stand with all four feet on the grid through which the shock was delivered, and to lurch back when shocked. These Ss were slowed down by shock, with stronger shocks producing greater decrements in performance. The Ss in the faster half of each shocked group tended, however, to stand with their forepaws off the grid upon receipt of food at the goal and to lurch forward when shocked. With these Ss, all but those of the strongest shock group were speeded up by shock, so that the relationship between performance and strength of punishment was reliably quadratic.

The above data, including those reported by Sheffield (1948, 1949), fit well with S-R reinforcement theory (e.g., Dollard & Miller, 1950; Miller, 1951). Shock for the slow Ss, being delivered to their forepaws, tended to produce a lurching back from the food cup. Reinforced by escape from pain and being incompatible with approach to the goal, this withdrawal response would tend to become anticipatory and thus interfere with running. With the fast Ss, however, shock was delivered only to their hindpaws, causing not a response of withdrawal, but one of lurching forward. Seemingly compatible with approach to the goal and also reinforced by escape from pain, this response of lurching forward would serve to promote faster running.[1]

The above findings, because of their correlational nature, are open to alternative interpretations. For example, if shock, per se, is facilitating at intensities slightly above threshold and aversive at stronger intensities, the obtained performance differences may have resulted from the slow, shocked Ss' receipt of shock on their less calloused and more sensitive forepaws, making the effective intensities for these Ss greater than those for the fast, shocked Ss which received shock only on their hindpaws. To assess these alternative

---

[1] Although a reinforcement interpretation is offered, it should be obvious that the data could also be treated within the framework of contiguity theory.

interpretations and to demonstrate experimentally the previously obtained facilitation and inhibition of performance produced by punishment, the present study manipulated both the type (hind- vs. forepaw) and intensity of shock (0–75 v.) administered at the goal on each trial to hungry rats being trained to run for food.

Method

Subjects

The Ss were 63 naive, male albino rats of the Sprague-Dawley strain, about 100 days old at the beginning of the experiment. The Ss were caged individually in the experimental room where a reversed day-night cycle was artificially maintained.

Apparatus

The Ss were run in a straight alley which was 8 ft. long, 4 in. wide, and 5 in. high (inner dimensions). The alley had a clear Plexiglas top, wooden sides and walls painted a flat black, and a stainless grid floor. The stainless steel rods of the grid were 1/16 in. in diameter and were separated by 3/8 in.

The first seven and the last 11 in. of the alley were separated from the remaining portion by guillotine doors, and served as start and goal compartments, respectively. A triangular Plexiglas food tray (1/2 in. thick, 1 1/2 in. long, 2 in. wide at the base, and tapered to 1/2 in. at the rounded apex) with a recessed concave metal foodwell at the apex, was attached on the grid floor to the far wall of the goal compartment. An unfrosted, 6 w. light bulb was recessed into this wall which was covered completely by a sheet of frosted Plexiglas. Raising of the start-box door operated a microswitch which started a precision timer. When S made contact with the pellet of moist food in the metal food cup, an electronic relay was activated, interrupting the timer and delivering a 60 cps, ac shock for .2 sec. through a .25 megohm resistor to alternate rods of the grid floor. A switching system permitted the shock to be delivered either to the first 7 or last 4 in. of the goal-box grid.

The entire alley was housed in a sound-reducing box (10 ft. long, 3 ft. wide, and 2 1/2 ft. high) constructed of homasote siding and lined with fiberglass insulation. The entire apparatus was supported 1 ft. off the floor of the laboratory by balloon tires which served to reduce building noises.

Procedure

Fifteen days prior to the beginning of training, Ss were started and maintained for the duration of the experiment on a daily wet mash food diet of 12 gm. ground Purina laboratory chow mixed with 12 gm. water. The Ss had continuous access to water in their home cages.

Each S was run during the dark phase of a day-night cycle and for a total of 50 training trials, administered two per day with an intertrial interval of 1½ hr. On every trial, S was placed in the start compartment and, when S oriented toward the goal, the start-box door was raised turning on the timer. The S could then run to the goal to receive a .3 gm. pellet of wet mash composed of equal parts by weight of ground chow and water. When S touched the food pellet, the electronic relay was activated, the timer stopped, and a single shock of a specified voltage was delivered via the grid. The S was removed from the goal box after it consumed the food pellet or after 30 sec. had elapsed and then was returned to its home cage. If, after the opening of the start-box door, S failed to run and touch the food pellet within 350 sec., the trial was terminated. At the end of each trial, S's running time was recorded to the nearest .01 sec. and then converted to a speed score (100/time in seconds). Those Ss which failed to complete a trial within the 350 sec. criterion received a speed score of .29. Approximately 1 hr. after S's second trial for a day, it received its daily portion of wet mash.

Design

For training, the 63 Ss were randomly assigned to seven groups of nine Ss each. The Ss of two of these groups received different intensities of shock at the goal (60 or 75 v.) but only on their hind-paws, i.e., current was delivered to the first 7 in. of the goal-box grid. The Ss of four other groups received different intensities of shock at the goal (30, 45, 60, or 75 v.) but only on their forepaws, i.e., current was delivered only to the last 4 in. of the goal-box grid. The final, control group of Ss received no shock (0 v.) at the goal.

Results and Discussion

Mean speeds for the several groups are presented in Figure 9.1 in blocks of 5 trials over the 50 trials of the experiment. As shown, group performance curves diverged over the course of training and approached different asymptotic levels. By the end of training, the hindpaw shock Ss were running faster and the forepaw shock Ss slower than the no-shock Ss. Group mean speeds for the forepaw shock Ss were also slower, the greater the intensity of shock these Ss received.

The obtained relationship between speed and both type and intensity of shock is more clearly evident in Figure 9.2, where group mean speeds over the last 20 training trials are presented as a function of goal-shock intensity. Both the faster speeds of the hindpaw shock Ss and the slower speeds of the forepaw shock Ss were positively related to goal-shock intensity. Because of the orderly progression of the performance curves over training (see Figure 9.1), only these data over the last 20 training trials were subjected to statistical analysis.

Analysis of variance of group mean speeds over the last 20 training trials shows that the overall differences among the groups are highly reliable ($F = 5.17$, $df = 6/56$, $p < .001$). However, when separate analyses are performed comparing the no-shock Ss with either the hind- or forepaw shock Ss alone, only the differences among the no-shock and hindpaw shock groups are significant ($F = 7.17$, $df = 2/24$, $p < .005$). Trend analysis of these data for the 0 through 75 v. hindpaw shock Ss shows further that speeds for these groups were positively related to shock intensity; the linear trend in the means is highly reliable ($F = 13.74$, $df = 1/24$, $p < .005$), with residual trend components being nonsignificant ($F < 1$).

Comparison of the no-shock and 75 v. forepaw shock groups alone shows that the difference between them is significant ($F = 6.54$, $df = 1/16$, $p < .025$), even though both the overall differences among the 0 through 75 v. forepaw shock groups and the trends in the data are not. These nonsignificant overall differences, being due in part to relatively large within-group variability for the weaker of

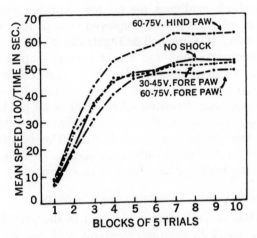

Figure 9.1   Group mean speeds for the no-shock and hind- and forepaw shock Ss in blocks of 5 trials over the 50 trials of the experiment. (The means for the 60 and 75 v. hindpaw Ss, for the 30 and 45 v. forepaw Ss, and for the 60 and 75 v. forepaw Ss have been combined in order to reduce the cluster of curves.)

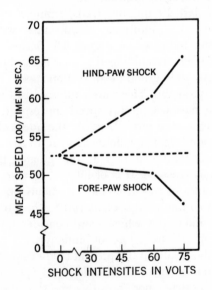

Figure 9.2   Group mean speeds over the last 20 trials as a function of both type (hind- vs. forepaw) and intensity of shock

the forepaw shock conditions, are not too surprising. Since 30–45 v. from the type of shock source employed is at or near the average threshold for Ss (cf. Campbell & Teghtsoonian, 1958),[2] small individual differences in threshold would tend to amplify between S variability in running speed under these weak shock conditions. Moreover, forepaw shock Ss may have occasionally avoided the shock by raising their forepaws off the grid or by placing them on the food cup, even though the triangular shape and floor location of this cup was designed to preclude such. This possibility would also account for the small, albeit significant, difference obtained between the no-shock and 75 v. forepaw shock groups.

The "Approach" Gradient Produced by Punishment

The facilitation of performance obtained in the present study for the hindpaw shock Ss contrasts markedly with the inhibition and underlying avoidance gradient typically produced by punishment at a goal (e.g., Karsh, 1962; Miller, 1959). For this reason an attempt was made in the present study to assess the possible gradient of facilitation produced by punishment.

Over the last 10 training trials, running speeds were also recorded (by means of additional photobeams) within the successive alley sections indicated in Figure 9.3. Because of the nonsignificant overall differences obtained among the 0 through 75 v. forepaw shock groups, only group mean section speeds for the hindpaw shock Ss were considered. These are expressed in Figure 9.3 as percentages of the no-shock group speed in respective sections. As shown, the section-speed ratios between the no-shock and the hindpaw shock Ss were larger the closer Ss were to the goal, with these "approach" gradients being higher, the greater the intensity of hindpaw shock Ss received. It is of interest to note that these data are inverted images of the avoidance gradients obtained by Karsh (1962) for comparable groups of Ss run in the same apparatus to food and shock intensities which were considerably stronger (75–300 v.), but not specific to S's fore- or hindpaws.

In total, the results of the present study cannot be interpreted in terms of a facilitating effect of mild shock, per se. Even though S's forepaws are perhaps more sensitive and thus the effective shock

---

[2] [See Campbell and Masterson (1968) for more extensive research on the behavioral effects of electric shock.—Eds.]

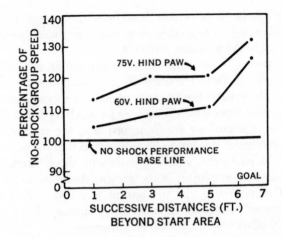

Figure 9.3 Group mean section speeds for the 60 and 75 v. hindpaw shock Ss over the last 10 trials, expressed as percentages of the no-shock group speed in respective alley sections. (Section speeds were recorded within successive 2 ft. distances beyond the start area—first 12 in.—and within the goal area—last 12 in.)

intensities for 60–75 v. forepaw shock Ss greater than those for hindpaw Ss, the performances of 30–45 v. forepaw shock Ss certainly do not suggest any facilitation with weaker shock intensities. Hence, the present results would seem to indicate that the facilitation or inhibition of performance produced by punishment relates to the nature of the response which is elicited by shock and conditioned to the cues of the situation.

In accord with observations noted previously (Fowler, 1963), hindpaw shock tends to elicit a response of lurching *forward,* and forepaw shock one of lurching *back.* Seemingly compatible with approach to the goal and reinforced by escape from pain, the response of lurching forward would serve, through its anticipatory occurrence, to promote faster running; conversely, the response of lurching back, also reinforced by escape from pain but incompatible with approach to the goal would tend to interfere with running. It seems plausible that the former effect might also be attributed in part to response generalization, with reinforcement of the response of lurching forward tending to strengthen further the similar response of running forward; or, perhaps to the tendency on the part of the hindpaw shock Ss to lurch forward as they approach the goal, in contrast to no-shock Ss which presumably slow down to avoid bumping into the back wall of the goal compartment.

The present results also indicate that, within the limits tested, the magnitudes of the conditioned effects of hind- and forepaw shock are greater, the greater the intensity of shock S receives and thus the strength of pain from which it escapes by lurching forward or back. While these relationships are in accord with the reinforcement interpretation offered, it is not to be anticipated that the effect of hind-paw shock, in particular, will be greater with shock intensities much higher than those employed in the present study. As suggested previously (Fowler, 1963), the strength of fear and consequent tendency to "freeze" conditioned under more intense shock conditions could easily offset any facilitation of performance.

Summary

Correlational data from several studies indicate that a punished act may be facilitated or inhibited depending on the nature of the response elicited by punishment. To demonstrate these effects experimentally and to assess alternative interpretations of them, 63 hungry rats were trained to run down an alley to food and different intensities of hind- or forepaw shock (0–75 v.) at the goal. The hindpaw shock Ss were speeded up and the forepaw shock Ss slowed down, with these effects being generally greater, the greater the shock intensity. These results fit well with drive-reduction theory in that responses elicited by hind- and forepaw shock and reinforced by escape from pain tend to be compatible and incompatible, respectively, with running.

10   Negative conditioning and periodic reinforcement

B. F. Skinner

The procedure of periodic reconditioning is also valuable in studying the hypothetical case of "negative conditioning" discussed in the
preceding chapter. In experiments now to be described the form of
negative reinforcement[1] used was a sharp slap to the foot or feet
used in pressing the lever, delivered by the lever itself in the course
of being depressed. The apparatus consisted of an electrically oper-

[As noted earlier, Thorndike abandoned the negative law of effect in favor
of a competing response theory of punishment that included both competing
emotional and skeletal responses. Guthrie subsequently denied the relevance of
competing emotional responses and attributed the entire behavioral effect of
punishment to competing skeletal responses. In contrast to Guthrie, Skinner
proposes that emotional consequences of punishment mediate its effect. According to Skinner, punishment results in the conditioning of a temporary emotional response to "the lever itself and incipient movements of pressing the
lever," which interferes with the punished response and thereby depresses its
rate. This interpretation of punishment may be called the fear hypothesis.—Eds.]

[1] [In terms of current usage, the word "punishment" should be substituted
for the phrase "negative reinforcement" throughout this selection. Skinner
(1953), as well as others, now refers to the operation of response contingent
termination of aversive stimulation as negative reinforcement. Punishment refers to response contingent *onset* of aversive stimulation.—Eds.]

ated double hammer striking upward against the two shafts of the lever behind the panel. The slap could be administered or omitted at will. Since a rat presses the lever with nearly the same force each time, the effect of the slap given by the sudden upward movement of the lever was relatively constant and was therefore to be preferred to an electric shock, which is the commonest form of negative reinforcement. The only stimulation in addition to the slap arising from the apparatus was a fairly loud click.

The first experiment concerns the effect of negative reinforcement upon extinction. Extinction curves after periodic reinforcement with food were obtained from four rats. On the third day the slapper was connected for the first time at the end of twenty minutes, and all responses made during the rest of the hour and on the following day were negatively reinforced. On the fifth day the slapper had been disconnected, and on the sixth and seventh the response was again periodically reinforced with food.

The results are shown in Figure 10.1. The first effect was an immediate strengthening of the reflex. A second quick response followed the first slap, and for the next two or three minutes a relatively rapid responding in the face of sustained negative reinforcement was observed. A second quick response was found to be the rule in some exploratory experiments in which a shock strong enough to cause a violent jump was administered, and in general an initial strengthening of the reflex is clearly indicated. This phase was followed by practically complete suppression. On the following day only a few scattered responses occurred and were negatively reinforced with the slap. On the next day (Day 6 in the figure) no responses were negatively reinforced, but *a very low rate was nevertheless maintained.* When the response was later reconditioned, the rate rose very much as in original periodic reconditioning.

Figure 10.1 suggests that a reduction in the size of the reserve of the reflex was brought about by the slap, such as might be expected if there were a process of negative conditioning exactly opposed to that of positive conditioning, in which each negative reinforcement subtracted a number of responses from the reserve. According to this view the low rate on the last day of extinction, when there was no negative reinforcement, was due to the emptiness of the reserve and was comparable with the rate at a much later stage of ordinary extinction. It will be seen in the experiments that follow

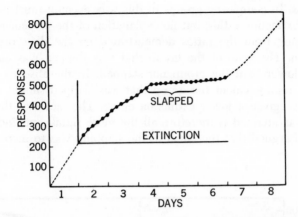

Figure 10.1   Effect of negative reinforcement upon the extinction curve. The extinction curve is the solid line. The part during which all responses were slapped is indicated. There is little or no recovery on the last day of extinction without slaps. The dotted lines give the slopes under periodic reinforcement.

that this conclusion is unjustified and that a conditioned emotional state is probably responsible for the suppression of activity on the last day of extinction in this experiment. The present interpretation is inconclusive for two reasons: (1) the use of the slapper was so prolonged that the emotional state could become almost maximally conditioned, and (2) the responses occurring on the last day without the slap were too few to permit an adequate extinction of this effect.

In an experiment in which the negative reinforcement was brief and the chance for extinction of an emotional effect increased, no reduction in reserve was discovered. Two groups of four rats each with no previous experience with the slapper were periodically reconditioned for three days. The reflex was then extinguished in both groups for two hours on each of two successive days. In one group all responses were slapped during the first ten minutes of the first day.

The result is shown in Figure 10.2. The effect of the slap in depressing the rate is obvious, but a full recovery when the negative reinforcement is withheld is also plain. At the end of the second day the two groups had emitted practically the same mean number of responses. In comparing groups in this way account must be taken of their extinction ratios, but no explanation of the present result is forthcoming from the ratios demonstrated on the days preceding extinction. The ratio of the group that was slapped was about 25 percent lower than the group not slapped. In the absence of any negative reinforcement the group that was slapped should accordingly have given a lower extinction curve. The fact that the same height was attained is therefore all the more significant; indeed, it might be argued that the effect of the slapping was to increase the reserve.

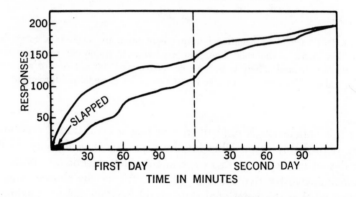

Figure 10.2   Effect of negative reinforcement upon extinction. The two curves are from groups of four rats each, with the same experimental history. All responses made by one group during the first ten minutes of extinction were slapped. The rate is depressed for some time but eventually complete recovery is made.

Figure 10.2 must lead us to revise the conclusion based upon the preceding figure. It is true that there is a temporary suppression of responses, but all responses originally in the reserve eventually emerge without further positive reinforcement. Such an effect is, by definition, emotional. It is an effect upon the relation between the reserve and the rate, not upon the reserve itself. In this experiment there is no evidence whatsoever for a process of negative conditioning directly the opposite of positive conditioning. The behavior of the rat, on the other hand, is quite in accord with the assumption that the slap establishes an emotional state of such a sort that any behavior associated with feeding is temporarily suppressed and that eventually the lever itself and incipient movements of pressing the lever become conditioned stimuli capable of evoking the same state. The effect was not clearly shown in Figure 10.1 for reasons already given.[2]

[2] [See Skinner (1953) for an extension of his views on punishment to human behavior.—Eds.]

11   An experimental study of punishment

William K. Estes

I. Introduction

The setting

It is a matter of everyday observation that a response which is followed by a disturbing or traumatic stimulus will tend to be weakened in strength and to be less likely to occur on subsequent occa-

Reprinted from *Psychological Monographs*, 1944, 57 (3, Whole No. 263) by permission of the author and the American Psychological Association. This monograph is a revision of a doctoral dissertation submitted to the graduate faculty of the University of Minnesota in June, 1943.
[The results of this widely cited research are usually interpreted as support for the fear hypothesis. In addition to replicating Skinner's major experimental finding of complete compensatory recovery under one condition (Experiment A), Estes produced evidence for the conclusion that most of the fear conditioning occurs to environmental stimuli and little to response-produced stimuli. A direct implication of this conclusion is that punishment does not have to be correlated with an operant response, but only with stimuli that provide the occasion for that response. Under most conditions, however, complete compensatory recovery from the suppressing effects of punishment did not occur, and under some conditions greater response suppression was produced when aversive stimulation was contingent upon responding than when it was not (Experiment L). Although rejecting the negative law of effect, Estes describes some mechanisms of response suppression, such as competing skeletal responses based upon escape from shock, in addition to the fear hypothesis.—Eds.]

sions. In his original formulation of the law of effect, Thorndike stated that an annoying after-effect exerts a weakening effect upon the punished stimulus-response connection. As a general descriptive principle, this statement has never been seriously questioned. Most experimenters have found that punishment for "errors" in learning situations tends to improve performance (Barlow, 1935; Bernard, 1941; Bernard & Gilbert, 1941; Bunch, 1928, 1935; Bunch & Hagman, 1937; Bunch & McTeer, 1932; Crafts & Gilbert, 1934; Dodson, 1932; Jenson, 1934; McTeer, 1931; Ni, 1934; Valentine, 1930; Vaughn & Diserens, 1930; Warden & Aylesworth, 1927; Warden & Diamond, 1931; Wood, 1934).[1] Likewise, in the classical conditioning situation, it has been shown that a conditioned response is weakened by punishment (Brogden, Lipman, & Culler, 1938).

Although the general tendency for punishment to weaken a response has been clearly established, the specific mechanism through which it acts has been a matter of dispute for more than a decade. As a result of a long series of experiments, Thorndike has revised his original formulation, and now believes that an annoying after-effect of a connection does not exert a direct weakening comparable to the strengthening effect of a reward; when a response appears to have been weakened by punishment, it is only because the organism has been forced to learn some alternative response to the situation (Thorndike, 1935). Unfortunately, however, the evidence on which Thorndike has based this conclusion is not entirely unequivocal; he has generally used very mild "punishments" (frequently mere lack of reward) and has dealt only with complex situations involving many alternative responses. Although Thorndike's revised formulation has been generally accepted, several recent investigators have produced evidence favoring the original law of effect (Brown, 1937, 1939; Stephens, 1934, 1940). Hilgard and Marquis (1940) summarize the present status of the problem as follows:

> The action of punishment is a subject urgently needing additional research. It is not clear at present whether inhibition by punishment can be accounted for in terms of interference from responses established by the noxious stimuli or whether it represents a different and independent form of inhibition (p. 126).

[1] [Part I on the role of punishment in discrimination learning is largely devoted to the punishment of errors.—Eds.]

The problem

The first question to be investigated in the present study will be the effects of punishment upon the dynamic properties of the punished response. As we have already noted, it is well known that a response can be weakened in strength as a result of an annoying after-effect regardless of the mechanism involved. But it remains to be determined whether the weakened response is actually eliminated from the organism's repertoire by punishment, or merely suppressed and capable of being released at its full original strength after punishment is discontinued. An exploratory investigation of negative reinforcement reported by Skinner (1938)[2] favors the latter possibility. And the clinical psychologist has long been aware of the significance of behavior which is prevented from occurring overtly ("repressed") because of its consequences, but which continued to exist in the organism's repertoire at a considerable state of strength. A number of the experiments which will be reported on the following pages deal with the changes in strength of a single isolated response produced by various combinations of positive and negative after-effects.

In the second portion of the investigation we shall be concerned with the clarification of the mechanism of action of punishment by means of an experimental analysis of the functional interrelationships of the variables operating in situations involving punishment.

After the derivation of the empirical principles governing the action of punishment upon a single response, an attempt will be made to determine whether additional principles will be required to account for the effects of punishment in more complex situations.

A note on method

The results of an experiment can be evaluated only in the light of the measures which have been taken to ensure functional isolation of the variables under consideration. The only completely satisfactory method of achieving such isolation is control of irrelevant variables. However, psychologists have frequently been unable to secure

[2] [See Selection 10.—Eds.]

satisfactory control of experimental conditions and have resorted to
the use of large numbers of subjects in the hope that the effects of
uncontrolled factors would tend to average out. In the present study
it has been necessary for several reasons to rely principally upon
experimental control. It appeared likely that many important quantitative properties of punishment would be revealed only under conditions of rigorous experimental isolation of the behavior studied.
And in order to investigate the relatively permanent effects of
punishment under varying conditions it was necessary to obtain a
large number of responses from each subject over a considerable
period of time, a procedure which was for practical reasons incompatible with the use of a large number of subjects.

In addition to the techniques of experimental control, which
will be described in detail later, the general design of the investigation and the statistical analysis of the data are pertinent to an evalu-
ation of the results. The various experiments described are "inter-
locking" in character, so that nearly every conclusion drawn from
the entire study is supported by the results of at least two different
experiments. Wherever feasible, statistical tests of significance, usually Student's "t" test, have been applied. It has been assumed that
whenever the probability attaching to the value of "t" yielded by
two sets of measures is less than 0.05 the possibility that the observed
difference is due solely to sampling errors can be safely disregarded.

Subjects and apparatus

The subjects in all of the experiments to be reported were albino rats
from the Minnesota laboratory stock. The groups of animals used in
different experiments varied somewhat with respect to age, sex, and
genetic history. Within each experiment, however, the experimental
and control groups have been equated with respect to all of these
factors.

The apparatus used has been described in detail by Heron
and Skinner (1939). During each experimental period each rat was
enclosed in a light-proof and nearly sound-proof box containing a
retractable lever which could easily be depressed and a magazine
which could be set to reinforce responses to the lever by releasing
small (0.05 gr.) pellets of food into a food tray at one end of the
box. A curve, number of responses vs. time, was recorded kymo-

graphically for each rat. An electric shock, the "punishment" in these experiments, could be delivered by a condensor through the wire grid which formed the floor of the experimental cage. The duration of the shock was but a fraction of a second. The tone used in one experiment was produced by phones attached to a sixty cycle AC transformer.

General procedure

While on an experimental routine, the animals were always fed dry Purina dog food for one hour immediately after the day's experimental session. Experimental periods were one hour long except where otherwise specified. Water was available in the living cages at all times. It was not possible to control the temperature of the living quarters completely; therefore comparisons of results of different experiments have been made only in cases where temperature variations could safely be assumed to be inconsequential.

The lever-pressing response is routinely conditioned under the following procedure. The rat is first placed in the experimental box for a one-hour period during which food pellets are periodically released by the magazine and the rat learns to respond promptly to the click of the magazine by approaching the food tray and seizing the pellet. On the day of conditioning, the rat is again placed in the box; the lever is now present and connected with the magazine so that responses to the lever will be reinforced with food. When, in the course of exploratory activity, the rat "accidentally" moves the lever, a pellet of food is released into the food-tray, and typically the rat soon comes to respond at a constant rate. It should be noted that any movement which results in depression of the lever counts as a response. Most rats form the habit of rising and striking the lever with the fore-paws.

After preliminary conditioning, each rat was given several hours of periodic reinforcement before being used in an experiment. Under this procedure, a control clock is set to reinforce single responses to the lever every four minutes, intervening responses going unreinforced. Except where specified otherwise, the preliminary training of all rats used in the following experiments consisted of initial conditioning and two or three hours of periodic reinforcement (just enough to produce a stable rate of responding).

Symbolic notation

The following notation will be used throughout the paper. R, response; S, stimulus; S^D, discriminative stimulus; S^R, reinforcing stimulus; S^P, disturbing or traumatic stimulus; $\overline{x}_E$, mean number of responses for experimental group during a given period; $\overline{x}_C$, mean number of responses for control group during a given period; "t", Student's "t-ratio", i.e., the ratio of a mean difference to an estimate of its standard error; P_t, the probability that a value of "t" as large as that observed would occur in a random sampling distribution; N, number of subjects; Pr., periodic rate (in terms of number of responses per hour); T_{1-x}, total number of responses during the first x experimental periods.

II. Basic Experiments

Outside of the laboratory, punishment occurs in two general types of situation. In the first, the punishment results mechanically from every occurrence of the response during the lifetime of the organism (e.g., the negative reinforcement produced by touching a hot radiator). In the second, punishment is administered, usually through the mediation of another organism, for making some specific response during a limited period of time (e.g., punishment of a child for going into the street). Since the former situation involves no peculiar theoretical problems, only the latter, and probably more general, case will be subjected to experimental study.

In the practical control of behavior, reward is usually discontinued when punishment is administered; however, in some instances, this is difficult or impossible (e.g., in the punishment of criminals), so both conditions will be considered in this chapter.

Section 1. The effects of varying conditions of punishment of a response upon the course of subsequent extinction

The experiments to be described in this section were designed to provide at least partial answers to these questions:

1. What are the effects of punishing a response upon the course of subsequent extinction?

2. To what extent are these effects a function of the conditions of punishment and the initial strength of the response?

    In the first situation to be considered, a response which was previously positively reinforced is punished during a limited period of time, then during subsequent periods is neither punished nor reinforced. Some of the problems which arise are illustrated by the diagram in Figure 11.1. Let us assume that two groups of animals have been positively reinforced for emitting some specific response and that they have attained equal mean rates of responding under periodic reinforcement as shown on Day 1 in Figure 11.1. Then, beginning on the following day, reinforcement is discontinued for the control group and all responses go unreinforced thereafter. Skinner's studies (1938) show that the rate of responding during subsequent periods will decline regularly for this group in a negatively accelerated curve and will continue to decline until a permanently low rate (slightly above zero) is reached and the response is said to be

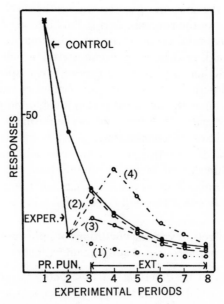

Figure 11.1   Paradigm of possible effects of a single period of punishment upon the course of subsequent extinction

extinguished. That is, effectively it is no longer a part of the organism's repertoire.

Now let us turn to the experimental group. On Day 2 (Figure 11.1) the experimental animals are severely punished for each response and the rate quickly falls to nearly zero. Superficially, it appears that by the use of punishment a state of extinction of the response has been reached in one day which required more than eight days for the control group under conditions of simple non-reinforcement. But in the case of the experimental group is the strength of the response at the end of Day 2 a reliable index of the true state of its dynamic properties? That is, if these rats are returned to the situation on subsequent days as were those of the control group, will the rate of responding (1) continue at a low value; (2) rise immediately after the termination of punishment to the rate which would have obtained if no punishment had been administered; (3) recover gradually on subsequent days until at some later point the curve rejoins that of the control group; or (4) during recovery rise above the rate of the controls for a time so that the total number of responses occurring during extinction is equal to that which would have appeared if no punishment had been administered?

Only if alternative (1) proves to be correct will we be able to conclude that punishment accelerates the process of extinction of a response from an organism's repertoire. Any other result will indicate that punishment results in a suppression rather than an elimination of behavior. The other possible continuations do not affect the total amount of time required for extinction, and differ among themselves chiefly in the extent of reduction in the total number of elicitations of the response necessary for extinction.

Experiment A. Effects of Mild Punishment upon Extinction

Throughout the present study, the severity, or intensity, of the punishment is judged by its momentary effect upon the animal's behavior. In the present stage of our knowledge, physical measures of the intensity of a negatively reinforcing stimulus have relatively little psychological meaning. Two widely separated intensities of shock are studied in this investigation. The "mild" punishment is a shock just strong enough to produce a reliable depression in the rate of responding and not strong enough to produce complete inhibition of the response, even when continued for an hour or more. The "severe" punishment is a shock which results in a decline in rate of responding to virtually zero within a few minutes. The following experiment investigates the effects of a short period (15 minutes) of mild punishment.

Subjects and procedure. The subjects, sixteen male rats, were divided into an experimental and a control group of eight rats each after preliminary conditioning and periodic reinforcement. On the first day of the experiment proper, both groups received one hour of extinction of the pressing response. From the fifth through the twentieth minutes of this period, the experimental animals were punished for responding. The condensors were connected in circuit with the levers and the grid floor of the experimental boxes so that when the condensors were set, depression of the lever released a shock through the grid. During the fifteen-minute period of punishment, the shocking apparatus was reset every thirty seconds.[3] Thus, not all responses were punished, but many were. A second hour of extinction without punishment was given both groups twenty-four hours after the first and a third forty-eight hours after the second.

Results. The course of the experiment is shown graphically in the left hand panel of Figure 11.2, and the quantitative results are summarized in Table 11.1. It will be noted that the experimental rats had a somewhat higher mean periodic rate than the controls.

The immediate effect of the shock was a gradual decrease in rate of responding. By the end of the interval of punishment, the rate for the experimental rats had dropped considerably below that of the controls. After termination of the shock, the strength of the response began to recover within a few minutes, and by the end of the hour was about equal to that of the controls. These effects are illustrated by a mechanically averaged kymograph record for four of the experimental rats reproduced in Figure 11.2a. The two groups produced about the same numbers of responses on the second day of extinction; on the third day the experimentals exceeded the controls by an amount sufficient to compensate fully for the deficit incurred on the day of punishment.

The higher periodic rate of the experimental rats indicates that they probably had a slightly higher average motivational level

---

[3] [This is an intermittent punishment procedure. Skinner (Selection 10) used continuous punishment (i.e., each lever press was punished).—Eds.]

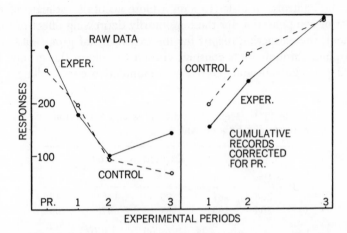

Figure 11.2 Effects of a short period of mild punishment upon extinction. Punishment was administered to the experimental rats from the fifth to the twentieth minute of Period 1. The left hand panel shows the mean periodic rates and extinction records in terms of the raw data; in the right hand panel the mean extinction curves have been corrected for differences in periodic rate and plotted cumulatively (Experiment A).

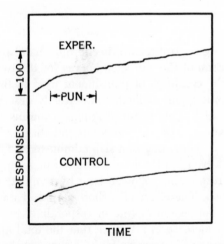

Figure 11.2a Reproduced from photostatic copies of mechanically averaged kymograph records of four experimental and four control rats for Period 1. The interval during which the experimental animals were punished is indicated (Experiment A).

than the controls. In order to gain a more accurate estimate of the extent of compensation for the temporarily depressing effect of punishment, the extinction record for the experimental group has been multiplied through by a constant chosen to equate the groups for initial periodic rate and plotted as a cumulative curve, along with

Table 11.1   Mean periodic rates and extinction records for Experiment A

		Extinction periods			
	Pr.	1*	2	3	T
$\bar{x}_E$	308	181	99	145	425
$\bar{x}_C$	264	198	97	67	362
t		.34	.06	3.02	
P_t		.72	.90	.01	

*During the fifteen-minute interval of punishment in Period 1, the mean number of responses for the experimental group was 45, of which 9.25 were punished; the corresponding value for the control group was 58 responses.

the corresponding control record, in the right hand panel of Figure 11.2. A comparison of the corrected curves for the two groups indicates that for the condition of punishment used in this experiment, the course of subsequent extinction is correctly described by Curve (4) in Figure 11.1. This result strikingly confirms an experiment reported by Skinner (1938). Skinner found that a short period of mild punishment (consisting of a slap administered to the rat's forepaws by a "kick-back" of the lever) resulted in a temporary depression in rate of responding followed later by complete compensation.

Conclusion. The effect of a short period of mild punishment is a temporary depression in rate of responding, followed later by a compensatory increase in rate such that the total number of elicitations of the response necessary for complete extinction is equal to that which would have been required if no punishment had been administered.

Experiment B. Effects of a Short Period of Severe Punishment upon Extinction

The interval of punishment used in this experiment was just long enough to allow the mean rate of responding of the punished animals to drop to virtually zero. Judged by its effect upon the momentary behavior of the rats, the shock was distinctly more severe than that used in Experiment A. This intensity was held constant throughout the remainder of the investigation, since it appeared that important properties of punishment would be revealed more clearly at high intensities.

Subjects and procedures. Nineteen rats were subdivided as follows after preliminary training:

Group	N
Part 1	
A (Experimental)	5
B (Control)	5
Part 2	
C (Experimental)	5
D (Control)	4

In the present discussion, the two parts of the experiment will be treated as essentially two replications of the same experiment. The significance of a minor difference in procedure on the day of punishment will be taken up in the next section of the paper. On the first day of the experiment proper, all four groups were placed in the boxes for a ten-minute period[4] during which they were subjected to the following procedures:

Group A: Punishment of all responses in addition to continued periodic food reinforcement

Group B: Periodic food reinforcement

Group C: Extinction with all responses punished

Group D: Extinction.

[4] Preliminary experimentation showed that with the intensity of shock used a ten-minute interval of punishment was long enough to produce temporary suppression of the responses in all cases but not long enough to permit any perceptible recovery from the initial effect.

From the second through the seventh day of the experiment, all four groups were returned to the boxes daily for one-hour periods of simple extinction.

Results. The results of the experiment are summarized in Table 11.2 and illustrated graphically in Figure 11.3. The immediate

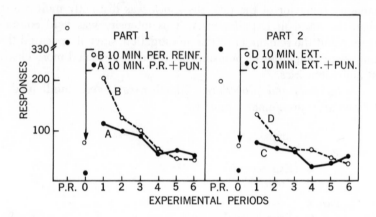

Figure 11.3   Effects of a short period of severe punishment upon extinction. The initial depression in rate of responding resulting from punishment is followed by gradual recovery until the experimental curves rejoin those of the controls (Experiment B).

effect of the punishment was a rapid decrease in the rate of responding until all of the experimental animals had ceased responding entirely by the end of the ten-minute period of punishment. The initial effect is illustrated by the individual record for one of the experimental rats of Part 2 reproduced in Figure 11.3a. It will be noted that the total number of responses made by the experimental rats was only a small fraction of the number produced by the controls during this period. On the first subsequent day of extinction, the rate of responding of the experimental animals was still markedly depressed. By the fourth day, however, the momentary strength of response for the experimentals was approximately equal to that of the controls. During the last three days of extinction, the experimental and control groups did not differ significantly. Although both experimental curves exhibit slight compensatory increases during the

Table 11.2   Mean number of responses per experimental period under conditions of periodic reinforcement, punishment, and extinction (Experiment B)

	N	Pr.	Pun.	Extinction periods					
				1	2	3	4	5	6
Part 1									
$\bar{x}_A$	5	336.6	15.8	115.2	103.2	91.0	57.0	60.6	51.0
$\bar{x}_B$	5	365.0	76.4	207.6	124.4	102.6	63.0	43.8	42.6
t			4.10	2.14	.51	.30	.24	.65	.74
P_t			.003	.07	.64	.77	.82	.53	.49
Part 2									
$\bar{x}_C$	5	260.9	20.0	79.4	66.6	58.6	28.0	32.2	32.2
$\bar{x}_D$	4	196.6	70.8	133.3	78.5	58.8	61.0	43.8	37.8
t			1.47	1.29	.43	.01	1.32	.90	.45
P_t			.18	.24	.68	.90	.22	.40	.57

latter stages of extinction, compensation is by no means complete, and the total heights of the experimental curves are somewhat reduced as compared to the control records. The general picture corresponds to Curve (3) of Figure 11.1.

The close agreement of the two parts of the experiment with

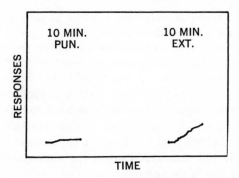

Figure 11.3a   Reproduced from photostatic copies of the curves of an experimental and a control rat on the day of punishment (Experiment B, Part 2).

respect to the course of recovery from punishment suggests that the form of the process may be well enough established by these data to permit a mathematical description.

Let us take as a convenient index of the effect of punishment during any given extinction period the difference between the heights of the experimental and control curves, expressed as a proportion of the latter. That is,

$$p = \frac{\bar{x}_C - \bar{x}_E}{\bar{x}_C}$$

Although this index is not entirely satisfactory, it is probably the best one available at present. It is to be expected that the extent to which a mathematical analysis of the effects of punishment can be fruitfully carried will be limited until an extensive mathematical treatment of conditioning and extinction has been completed. The observed values of p for the two parts of the experiment are plotted against time in Figure 11.4.

Choice of a simple mathematical function to describe the recovery process must be guided by several known conditions in addition to the trend of the empirical points in Figure 11.4.

1. The form of the recovery process is, in part, a function of the severity of punishment (Experiments A and B).
2. Recovery is affected by individual differences in constitutional "reactivity" or "sensitivity" to the punishing stimulus (observed in all of these experiments).
3. The rate of recovery is probably a function, in part, of the amount of positive reinforcement of the response prior to the period of punishment (for experimental confirmation of this assumption see Experiment F).

Unfortunately, it is not yet possible to obtain independent quantitative estimates of the effects of these factors upon the rate of recovery. However, their effects can be taken into account by incorporating into the equation a measure of the initial effect of punishment which is in turn a joint function of these factors.

A simple function which meets the above-mentioned conditions is an equation of the form

$$p_t = p_0 e^{-at} \tag{A}$$

where p_0 is the value of p for the period during which punishment is administered, t is a measure of time in terms of the number of periods of exposure to the situation in which the punishment was administered, e is the base of Naperian logarithms, and a is a constant.

A curve of this form in which

$$p_0 = 0.7932$$
$$a = 0.6772$$

has been fitted to the first four empirical values of p for Part 1 of the experiment in the lower panel of Figure 11.4. The function chosen is evidently descriptive of the trend of observed points.

A preliminary test of predictive significance of this function is afforded by Part 2 of the experiment, since, by means of the equation, it should be possible in the case of other experiments carried

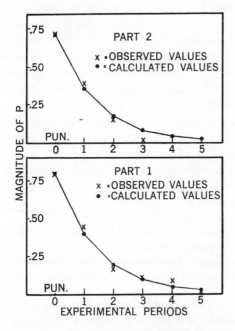

Figure 11.4 The course of recovery from the depressing effect of a short period of severe punishment, including both theoretical and observed values of p, an index of the current effect of punishment (Experiment B)

out under conditions similar to those of the original to predict the course of recovery from punishment if a measure of the initial effect of the punishment is available. The theoretical curve in the upper panel of Figure 11.4 represents an equation of the same form as equation (A), in which the value of the constant of decrement, a, *is taken from the curve of Part 1*. It will be observed that the predicted and observed values of p for Part 2 of the experiment are in fair agreement, especially considering the small number of subjects used. The empirical points have not been plotted beyond the point at which the difference between experimental and control groups once reaches zero in either case. The extinction curves become so low by the third or fourth day that for small groups of animals the observed values of p must become very unreliable beyond this point.

Equation (A) is to be treated as an empirical rather than a rational equation. It will be possible in later experiments, however, to test the descriptive power of this function beyond the limits of the data upon which it was based. It will be noted, for example, that according to Equation (A), recovery from the effects of punishment is never quite completed. With increasing time, the magnitude of p approaches zero asymptotically. It is impossible to confirm or refute this property of the equation in the present experiment since the effect remaining after three or four periods of extinction is so small as to be obscured by "chance" fluctuations. In Experiment C, in which the period of punishment is of considerably greater duration, it may be possible to test this implication of the equation, since the relatively permanent effect of punishment should in that case be large enough to be detectable under suitable conditions.

Conclusion. It appears that under the conditions of the present experiment, namely:

(a) that a response has been raised to a relatively high state of strength by periodic reinforcement; and

(b) that punishment is administered for a period of time just long enough to produce temporary suppression of the response;

the process of recovery from the effect of the punishment during subsequent periods in which the response is neither punished nor rewarded is described by the equation

$$p_t = p_0 e^{-at}$$

where p_t is an index of the effect of punishment remaining at time t, p_o is a measure of the initial effect of the punishment, and a is an arbitrary constant.

It is probable that, under the conditions stated, the process of recovery from punishment will always proceed more rapidly than extinction of the response; therefore the effects of punishment will be almost completely dispelled at some point prior to the time at which extinction would have been completed in the absence of punishment. Subsequent to this point, the strength of the response will equal or exceed that which would have obtained if no punishment had been administered. The total amount of time required for complete extinction of the response will not, then, be affected by the punishment, irrespective of its severity, although the number of elicitations of the response necessary for extinction may be reduced somewhat.

Experiment C. Effects of Prolonged Punishment upon Extinction

In Experiment B, the punishment was continued only until the rate of responding had dropped to approximately zero. In the present experiment, the punishment was carried beyond this point of temporary inhibition, so that when the response began to recover in strength later in the period, it was again punished. By the end of a sixty minute period of punishment, it appeared likely that the rate of responding would remain virtually at zero so long as the correlation of shock with response was maintained. In the vernacular, the animals had learned "that the administration of punishment was not merely a temporary matter."

Subjects and procedure. The subjects for the two parts of the experiment were twenty rats subdivided as follows:

Group	N
Part 1	
A (Experimental)	4
B (Control)	5
Part 2	
C (Experimental)	5
D (Control)	6

After the usual preliminary training, the animals were subjected to the following procedures.

Part 1. On the first day of the experiment, Group B received one hour of extinction while Group A received an hour of extinction with all responses punished. Subsequently each group received four periods of simple extinction. The intervals between experimental periods were varied: between the first and second, one day; between the second and third, two days; between the third and fourth, four days; between the fourth and fifth, twenty days.

Part 2. On the first day, Group D received simple extinction of all responses for one hour, while Group C received an hour of extinction with all responses punished. Eight days later, both groups were returned to the boxes for further extinction. The second and third periods were separated by one day, the third and fourth by twenty days.

After the last extinction period, all four groups of animals were reconditioned[5] and given two more days of periodic reinforce-

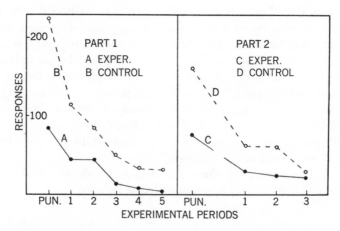

Figure 11.5   Effects of a sixty-minute period of punishment upon extinction. In Part 2, extinction was not begun until eight days after the period of punishment, the depressing effect of punishment was not dispelled by a mere lapse of time (Experiment G).

[5] During the period of reconditioning each animal was reinforced for the first five consecutive responses emitted, then periodically reinforced for the remainder of the hour.

ment followed by three days of extinction in order to test for any permanent effects of the protracted punishment.

Results. A comparison of the experimental and control records of Part 1 (Figure 11.5 and Table 11.3) reveals little recovery from the effects of the long period of punishment. The extinction curve for Group A approaches the form of Curve (1) in Figure 11.1. However, the fact that in Part 2, where the same amount of punishment was used, the experimental curve rejoins that of the controls on the fourth day, suggests that the recovery process in the case of Group A was not entirely absent, but for some reason was delayed. This hypothesis is supported by the results of the reconditioning, and second extinction. A relatively permanent effect of the protracted punishment is indicated by the fact that Groups A and C have lower periodic rates and smaller extinction curves *after reconditioning* than the control groups, although they had exhibited higher periodic rates prior to the period of punishment.[6] However, during the hour

Table 11.3 Quantitative data of Experiment C in terms of group means, including number of responses per hour during original periodic reinforcement, punishment, and extinction; total number of responses during first extinction; number of responses during the hour of reconditioning; periodic rate after reconditioning; total number of responses during second extinction

	Pr.	1 (Pun.) 2	3	4	5	6	T	Rec.	Pr.	$T_{Ext.}$
			Part 1							
$\bar{x}_A$	453.1	84.8	46.0	47.5	15.8	8.5	5.8	208.4	236.5	140.8	188.8
$\bar{x}_B$	365.4	222.6	113.0	86.8	51.6	34.4	33.6	542.0	174.0	218.0	235.0
t	.54	1.41	3.31	2.27	2.20	5.52	2.84	2.26	.83	1.43	.67
P_t	.60	.20	.01	.06	.06	.001	.03	.06	.43	.19	.52
			Part 2							
$\bar{x}_C$	457.8	77.2	29.0	23.2	23.4			152.8	120.2	159.4	189.0
$\bar{x}_D$	378.2	161.5	63.5	63.0	28.2			316.2	239.2	242.9	239.0
t	.56	2.39	1.61	1.49	.48			2.50	1.25	1.14	1.31
P_t	.59	.04	.17	.17	.64			.03	.24	.30	.22

[6] This result confirms one implication of the equation developed in Experiment B, namely, that of a permanent effect of punishment.

of reconditioning after the first extinction (see Table 11.3), the animals of Group A averaged a considerably larger number of responses than the corresponding controls. This anomalous finding suggests that a number of responses which had been suppressed by the severe punishment and which had not recovered sufficiently in strength to appear during the extinction periods were released when reinforcement was re-introduced and produced a temporary spurt in rate of responding.

It appears likely that the extreme delay in recovery from punishment in this experiment may be accounted for at least in part by the temporal spacing of the extinction periods. In other experiments which involved long periods of punishment but in which the extinction periods were separated only by twenty-four hour intervals, recovery was considerably accelerated (e.g., Experiment F).

Except for the differences already noted, the results of Part 2 of the present experiment are similar to those of Part 1. The effects of punishment clearly were not dispelled by mere lapse of time between termination of punishment and the beginning of subsequent extinction. In fact it appears not unlikely that the affect of a lapse of time is to accentuate the effect of punishment.

Even with the amount of punishment used in this experiment, the strength of the response at the end of the period of punishment cannot be taken as an index of its true state. By the end of the hour of continuous punishment, it seemed almost certain that the rate of responding would remain very close to zero so long as punishment was continued. But during subsequent periods of extinction without punishment, the experimental animals emitted a substantial number of responses, even though the rate was considerably depressed as compared to the control record.

Conclusion. A response which has once been strengthened by periodic reinforcement cannot be eliminated from the organism's repertoire solely through the action of punishment. Although extreme instances may conceivably be found in which this principle breaks down, it is now well established for a wide range of conditions of punishment.

Clearly, punishment results in a suppression rather than a weakening of the response. If extinction is carried out while the response is depressed in strength as a result of prolonged punishment, a considerable saving may be effected in the total number of elicitations of the response necessary for extinction. However, there is no evidence that the *time* required for complete extinction can be reduced by the action of punishment. In cases where punishment has apparently accelerated the extinction process, the suppressed behavior can still be released under suitable conditions.

Experiment D. Effects of Several Short Periods of Severe Punishment upon Extinction

The results of the preceding experiment suggest that a response cannot be eliminated from an organism's repertoire by a single period of continuous punishment irrespective of its duration. However, it may be that repeated periods of punishment might accomplish what one period cannot. The following experiment was designed to test this possibility.

Subjects and procedure. After preliminary training, eight rats were divided into an experimental and a control group, each including two males and two females. On each of the first three days of the experiment proper, both groups were placed in the experimental boxes for a ten-minute period, during which the control rats received simple extinction while the experimental animals received extinction plus punishment for all responses. Both groups were given one hour of extinction daily on the fourth, fifth, and sixth days of the experiment.

Results. The immediate effects of punishment in this experiment (see Figure 11.6 and Table 11.4) are similar to those observed in Experiment B. During the first period of punishment, the rate of responding for the experimental group dropped to nearly zero. At the beginning of each of the next two periods, the strength of the response had "spontaneously" recovered somewhat but quickly dropped back to zero when punishment was continued. It is apparent that so long as punishment continues to follow all responses, the rate of responding can be held at a level equal to or less than that reached by the controls after six days of extinction.[7] When the punishment was finally discontinued, however, it was again demonstrated that punishment had not afforded a means of "shortcutting" the extinction process. The sharp rise in the experimental curve on

[7] The true difference between the two groups during the periods of punishment is probably greater than that indicated by Figure 11.6, since the experimental group had the higher rate under periodic reinforcement.

Estes

Table 11.4 Mean number of responses per experimental period under conditions of periodic reinforcement, punishment, and extinction (Experiment D)

	Pr.	Punishment			Extinction			$T_{Pun.}$	$T_{Ext.}$	T_{1-6}
		1	2	3	4	5	6			
		(10 min. periods)			(60 min. periods)					
$\bar{x}_E$	317.0	8.0	4.3	4.3	69.8	20.8	22.8	16.6	113.4	130.0
$\bar{x}_C$	268.5	28.3	23.8	16.3	76.0	37.3	27.3	68.4	140.6	209.0
t		2.73	3.35	6.03	.20	1.14	.63	4.34	2.68	1.31
P_t		.04	.01	.001	.85	.31	.62	.005	.04	.24

the fourth day might even suggest that the action of punishment is governed by a law of diminishing returns similar to that observed in the case of original positive reinforcement (Skinner, 1938), and that recovery from the initial effect of punishment was proceeding

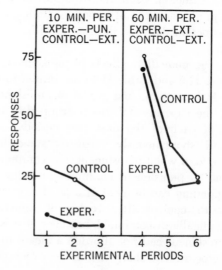

Figure 11.6 Effects of several short periods of punishment. Note the abrupt recovery in strength of the response when punishment is discontinued (Experiment D).

concomitantly with the continued punishment during the second and third periods.

Conclusion. The effect of repeated periods of severe punishment is a suppression of the response which is maintained as long as the punishment continues to be correlated with the response. After discontinuation of the punishment, the strength of the response recovers to an extent such that during subsequent periods of extinction the rate of responding is about equal to that which would have obtained at the same time if no punishment had been administered. The total number of unreinforced elicitations of the response required for extinction is reduced by this procedure by a number equal to the difference between the number occurring during the periods of punishment and the number which would have occurred during those periods under conditions of simple non-reinforcement. However, the *time* required for complete extinction is not altered by punishment.

When a response has once been reinforced, there are definite limits imposed by the structure of the organism upon the extent to which external agencies can control the behavior by supplying or withholding punishments and rewards. Conditions intrinsic to the organism govern the maximum amount of behavior which will be available for elicitation during any given period of time. By the application of punishment, one can modify, almost at will, the number of responses during any single period of exposure to the situation in which the response can be made, but the total number of such periods necessary for elimination of the response cannot be modified.

Experiment E. Effects of Periodic as Compared to Continuous Punishment of the Response upon the Course of Extinction

Skinner (1938) has shown that periodic positive reinforcement of a response produces much greater resistance to extinction than continuous reinforcement. The following experiment was designed to determine whether a similar principle governs the action of punishment.

Subjects and procedure. Two groups of rats, each including three males and two females, received the usual preliminary training before beginning the experiment proper. On the first day both groups were placed in the experimental boxes for a forty minute period, Group B receiving punishment for all responses while Group A was given periodic punishment under the following procedure. The period was divided into eight five-minute intervals. During the first, fourth, and seventh of these intervals, all responses were followed by shock, while responses occurring during the intervening intervals were neither punished nor reinforced. On the last five days of the experiment both groups were given one hour of simple extinction daily.

Results. The results are summarized in Figure 11.7 and Table 11.5. Clearly the procedure of continuous punishment produced a more rapid decline in rate of responding on the first day than periodic punishment, although the average number of punished responses was about the same for the two groups (Group A, 9.0; Group B, 8.5). During the subsequent extinction, on the other hand, Group A showed somewhat slower recovery. Since the two groups

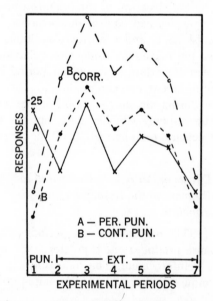

Figure 11.7   Periodic vs. continuous punishment. The corrected curve for Group B, which received continuous punishment on Day 1, has been multiplied through by a constant chosen to equate the two groups with respect to periodic rate (Experiment E).

Table 11.5   Mean periodic and extinction records for Experiment E

	N	Pr.	1 (Pun.)	2	3	4	5	6	7	T_{2-7}
			Extinction periods							
$\bar{x}_A$	5	152.6	23.8	15.0	24.8	14.8	20.2	18.6	13.0	106.2
$\bar{x}_B$	5	107.8	8.5	20.4	26.8	21.0	23.8	19.8	9.8	121.6

differed considerably in initial periodic rate, a curve corrected for periodic rate is included in Figure 11.7. The difference between groups on the first day yields a value of "t" which would be expected about nine times in a hundred through the operation of chance factors. On the remaining days of extinction, the trend is consistent although none of the individual mean differences are statistically reliable. Although the difference in the effects of the two conditions of punishment is not large, the observed difference can probably be accepted with confidence, since this result is confirmed by an independent experiment which will be reported later (Experiment K).

Conclusion. Continuous punishment produces a greater initial depression in strength of the response than periodic punishment; however, recovery from the effects of periodic punishment is clearly no more rapid than recovery from continuous punishment, and is probably somewhat slower. Again it is observed that the strength of a response at the end of a period of punishment is not a reliable index of its true state.

Experiment F. Effects of Punishment upon Responses which Differ in Initial Resistance to Extinction

In exploring the effect of various conditions of punishment, we have dealt in each instance with behavior which existed at a state of considerable strength prior to the period of punishment. This is the case of most general interest since in the practical control of behavior the use of punishment is usually unnecessary if the response in question is not strong to start with. Likewise, in clinical psychology, one is concerned over the "repression" of a response only if it is strong enough to be a source of conflict. At this point in the present investigation, however, it is necessary to determine whether the effects of punishment upon initially strong and initially weak responses differ in kind or only in degree. The following experiment was designed to measure the effects of a period of severe punishment upon two responses which differ widely in amount of previous positive reinforcement.

Subjects and procedure. The subjects were twelve female rats. After preliminary conditioning they were divided into three groups of four rats each; then, Groups A and B were given one hour and Group C five hours of periodic reinforcement. On the first day of the experiment proper, all of the animals were placed in the boxes for a forty-minute period during which Group B received simple extinction, while Groups A and C received extinction plus punishment for all responses. On the remaining four days of the experiment all groups received one-hour periods of extinction.

Results. Group A, which had received only one hour of periodic reinforcement, clearly shows a greater initial depression in rate of responding during the period of punishment and a slower recovery from the effects of the punishment than Group C (Figure 11.8 and Table 11.6). Group A had recovered sufficiently by the

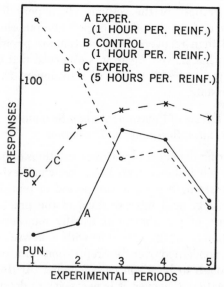

Figure 11.8 Effects of punishment as a function of initial strength of the response. Groups A and B had received one hour, Group C five hours, of periodic reinforcement prior to Day 1 (Experiment F).

Table 11.6   Mean periodic rates and extinction records for Experiment F

	Pr.	Extinction periods					
		1 (Pun.)	2	3	4	5	T_{1-5}
$\bar{x}_A$	210.3	16.5	23.0	74.3	68.5	38.3	220.6
$\bar{x}_B$	239.0	136.8	103.8	58.3	63.0	32.5	394.4
$\bar{x}_C$	291.8	44.3	75.0	84.8	88.5	80.5	373.0
B−A							
t	.37	6.41	4.47	.30	.18	.35	5.20
P_t	.72	.001	.004	.77	.86	.73	.002
B−C							
t	2.25	4.30	.92	1.08	.75	1.77	.25
P_t	.07	.005	.39	.32	.48	.13	.81

second day of extinction so that the rate of responding differed little from that of the control group during the remainder of the experiment. Group C recovered somewhat more rapidly and during the last three periods of extinction exhibited a compensatory increase in rate which partly made up the initial deficit caused by the punishment.[8] A comparison of these results with those of previous experiments indicates that the extent of later compensation for the initial depression in rate of responding resulting from punishment is dependent upon both the conditions of punishment and the amount of previous positive reinforcement. The proportion by which the total number of elicitations of the response necessary for extinction can be reduced by a given condition of punishment decreases with increasing amounts of previous periodic reinforcement. The greater the initial strength of a bit of behavior, the less effective is punishment as a means of controlling it. It appears likely that with sufficient periodic reinforcement a strength of response could be achieved such that no period of continuous punishment, regardless of duration or intensity, would affect the total number of elicitations of the response required for complete extinction.

[8] The last three points on the curve of Group C would probably represent a compensatory increase even if compared with a control group which had also received five hours of periodic reinforcement. An unpublished study conducted by the writer indicates that such a control curve would not lie very far above Curve B.

Conclusion. The extent to which the total number of unreinforced elicitations necessary for the complete extinction of a response can be reduced by punishment is a joint function of the amount of punishment and the amount of previous periodic reinforcement. With increasing amounts of periodic reinforcement, the resistance of a response to the effects of punishment probably increases more rapidly than the resistance to extinction.

Experiment G. Punishment of a Response After Establishment of a Discrimination

Since the preceding experiment demonstrated that the course of recovery from punishment is a function of the initial strength of the response when differences in strength have been produced by different amounts of periodic reinforcement, it is of interest to determine whether the same relations hold when differences in initial strength result from the formation of a discrimination. The latter procedure should provide a rather delicate test of the relationship since it produces very low but stable states of strength.

It has been shown by Skinner (1938) that a stimulus which characteristically precedes reinforcement of a response becomes an "occasion" for the occurrence of the response. For example, if a response is repeatedly reinforced when it occurs in the presence of a tone, but is never reinforced when the tone is absent, the response is gradually brought under the control of the tone (i.e., the tone becomes a discriminative stimulus for the response). If we designate the discriminative stimulus as S^D, the situation in the absence of S^D as S^N, and the response as R, then during discriminative training the correlation $S^N \cdot R$ decreases in strength while the correlation $S^D \cdot R$ increases, and the organism comes to respond at a much higher rate when the tone is sounding than when it is not. After several periods of discriminative training, $S^N \cdot R$ is virtually extinguished; $S^D \cdot R$ remains at considerable strength, but is much more readily extinguished than a response which has been merely periodically reinforced without differential correlation of the reinforcement with a discriminative stimulus.

The present experiment was designed to answer the following questions:

1. After the establishment of a discrimination, how will punishment ad-

ministered in the absence of S^D affect the strength of the response in its presence?

2. Will recovery from punishment under the two stimulating conditions differ as should be expected according to the relation between initial strength of response and resistance to punishment formulated above (Experiment F)?

Subjects and procedure. The subjects were eight rats divided into an experimental group of five rats and a control group of three. After preliminary training, the animals were given eight experimental periods of discriminative training under the following procedure. Every four minutes a tone was sounded in the experimental boxes; the next response to the lever released a pellet of food from the magazine and turned off the tone. Responses occurring during the silent intervals were unreinforced. By the end of the eighth day under this procedure, the discrimination was well established, as indicated by reduced latencies of response after onset of the tone and low terminal rates of responding in the absence of the tone (about 13 responses per hour per rat for the experimental group and 45 for the controls). After the completion of discriminative training, the experimental rats were given ten minutes in the boxes with all responses punished while the controls were given ten minutes of simple extinction. The tone was not present for either group during this period. On the following day both groups were given one hour of extinction without the tone. During three further periods of extinction, the tone was turned on for both groups according to the following schedule.

Second period	the last 25 minutes,
Third period	the last 45 minutes,
Fourth period	the last 45 minutes.

Results. The results are summarized in Table 11.7. The course of recovery from the effects of punishment is shown graphically in Figure 11.9 where the measure of the effect of punishment during each experimental period is again taken as

$$p_t = \frac{\bar{x}_C - \bar{x}_E}{\bar{x}_C}$$

The solid line in Figure 11.9 represents the values of p for silent pe-

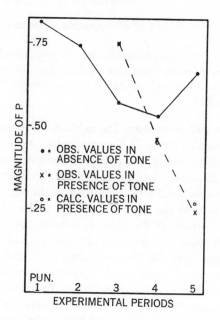

Figure 11.9 Recovery from punishment during silent intervals and intervals when the tone was sounding. The magnitude of p is an index of the current effect of punishment (Experiment G).

riods, while the broken line represents corresponding values of p for intervals when the tone was sounding.

The initial effect of punishment was apparently almost completely generalized from $S^N \cdot R$ to $S^D \cdot R$; the magnitude of P for the first interval of extinction when the tone was sounding (on Day 3 in Figure 11.9) was approximately equal to that for the first silent extinction period (Day 2 in Figure 11.9).

The course of recovery from punishment was quite different for the two stimulating conditions. There was little recovery in rate of responding in the absence of S^D. Recovery of strength in the presence of S^D, however, followed a course similar to that observed in Experiment B. Theoretical values of p for intervals when the tone was sounding have been calculated from equation (A) of Experiment B,

$$p_t = p_o e^{-at}$$

with the magnitude of the constant of decrement e^{-a} taken as 0.6
There is fair correspondence of observed and calculated values for
the last two extinction periods; unfortunately, however, extinction
was not carried far enough to provide an adequate test of the good-
ness of fit. On the last day of extinction, $S^D \cdot R$ had completely recovered from the effect of punishment, while $S^N \cdot R$ remained at a
very low strength.

Table 11.7   Mean number of responses during silent intervals and
intervals when the tone was sounding (Experiment G)

	N	1: Pun. S^N	2: Ext. S^N	3: Ext. S^N	3: Ext. S^D	4: Ext. S^N	4: Ext. S^D	5: Ext. S^N	5: Ext. S^D
$\bar{x}_E$	5	5.4	44.2	28.2	16.2	12.6	33.6	7.2	23.6
$\bar{x}_C$	3	28.3	170.0	65.0	64.7	26.7	62.3	21.3	31.0
t		4.26	2.71	3.71	5.81	1.62	1.85	1.47	.68
P_t		.005	.04	.01	.001	.15	.12	.20	.52

Conclusion. After the establishment of a discrimination between two stimulating conditions S^D and S^N, the initial effect of a
short period of severe punishment of the response in the absence of
S^D (i.e., condition S^N) is almost completely generalized to the
strength of the response in the presence of S^D. Recovery in strength
of the connection $S^D \cdot R$ follows a course similar to that observed in
the case of a response which had received simple periodic reinforcement prior to punishment. The strenth of $S^N \cdot R$ exhibits very little
recovery from the effects of punishment.

Section 2. Conflicting effects of concomitant punishment and reward

A comparison of the effects of punishment administered after the
discontinuance of reinforcement with the effects of punishment administered while the response is still being periodically reinforced is
afforded by the two parts of Experiment B. On the first day of that
experiment, one experimental Group (A) was given the usual pe-

riodic food reinforcement for pressing the lever and in addition was punished for all responses; in the case of the other experimental group (C), food reinforcement was discontinued while all responses were punished; the control groups (B and D) received simple periodic reinforcement or extinction. The results of the two procedures can be seen in Figure 11.3. It is clear that with the intensity and duration of punishment used in that experiment it makes little difference whether or not periodic positive reinforcement continues during the period of punishment. The extent of initial depression in strength of response was approximately the same for the two procedures. Moreover, the mathematical descriptions of the course of recovery from punishment in each instance indicates a similar form of the process in the two cases.

The course of recovery from punishment when the response continues to receive periodic reinforcement after the discontinuation of punishment is investigated in the following experiment. This case is of particular practical interest because punishment is most commonly resorted to as a means of influencing behavior when the factor of reward cannot easily be brought under control.

Experiment H. The Acceleration of Recovery from Punishment by Positive Reinforcement

Subjects and procedure. The subjects were five male rats. After preliminary training the animals were subjected to the following procedure during a one-hour period. The control clock was set to reinforce single responses with food at four-minute intervals during the entire period (i.e., the usual procedure of periodic reinforcement); from the fifteenth to the thirtieth minutes of the hour all responses were punished.

Results. The effects of the punishment and the course of subsequent recovery are shown in Figure 11.10. The initial effect of punishment under periodic positive reinforcement is a sharp decline in rate of responding similar to that observed in Part 1 of Experiment B. However, the recovery in strength following discontinuation of the punishment is greatly accelerated in the present experiment where the after-effects of the punishment are in conflict with continuing positive reinforcement. The amount of time subsequent to the termination of punishment required for the rate of responding to regain the level which obtained before punishment is, in this case,

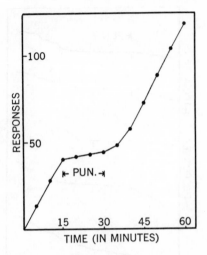

Figure 11.10 Acceleration of recovery from punishment by positive reinforcement. Periodic food reinforcement at four minute intervals was given throughout the hour (Experiment H).

approximately equal to the interval during which punishment was administered.

An important property of punishment is revealed by the behavior during the interval when the response was both punished and periodically reinforced. The rate of responding dropped sharply to a low value, about one-tenth of its former magnitude,[9] *it then remained constant* at this new low value until punishment was discontinued. The effect of punishment upon the periodic curve is simply a change in slope, in contrast to the negatively accelerated extinction curve which results from mere non-reinforcement. Although Thorndike (1932b, 1935) and many of his followers (e.g., Lorge, 1933a; Lorge & Thorndike, 1933; Stephens, 1940) have frequently used the terms "punishment" and "non-reward" almost interchangeably, it is clear that the two procedures may produce quite different effects upon the dynamic properties of the response.

In an earlier study reported by Skinner (1938) a group of rats received periodic punishment (consisting of a slap to the forepaws

[9] This effect can be seen most clearly in the individual curves of Figure 11.10a.

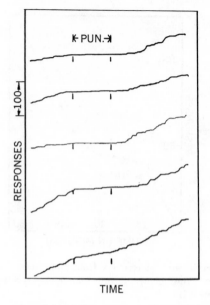

Figure 11.10a   Reproduced from photostatic copies of the individual curves for the period which included the fifteen-minute interval of punishment (Experiment H)

administered by a "kick-back" of the lever) simultaneously with periodic food-reinforcement of a lever-pressing response throughout several experimental periods. The result was a temporary reduction in periodic slope, followed by a return to the slope which had obtained under periodic food-reinforcement alone. The differences between the results of Skinner's experiment and the present one are probably due to differences in severity of punishment. In the former case, the punishment was mild and the animals quickly became adapted to it; in the latter, the punishment was severe enough so that little adaptation would be expected.

The effects of punishment upon the strength of a response are very similar to those of a change in level of drive. Punishment of a periodically reinforced response results simply in an adjustment of the rate of responding to a lower, but still constant, value which is determined jointly by the conditions of reinforcement and the severity of the punishment. Likewise during extinction, punishment produces a depression in strength of the response which is maintained so long as the effects of the punishment persist. However progress toward complete elimination of the response is not accelerated while the strength is depressed because of punishment.

Conclusion. Concomitant punishment and reward of a response produce essentially the same changes in its dynamic properties as punishment after discontinuation of reward. The immediate effect of punishment upon a periodically reinforced response is a change in slope similar to that effected by a change in level of drive. If reinforcement continues after the discontinuation of punishment, the effect of punishment is quickly dissipated.

III. Analysis of the Action of Punishment

In any situation involving punishment, at least three principle variables can be distinguished: the response, R, discriminative stimuli for the response, S^D, and a disturbing or traumatic stimulus, S^P. The experiments reported in the earlier sections of this paper have, like most other psychological studies of punishment, investigated only the correlation between S^P and R or between S^P and $S^D \cdot R$ where the latter connection is taken as a unit. They have been concerned with punishment for doing something, the implicit assumption being that the effects of punishment are entirely dependent upon the temporal contiguity of the punishment and a response, and upon the punishment's being strictly contingent upon the occurrence of the response. In this chapter an attempt will be made to secure experimental confirmation or refutation of these assumptions.

Experiment I. Effects upon Extinction of a "Punishment" not Directly Associated with the Response

The following experiment investigates the effects upon a response of correlation of a disturbing stimulus with the discriminative stimuli[10] for the response.

Subjects and procedure. An experimental and a control group, of four rats each, were subjected, after preliminary training, to the

---

[10] In this experiment the discriminative stimuli are merely the stimuli which are normally present in the experimental situation and which, after initial conditioning, provide the "occasion" for the occurrence of the response.

following procedure. Both groups were placed in the experimental boxes for a ten-minute period of extinction, during which the experimental group received periodic shocks at intervals of approximately thirty seconds.[11] Care was taken that the shock should not be given during or immediately following a response to the lever. Otherwise, the shocks were entirely uncorrelated with the response during this period. Beginning on the following day, each group was given six one-hour periods of simple extinction.

Results. A comparison of the extinction curves for the experimental and control groups of the present experiment (Figure 11.11) with the corresponding curves for Experiment B in which the experimental groups had received ten minutes of punishment (Figure

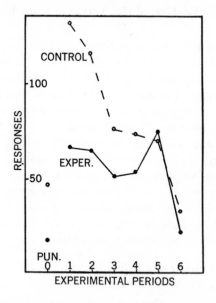

Figure 11.11   Effects of periodic shocks upon extinction. On the day of "punishment," the experimental animals were given a series of shocks which were not temporally contiguous with responses to the lever (Experiment I).

[11] [Noncontingent shock, as used here, may have effects similar to a punishment that occurs long after the response (Camp, Raymond, & Church, 1967). See Selection 22 for an experiment on the delay of punishment gradient, and Experiment II of Selection 12 and Selection 14 for additional data on the relative effects of punishment vs. noncontingent shock.—Eds.]

11.3) reveals a striking similarity between the effects of a negatively reinforcing stimulus which is uncorrelated with the response and one whose administration is contingent upon the occurrence of the response. In other words, merely being shocked in the experimental situation apparently has the same effect upon the animals' behavior with respect to the lever as being punished for making the response.

Table 11.8   Mean periodic rates and extinction records for Experiment I

	N	Pr.	Pun.	1	2	3	4	5	6	T_{1-6}
$\bar{x}_E$	4	266.3	17.3*	66.5	65.5	51.5	53.8	75.5	22.3	335.1
$\bar{x}_C$	4	266.3	46.8	132.8	116.8	76.0	74.3	70.5*	33.3	503.7
t			2.33	2.11	1.64	1.30	1.26	.18	1.13	2.41
P_t			.05	.08	.15	.24	.25	.88	.30	.05

*Record for one rat during this period lost because of mechanical difficulty with the recorder.

A more precise comparison of the two experiments is afforded by the mathematical descriptions of recovery from punishment in the two cases. In experiment B, it was found that recovery from punishment was described by an equation of the form:

$$p_t = p_o e^{-at}$$

where p_t is the magnitude of

$$\frac{\bar{x}_C - \bar{x}_E}{\bar{x}_C}$$

at the time t, p_o is the value of p for the period of punishment, and a is a constant. In Figure 11.12, an equation of this form with

$$p_o = .63$$
$$a = .21$$

has been fitted to the empirical values of p for the present experiment. The theoretical curve provides a good fit to the empirical points for the first four days of extinction. The last two points deviate from the expected value, but an average of the two would fall approximately on the curve. As noted above (Experiment B) this increased scatter toward the end of extinction is to be expected unless the number of subjects is very large because of the low terminal heights of the extinction curves. That is, on the fifth or sixth day, a chance deviation of only a few responses has a disproportionately large effect upon the value of p. And both in this experiment and in Experiment B, deviations from the theoretical curve tend to counterbalance each other in direction. That is, a marked deviation below the curve is followed by a compensatory rise above it. This phenomenon of compensation for deviations below a smooth curve representing the mean trend of a set of observed values has been frequently observed in connection with extinction curves (Skinner, 1938). In any case, the theoretical curve in Figure 11.12 provides a satisfactory description of the trend of the observed points and the correspondence of calculated and observed values is probably better than could be obtained with any other simple mathematical function without increasing the number of arbitrary constants.

Since the effect of a shock which immediately follows a response (a "punishment") upon the dynamic properties of that response is satisfactorily described by the same mathematical func-

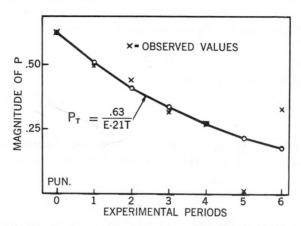

Figure 11.12   Recovery from the effects of "punishment" which was not correlated with the response. The magnitude of p is an index of the current effect of the "punishment" (Experiment I).

tion which most simply describes the effect of a shock which is independent of the response, the conclusion seems inescapable that at least a great part of the initial effect of punishment is due simply to correlation of the negatively reinforcing stimulus with the experimental situation. The important correlation appears to be that between the shock and the stimuli which normally act as the occasion for the occurrence of the response rather than between the shock and the response per se.

These results clearly confirm the contention of Thorndike (1935) that the action of punishment is not a direct "weakening" of the punished stimulus-response connection. Rather it appears that some part of the reaction to punishment becomes conditioned to the same stimuli which previously formed an occasion for the occurrence of the punished response, and that the empirical points of Figure 11.4 and 11.12 actually represent extinction curves for this conditioned reaction.

Conclusion. The temporal contiguity of a disturbing stimulus and stimuli which normally act as an occasion for the occurrence of a response yields a depression in rate of responding during subsequent periods of extinction very similar to that produced by actual punishment of the response.

Experiment J. Extinction of the Effects of Punishment Without Elicitation of the Response

The fact that little difference can be detected between the effects of a short period of punishment of a response and the effects of a comparable period during which the disturbing stimulus was administered independently of the response upon the course of subsequent extinction, indicates that a great part of the initial effect of punishment is attributable to the conditioning of a state of anticipation of the shock to the experimental situation and does not depend upon a close correlation of the shock with the response. If this interpretation is correct, it should be possible to extinguish the greater part of the effect of punishment, without elicitation of the response. The following experiment was designed to test this possibility by measuring the effect upon the course of recovery from punishment of the interpolation of a period of adaptation to the experimental situation between the period of punishment and the beginning of subsequent extinction. Part 1 of the experiment is purely exploratory;

Part 2 is a replication with larger groups of animals and a slightly modified procedure.

Part 1—Subjects and procedure. The subjects were three groups of rats, each including two males and one female. After preliminary training, the animals were subjected to the following procedure. During a ten-minute period in the experimental boxes, Group A received simple extinction; Group B received extinction plus punishment for all responses; Group C was placed in the boxes with the levers removed, and shocks were administered at sixty second intervals. On the following day all nine animals were placed in the boxes for two hours *with the levers retracted* in order to permit adaptation of any "emotional" reaction to the experimental situation which had become conditioned as a result of the procedure of the preceding day. On the third day, the levers were returned to the boxes and each group was given an hour of extinction.

Part 1—Results. The mean heights of the extinction curves obtained on the third day of the experiment proper are as follows:

> Group A 77.5
> Group B 88.0
> Group C 66.3

The marked depression in rate of responding during the first period of extinction after punishment which was so clearly evident in Figure 11.3 is lacking in these data. All of the differences are statistically insignificant. Evidently the effect of a short period of punishment was dispelled by a period of exposure to the experimental situation.

Part 2—Subjects and procedure. Twenty-eight rats were first given the usual preliminary conditioning and periodic reinforcement. The animals were then subdivided into six groups matched as closely as possible on the basis of initial periodic rate and subjected to the following procedures during a ten-minute test period:

> Groups A_0 and A_1: extinction with all responses punished;
> Groups B_0 and B_1: periodic shocks, at sixty second intervals with levers retracted;
> Groups C_0 and C_1: extinction.

On the following day, Groups A_0, B_0, and C_0 remained in the living cages; Groups A_1, B_1, and C_1 were placed in the boxes with the levers retracted, for a one-hour period of adaptation. Beginning on the third day, each group received seven one-hour periods of extinction. The first six were on consecutive days; the seventh was delayed until a week after the sixth in order to permit spontaneous recovery from extinction. The number of rats in each group is given in Table 11.9, along with a summary of the procedure and the quantitative results.

Part II—Results. A comparison of the two sets of curves in Figure 11.13[12] indicates that the effect of the period of adaptation was an almost complete extinction of the effects of punishment. The results of punishment without adaptation, shown in the upper panel of

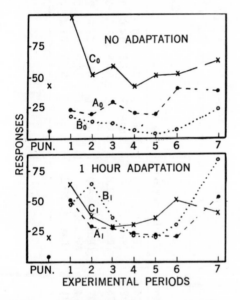

Figure 11.13   Effects of a period of adaptation upon the course of recovery from punishment. During the period of "punishment," Groups A_0 and A_1 were punished for responding, Groups B_0 and B_1 received random shocks, Groups C_0 and C_1 received simple extinction (Experiment J).

[12] This experiment was conducted during the summer at a time when day to day temperature variations were unusually great. The resulting irregularity of the extinction curves precludes a very detailed analysis of the data. The general result, however, may be accepted with confidence, since the two parts of the experiment are in complete agreement. Also, the conclusions drawn from these experiments will be subjected to an additional check in Experiment K.

Table 11.9 Summary of the procedure and quantitative results of Experiment J, part 2

	N	Pr.	10 min. period		Amt. Adapt.	Extinction periods						
						1	2	3	4	5	6	7
$\bar{x}_{A_0}$	5	215.6	(Pun.)	6.0	None	23.2	20.0	29.4	21.4	20.0	41.0	38.8
$\bar{x}_{B_0}$	3	222.0	(Shock)	–	None	17.7	14.0	12.7	6.0	3.3	7.3	24.0
$\bar{x}_{C_0}$	6	176.7	(Ext.)	42.8	None	99.8	52.3	59.2	42.3	52.2	57.7	64.2
$\bar{x}_{A_1}$	6	207.5	(Pun.)	4.0	1 hr.	51.7	28.8	27.5	23.8	22.8	21.2	53.8
$\bar{x}_{B_1}$	3	214.7	(Shock)	–	1 hr.	48.0	65.3	37.3	22.7	23.0	30.3	84.3
$\bar{x}_{C_1}$	5	201.0	(Ext.)	20.2	1 hr.	64.6	38.2	28.2	29.8	35.0	52.4	41.8

Figure 11.13, agree with those of earlier experiments (B, C, I) in showing a rather persistent depression in rate of responding during extinction. When an hour of adaptation is interpolated between punishment and extinction, however, the extinction curves of the three groups do not differ significantly (lower panel of Figure 11.13).

When extinction begins immediately, the group which had received periodic shocks exhibits a more prolonged depression in rate of responding than the group which had received punishment for responding; however, more complete recovery is effected after a period of adaptation in the boxes for the animals which received periodic shocks than for those which were punished. Therefore, it appears that not quite all of the effect of actual punishment is attributable merely to the correlation of the disturbing stimulus with the general stimulation from the experimental situation. The essential difference between the two procedures may lie mainly in the fact that when the shock is closely correlated with the response, the "anticipatory" reaction to shock may be conditioned to tactual stimulation from the lever and the proprioceptive stimulation from the movements involved in pressing the lever as well as to general stimulation from the experimental situation. During the period of adaptation, then, only the latter connections are extinguished. Conditioning to specific stimulation from the lever cannot be extinguished until subsequent extinction, involving repeated elicitation of the response, is carried out. The results of the present experiment indicate, however, that during a short period of severe punishment, the conditioning of the reaction to punishment tends to be rather generalized to the whole complex of stimuli acting at the time and that little specific connection between the punishment and the response is established. Of course it does not follow from the results of this experiment that the correlation of punishment with the punished response is unimportant. Experiment K will investigate conditions under which a closer connection between the effect of punishment and the punished response can be established.

Part III—Conclusion. The effects of a short period of severe punishment upon the dynamic properties of a response are almost completely dispelled by a period during which the organism is exposed to the experimental situation but is unable to make the response. The interpretation of punishment as a process of suppression rather than extinction of the response is substantiated by the present demonstration that the principal effects of a short period of punishment can be conditioned or extinguished quite independently of the elicitation of the response.

Experiment K. Periodic and Continuous Punishment Compared with Respect to the Specificity of their Effects to the Punished Response

In an earlier experiment (Experiment E) it was shown that the effects of periodic punishment tend to be more persistent than the effects of continuous punishment. In view of the results of Experiments I and J, it is possible that the greater persistence of the effect of periodic punishment may be due to the greater opportunity afforded for strong conditioning of part of the reaction to the disturbing stimulus to tactual stimulation from the lever and to proprioceptive stimulation from the movements involved in pressing the lever. (It has been well established (Skinner, 1938) that periodic reinforcement of a response produces much greater resistance to extinction than continuous reinforcement.) If this interpretation is correct, then the interpolation between the period of punishment and the beginning of subsequent extinction of a period of adaptation to the general stimulation of the experimental situation should be expected to increase the disparity between the effects of the two procedures of punishment.

Subjects and procedure. The eighteen rats serving as subjects in this experiment were divided after preliminary training into one control and two experimental groups of six rats each. On the first day of the experiment all three groups were placed in the experimental boxes for a forty-minute period during which Group C received extinction, Group B, extinction plus punishment for all responses, and Group A, extinction plus periodic punishment. Under the latter procedure, the condensors were connected in circuit with the levers for one minute out of every four, during which all responses were punished; during the intervening intervals responses were neither punished nor reinforced. On the following two days, all groups were placed in the boxes for one-hour periods with the levers retracted. Beginning on the fourth day, each group received six one-hour periods of extinction.

Results. The quantitative results of this experiment are sum-

Table 11.10 Mean periodic rates and extinction records for Experiment K

	N	Pr.	Pun.	Raw data extinction periods						Pun.	Data corrected for periodic rate extinction periods					
				1	2	3	4	5	6		1	2	3	4	5	6
$\bar{x}_A$	6	265.2	37.5	18.3	65.5	26.3	14.5	28.7	26.3	48.2	19.7	60.7	36.3	18.0	33.3	36.3
$\bar{x}_B$	6	223.3	16.5	50.8	63.7	39.5	17.2	39.2	40.0	24.2	76.2	91.5	53.5	25.3	53.7	56.0
$\bar{x}_C$	6	448.0	158.0	118.5	78.3	88.0	49.3	59.2	45.2	95.5	60.7	60.8	43.5	24.0	36.8	24.8
A—B																
t		.78	2.02	2.07	.09	1.33	.49	.74	.37	1.60	2.79	.99	1.47	1.06	.99	1.04
P_t		.45	.07	.06	.92	.20	.64	.48	.71	.14	.02	.35	.17	.31	.35	.32
A—C																
t		1.17	1.67	1.34	.51	1.09	1.07	1.07	.82	2.58	1.98	.01	.48	.76	.20	.92
P_t		.27	.13	.21	.62	.30	.31	.31	.42	.03	.08	.99	.64	.46	.85	.37
B—C																
t		1.44	1.96	.89	.56	.85	1.00	.67	.21	3.86	.57	1.24	.72	.15	1.09	1.83
P_t		.18	.08	.39	.59	.42	.34	.52	.84	.003	.59	.24	.48	.88	.30	.10

marized in Table 11.10. Since Group C has a disproportionately high periodic rate, all comparisons are made both for the raw data and for data corrected for differences in motivational level. Although the results are not greatly different with or without the correction for motivational level, the corrected data probably give a truer picture of the influence of the variables under consideration.

Group B, which received continuous punishment on the first day of the experiment proper, exhibited the greater depression in rate of responding during the period of punishment. After the two periods of adaptation to the experimental situation, however, the effects of the punishment had been almost completely dispelled, as indicated by the fact that the curve of Group B (Figure 11.14) nearly

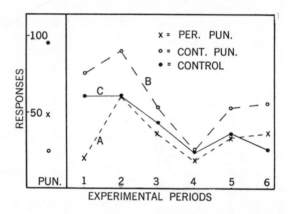

Figure 11.14   Effects of a period of adaptation upon recovery from periodic as compared to continuous punishment mean curves correlated for periodic rate (Experiment K)

rejoins the control curve on the first day of extinction. The group which received periodic punishment (Group A), showed less initial effect of punishment, but exhibited little recovery from the punishment on the first day of extinction indicating that the effects of periodic punishment are more closely associated with the punished response than those of continuous punishment.

Conclusion. The results of this experiment, with those of Experiment E, show that while continuous punishment of a response produces greater initial depression in strength, periodic punishment results in a more persistent inhibitory effect during subsequent extinction. The effects of periodic punishment are more specific to the punished response than those of continuous punishment.

IV. Induction of Punishment Between Dynamically Related Responses

The preceding experiments have investigated the principles governing the effects of punishment upon a single isolated response. Now, it is of interest to determine whether or not additional principles will be required to account for the action of punishment in a more complex case involving more than one response. The greatest part of the literature on experimental studies of punishment has been concerned with situations in which two alternative responses are available, one of which is arbitrarily considered "right" and the other "wrong," for example, studies of the effect of punishment for "errors" in maze learning. It is likely that the apparently conflicting results of many of these studies (see, for example, Brown, 1937; Tolman, Hall, & Bretnall, 1932) on the question of the effectiveness of punishment are due to the fact that the experiments have typically been set up merely to determine which of two alternative responses is "learned" rather than to trace the changes in strength of each response resulting from the punishment. In the following experiment the animals first learned to press two different levers for food reinforcement, then one response was punished, and the resulting changes in strength of both were traced through subsequent periods of extinction.

Experiment L. Effects of Punishment in a Situation Involving More Than One Response

Subjects and procedure. The subjects were two groups of four rats. The apparatus was the same as that used in preceding experiments except for the addition of a second lever. The two levers were about two inches apart on one wall of the experimental box, one situated to the left and one to the right of the food tray. Both levers were retractable so that either could be presented alone. After preliminary conditioning, each rat was given two hours of periodic reinforcement on each lever. Since the mean rates of responding under periodic reinforcement were 152.0 responses on the left lever and 150.4 on the right lever, it can safely be assumed that the strengths of the two responses were equal. The remainder of the experiment was carried out according to the following schedule:

Group	10 min. pun.	Four extinction periods	Fifth extinction period
A	Left lever	Right lever	Left lever
B	Left lever	Left lever	Right lever

Results. The results of the experiment are presented in Figure 11.15 and Table 11.11. Records corrected for differences in initial periodic rate are included along with the raw data in both cases. A comparison of the heights of the two curves on the first day in Figure 11.15 indicates that the initial effect of punishment is completely generalized to the unpunished response. The course of recovery dur-

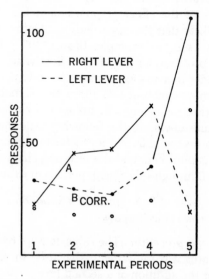

Figure 11.15 Effects of punishment in a situation involving alternative responses. Prior to Day 1, each group had received periodic reinforcement on both levers, then punishment on the left lever. The corrected curve for Group B has been multiplied through by a constant chosen to equate the two groups for periodic rate. Uncorrected values for Group B are indicated by the open circles (Experiment L).

Table 11.11   Mean periodic rates and extinction records for Experiment L

	N	Pr.	1	2	3	4	5	D_{4-5}
			Extinction period					
			Raw data					
			R	R	R	R	L	
$\bar{x}_A$	4	220.3	22.5	46.0	47.3	67.8	48.3	+19.5
			L	L	L	L	R	
$\bar{x}_B$	4	134.9	20.8	18.3	17.0	24.8	65.3	−40.5
t		1.95	.12	1.30	1.41	1.10	.51	2.58
P_t		.10	.91	.34	.21	.31	.63	.04
			Corrected for periodic rate					
			R	R	R	R	L	
$\bar{x}_A$	4	220.3	22.5	46.0	47.3	67.8	48.3	+19.5
			L	L	L	L	R	
$\bar{x}_B$	4	220.3	33.9	29.8	27.7	40.4	106.4	−66.0

ing the next three periods is quite different for the two responses, however, being considerably accelerated for the unpunished response, R_R. On the fifth day of extinction, when the previously retracted lever was presented to each group, the result was a sharp rise in rate of responding for Group B which had been receiving extinction on the punished response, R_L, and a sharp decline in rate for Group A which had been receiving extinction on the unpunished response, R_R. A comparison of the differences between rates on the fourth and fifth days for the two groups yields a value of "t" which would occur only four times in a hundred in a chance distribution. An X^2 test applied to the mean rates on the same two days yields a value of X^2 which would occur less than one time in a thousand in a chance distribution. The result is the same for the data corrected for initial periodic rate as for the raw data.

Two relatively distinct effects of punishment can be distinguished. The first is not specific to the punished response but affects to about the same extent any behavior which would normally occur in the situation in which the punishment was administered. In this experiment, the punishment initially affected the two responses equally. But the subsequent course of recovery, and the marked changes in strength when the previously retracted levers were presented on the fifth day of extinction, show that a part of the effect of punishment is quite specific to the punished response. The recovery in strength of R_R during the first four days of extinction in the case of Group A together with the sharp rise in rate of responding for Group B on the fifth day when the right lever was presented for the first time during extinction, show that the generalized effect of punishment upon R_R adapts out at about the same rate during subsequent periods in the experimental situation whether the response is elicited or not. On the other hand, the drop in the curve of Group A on the fifth day demonstrates that part of the effect of punishment is specific to the punished response and cannot be extinguished without unpunished elicitations of that response. It appears, then, that the effects of punishment in this situation can be completely accounted for by the principles developed in Chapters II and III.

Conclusion. If of two equally strong responses, R_1 and R_2, which have previously been reinforced in a given situation one, R_1, is punished to the point of temporary suppression, the initial effect of the punishment is completely generalized to R_2. During subsequent periods of extinction, the recovery of R_2 from the effects of punishment is considerably accelerated over that of R_1 and appears to proceed at about the same rate during periods of exposure to the experimental situation whether R_2 is actually elicited or not. As for the effect of punishment upon the punished response itself, the results of this experiment confirm the conclusion drawn from Experiment J—that partial recovery from punishment occurs during subsequent periods of passive exposure to the experimental situation but that complete recovery is contingent upon a sufficient number of actual elicitations of the response.

V. Summary of Empirical Principles

I.

When the disturbing stimulus is of sufficient intensity and is temporarily contiguous with a response and with the discriminative stimuli for the response, the immediate effect of punishment is regularly a depression in strength of the response. This effect is maintained so long as the punishment continues to be correlated with the response.

However, the rate of responding at the end of a period of punishment, regardless of severity or duration, is not a reliable index of the true latent strength of the response. Discontinuation of punishment is always followed by some recovery in strength.

II.

The effects of punishment are contingent upon a close association of the disturbing stimulus with the stimuli which normally provide an occasion for the occurrence of the response (discriminative stimuli). There is no evidence that the correlation of the punishment with the response per se in the role of a "negative reinforcement" is important.

III.

The extinction of a response which has been positively reinforced cannot be accelerated by the application of punishment; the total amount of time necessary for extinction is evidently determined by the conditions of previous positive reinforcement and cannot be reduced by punishment.

IV.

The extent to which the total number of unreinforced elicitations of a response necessary for extinction at a given level of drive can be reduced by punishment is a joint function of the conditions of punishment and the conditions of previous positive reinforcement.

A. When a response which has been strengthened by periodic reinforcement is punished for a time and then during subsequent periods is neither punished nor reinforced, the following relationships hold:

1. A period of mild punishment produces a temporary depression in rate of responding which is followed by a compensatory increase so that the total number of unreinforced elicitations necessary for complete extinction is not altered.

2. When a severe punishment is continued to the point of temporary suppression of the response, the process of recovery from the initially depressing effect of the punishment is described by an equation of the form

$$p_t = p_0 e^{-at}$$

where p_t is an index of the effect of punishment remaining at time t, p_o is the magnitude of p during the period of punishment, and a is a constant. After recovery from the effects of punishment, there is only partial compensation for the previously depressed rate of responding.

3. When severe punishment is prolonged beyond the point of temporary inhibition, a considerable saving may be effected in the total number of unreinforced elicitations of the response necessary for extinction.

B. The proportion by which the total number of unreinforced elicitations of the response necessary for extinction can be reduced by a given condition of punishment decreases with increasing amounts of previous positive reinforcement.

V.

After the establishment of a discrimination, the initial effect of punishment of the response in the absence of the discriminative stimulus (the stimulus which provides the occasion on which the response will be reinforced) is almost completely generalized to the strength of the response in its presence. Recovery in strength of the response in the presence of the discriminative stimulus follows a course similar to that observed in the case of a response which was simply periodically reinforced for a time prior to the period of punishment. The strength of the response in the absence of the discriminative stimulus exhibits little recovery from the effects of punishment.

VI.

The immediate effect of punishment upon a periodically reinforced response is a simple change in slope of the periodic curve (i.e., a decline in strength); if reinforcement continues after the discontinuation of punishment, the effects of punishment are quickly dissipated. The effects of punishment of a response upon the course of subsequent extinction are about the same whether or not positive reinforcement continues during the period of punishment.

VII.

The result of a period during which a disturbing stimulus is associated with the stimuli which normally act as an occasion for the occurrence of the response is a depression in strength of the response during subsequent periods of extinction very similar to that produced by a period of actual punishment of the response.

VIII.

The effects of a period of severe punishment are almost completely extinguished by a period during which the organism is exposed to the experimental situation but is unable to make the response.

IX.

The effects of periodically administered punishment are more specific to the punished response than those of punishment which follows every occurrence of the response.

X.

If of two alternative responses to a situation, R_1 and R_2, which are initially of equal strength, one, R_1, is punished, the initial effect of punishment is completely generalized to R_2. During subsequent periods, the recovery of R_2 from the effect of punishment is considerably accelerated over that of R_1 and proceeds at about the same rate during periods of exposure to the experimental situation whether R_2 is actually elicited or not. As for the recovery from punishment of the punished response, R_1, it appears that partial recovery occurs during periods of passive exposure to the experimental situation, but complete recovery is contingent upon a sufficient number of actual elicitations of the response.

VI. Theoretical and Practical Implications

An interpretation of punishment in terms of emotional conditioning and conflict[13]

The results of the present investigation tend, in general, to confirm Thorndike's most recent formulation of the law of effect (Thorndike,

---

[13] [See Estes (1969) for a more recent theoretical treatment of punishment.—Eds.]

1935). It appears that the effects of punishment upon the punished response are due to competing reactions aroused by the noxious stimulus. No evidence has been forthcoming to indicate that punishment exerts a direct weakening effect upon a response comparable to the strengthening produced by a reward. The term "reinforcement" can best be reserved for the latter class of stimuli.

The observed facts concerning the action of punishment can be accounted for in terms of conditioning principles established by investigations of the effects of a noxious stimulus which is not correlated with a response in the role of a punishment. An experiment reported by Estes and Skinner (1941) demonstrated that a tone which precedes a disturbing stimulus acquires the capacity to depress the strength of behavior normally occurring in the situation even though the behavior has never been directly associated with either stimulus. It was concluded that the tone becomes an occasion (a conditioned stimulus) for a state of "anxiety" or anticipation of the shocks.

In an earlier investigation, Warner (1932) subjected rats to repeated presentations of a CS (buzzer or light) followed by shock, under a variety of conditions and observed the reaction to the buzzer or light resulting from the conditioning. He found that no specific parts of the original response to the US, with the possible exception of autonomic reactions, such as change in breathing rate, are regularly conditioned. About all that can be said with confidence about the conditioned state of anticipation which comes to be aroused by a stimulus (S_1) which characteristically precedes a disturbing stimulus (S_2), is that it commonly involves parts of the original unconditioned reaction to S_2 together with some apparently random activity, and that it results in the disruption of the "normal" behavior of the organism, in the situation in question so long as S_1 is present.

It is clear, then, that a disturbing or traumatic stimulus arouses a changed state of the organism of the sort commonly termed "emotional" and that any stimulus present simultaneously with the disturbing stimulus becomes a conditioned stimulus capable of itself arousing the state on subsequent occasions. From the results of the present investigation, we may conclude that a great part of the initial effect of punishment is due to this sort of emotional conditioning. In Experiment G, in which the rats were merely given shocks while in the experimental situation, the stimuli which normally provided an occasion for the occurrence of the lever-pressing response became conditioned stimuli for anticipating the shock. When punishment is correlated with the response, emotional reaction can also become conditioned to the incipient movements of making the response. (This interpretation has been anticipated by Skinner [1938].) During periods following discontinuation of punishment when the organism is exposed to the situation in which punishment occurred but is unable to make the response, the connections between the conditioned emotional state and the stimuli present in the situation are extinguished.

In addition to a generalized emotional reaction, a disturbing stimulus usually arouses a withdrawal response, R^w. It has been shown (Bugelski & Miller, 1938; Hilgard & Marquis, 1940; Holt, 1931) that R^w becomes conditioned to any stimulus which is contiguous with the disturbing stimulus. In many situations involving punishment there is opportunity for R^w to become conditioned to the same stimuli which previously aroused the punished response. Part of the effect of punishment in these cases is probably a result of conflict between the competing responses. If the disturbing stimulus is of sufficient intensity, R^w becomes prepotent and the original response temporarily ceases to occur. When a child touches a hot radiator, for example, the painful stimulation causes a vigorous withdrawal from the hot object. On subsequent occasions, the sight of the radiator alone will suffice to arouse the withdrawal response which, being directly in conflict with the response of touching the radiator, prevents the occurrence of the latter. However, the present investigation has demonstrated that the original response is not eliminated from the organism's repertoire, but continues to exist at a state of considerable latent strength. Whenever punishment is discontinued, experimental extinction of R^w begins; and as R^w is weakened, the original response recovers in strength. It is likely that the superiority of periodically administered punishment over punishment which follows every occurrence of a response (noted in Experiments E and K) is due to the resulting periodic reinforcement of the response of withdrawal from the region of the lever. Skinner (1938) has shown that periodic positive reinforcement of a response produces much greater resistance to extinction than continuous reinforcement. In this situation, termination of the shock presumably acts as reinforcement for the response of withdrawal from the lever.

The generalized effects of punishment are probably mediated largely by the "emotional" reaction aroused by the noxious stimulus. This reaction should be expected to affect any behavior normally occurring in the situation and accounts for the initially complete induction of the effects of punishment between dynamically related responses noted in Chapter IV. During a period of adaptation to the situation in which punishment occurred, the connections of the conditioned emotional state to the general stimulation from the experimental situation and to stimuli produced by movements of making the response are extinguished, the former directly, the latter through induction.

Punishment in the practical control of behavior

Probably the most important practical implication of the present study is the demonstration that a response cannot be eliminated from an organism's repertoire more rapidly with the aid of punishment than without it. In fact, severe punishment may have precisely the opposite effect. A response can be permanently weakened only by a sufficient number of unreinforced elicitations and this process of extinction cannot proceed while a response is suppressed as a result of punishment. The punished response continues to exist in the organism's repertoire with most of its original latent strength. While it is suppressed, the response is not only protected from extinction, but it also may become a source of conflict. An emotional state, such as "anxiety" or "dread," which has become conditioned to the incipient movements of making the response will be aroused by any stimuli which formerly acted as occasions for the occurrence of the response.

Another disadvantage of severe punishment lies in the generalization of the conditioned emotional reaction aroused by the disturbing stimulus to other stimuli acting at the time. Whipping a dog, for example, is quite as likely to result in the conditioning of fear and withdrawal reactions to the sight of the trainer as in the weakening of the undesired behavior. And the emotional state is as effective in depressing the strength of other behavior which would normally occur in the situation in question as in depressing the strength of the punished response.

Punishment can be used profitably as an aid in the elimination of an undesired response only if the severity of the punishment is adjusted in such a manner that the response continues to occur, but at a reduced rate; under this condition, a considerable saving may be effected in the number of unreinforced elicitations of the response necessary for extinction, although the total amount of time required cannot be reduced.

In cases where the factor of reward cannot be brought under control, punishment of suitable intensity can be used to hold the response at a low strength, provided that the correlation of punishment with the response can be maintained indefinitely. It was shown in Chapter II, Section 2, that the result of directly opposed punishment and reward is an equilibrium with the resultant strength of the response a function of the relative intensities of the two factors. For any given condition of reinforcement, a condition of punishment can probably be found that will reduce the rate of responding to a very low value. The principle difficulty with this procedure is that whenever punishment ceases to be correlated with the response, the effects of the punishment are quickly dissipated.

In many instances one is interested not so much in actually eliminating a response as in supplanting an undesired response to a situation with a more acceptable one. Punishment can be usefully employed as a means of temporarily suppressing the original response while some other response is strengthened by reinforcement.[14]

In all of these cases, punishment can be expected to weaken a response only if it is temporally contiguous with the discriminative stimuli for the response and with the movement involved in making it, or with both. Many a dog-owner has learned the futility of attempting to break the habit of chasing cars by punishing the animal when he returns from the chase and the car is out of sight. Educators and animal trainers have frequently observed that punishment is usually ineffective if delayed too long after the occurrence of the response. However, the present study has shown that it is not the correlation of the punishment with the response per se that is important, but the contiguity of the punishment with the stimuli which formerly aroused the response.

14 [See Selection 6 for data supporting this conclusion.—Eds.]

12 Permanent effects of punishment during extinction

Erling E. Boe and Russell M. Church

The results of two experiments (Estes, 1944, Experiment A; Skinner, 1938, p. 154)[1] indicate that a brief period of punishment at the beginning of extinction will not reduce the total number of responses emitted during the course of extinction, even though the immediate effect of punishment is to depress response rate. For these results to

Reprinted from the *Journal of Comparative and Physiological Psychology*, 1967, 63, 486–492 by permission of the American Psychological Association. This investigation was supported by a United States Public Health Service Fellowship (PHS 1-F2-MH-28233) and Research Grant MH-08123 from the National Institute of Mental Health.

[The two experiments reported here extend some of the research reported by Estes (Selection 11) on the compensatory recovery phenomenon and on the importance of contingency between a response and aversive stimulation. The failure of complete compensatory recovery to occur under even mild levels of shock intensity following the discontinuation of punishment indicates that the phenomenon is either unreliable or else occurs under a very narrow range of conditions. Further evidence is reported of the greater suppressing effect of punishment than noncontingent shock both during the period of its application and following its discontinuation. Although the results do not support the negative law of effect to the exclusion of other hypotheses, the authors point out that it is not as untenable as has been generally assumed since Thorndike discounted it in 1932.—Eds.]

[1][See Selections 10 and 11.—Eds.]

occur, punished Ss must emit more responses than control Ss during postpunishment extinction sessions to compensate for their reduced output during punishment. For convenience, this phenomenon will henceforth be referred to as compensatory recovery.

On the basis of other experiments (B, C, D, F, G, & J) in which compensatory recovery did not occur, Estes (1944) drew the general conclusion that "The extent to which the total number of unreinforced elicitations of a response necessary for extinction at a given level of drive can be reduced by punishment is a joint function of the conditions of punishment and the conditions of previous positive reinforcement [p. 34]." Compensatory recovery was not found in other experiments (Akhtar, 1963; Boe, 1964) as well. Thus, the conditions under which it is observed appear to be much narrower than the conditions under which it is not. The present experiments were designed first to reproduce compensatory recovery, if possible, and then to identify various conditions necessary for its demonstration.

Experiment 1

Boe (1964) found that the extent to which punishment reduced the total number of responses during extinction was inversely related to punishment intensity and directly related to the number of training trials. In this experiment rats were trained to enter the right goal box of a modified Y maze and then, during the first 10 of 30 extinction trials, they were punished with a brief shock. Compensatory recovery was not found in any of the nine relevant groups in Boe's experiment, although it might be found in a free-responding situation, at least under optimal conditions. Consequently, Experiment 1 was designed to replicate as exactly as possible the procedures used by Estes (1944) in Experiment A where compensatory recovery has been previously reported. In addition to his "mild" shock group, several groups with higher voltage levels were added so that the range of shock intensities over which the phenomenon occurs could be observed.

Method

Subjects

The Ss were 60 naive, male, albino, Norway rats of hysterec-tomy-derived, barrier-sustained stock that arrived from the Charles River Breeding Laboratories at 49 days of age. They were about 125 days old at the beginning of the experiment and weighed 215–295 gm.

Apparatus

A force of about 15 gm. was required to operate the lever in six standard lever boxes. Electrical stimulation was applied through a grid floor with a matched-impedance ac source (150 K ohm in series with Ss).

Design

The 60 Ss were randomly assigned to six groups differing only in the intensity (0, 35, 50, 75, 120, or 220 v.) of the .1-sec. electric shocks. One S in the 50-v. group was eliminated because of failure to acquire the lever-pressing response. The Ss in a particular group were punished with the same voltage throughout the punishment phase. The least severe shock (35 v.) was barely strong enough to elicit a reliable UR in pilot animals that were stimulated noncon-tingently, while the 220-v. shock elicited a strong UR. According to Campbell and Teghtsoonian (1958), the threshold for aversion in rats is 30 v. for the matched-impedance source used here.

Procedure

The Ss were housed in individual cages with water always accessible, and were handled daily. For the first 7 days, food was available ad lib; thereafter, Ss were given daily feedings of about 12 gm. of dry Purina chow mixed with about 25 cc of water.

On the first experimental day all Ss were trained to approach the food cup following the activation of the pellet dispenser by auto-matically dispensing one 45-mg. Noyes food pellet each minute until 60 pellets had been delivered. On Day 2, each S was continuously reinforced for the first 30 lever responses and then returned to its home cage. Thereafter, all sessions were 60 min. long and each S was run at approximately the same time each day.

For the next three sessions, lever pressing was reinforced on a 4-min. FI schedule. Extinction commenced on the following (sixth) session and was continued for nine 1-hr. sessions in all. Shock was contingent upon lever pressing during Minutes 5–20 of the first extinction session only. During the 15-min. punishment phase, the stimulator was reset every 30 sec. and the next response was punished. Thus, a maximum of 30 shocks could be delivered to a particular S if sufficient responding were maintained.

Upon completion of the nine extinction sessions, three 1-hr. retraining sessions were scheduled. The first five responses during the first retraining session were reinforced with a food pellet; thereafter, reinforcement was delivered on the original 4-min. FI schedule.

The procedures employed from magazine training through the first three extinction sessions were identical to those reported by Estes (1944) for his Experiment A. In the present experiment, however, there were six additional extinction sessions, and then three retraining sessions that replicated the procedure used by Estes in his Experiment C.

Dependent Variable

The number of responses during the last session of reinforced training was highly correlated with the number of responses emitted during the nine sessions of extinction. The rank order correlations between these variables for the 10 Ss of each of the six groups of Experiment I and the six groups of Experiment II were computed separately. They ranged from .53 to .94 with a median of .76. A rank order correlation of .55 based on ten independent observations is significant at the .05 level (one-tailed). Since the purpose of the experiment was to examine performance differences during extinction as a function of punishment intensity, it was desirable to reduce the effect of performance level prior to treatment on performance level during extinction. Therefore, the number of responses during various segments of extinction for a particular S was divided by the number of responses that S made during the last session of reinforced training, and the ratio was then multiplied by 100. The resulting number is hereafter called the *response percentage*, and it is the dependent variable used for reporting most of the results. (The mean number of responses during the last session of reinforcement training was 722.) The correlations between number of responses during the last day of training and response percentage for the 12 groups of Experiments I and II had a median of $-.17$ and only 2 of 12 were greater than $\pm .55$. Thus, the response percentage measure is virtually independent of variation in reinforced response rate.

Results

Median response percentages for the six groups of Ss are presented in cumulative form for the nine sessions of extinction in Figure 12.1.

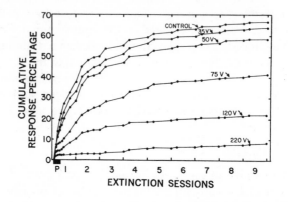

Figure 12.1   Cumulative median response percentage during extinction. (Punishment, *P*, was contingent upon lever pressing during Minutes 5–20 of the first extinction session.)

It is obvious that there was both an immediate (i.e., during the punishment period) and a permanent (i.e., during nine sessions of extinction) decrease in responding, with the amount of decrease depending upon punishment intensity. Although response rate increased somewhat upon discontinuation of punishment in the three most intensely punished groups, there was no evidence of compensatory recovery.

The relationship between response percentage during the 15-min. punishment period and voltage of the punishing shocks is shown in the upper section of Figure 12.2. An exponential curve was

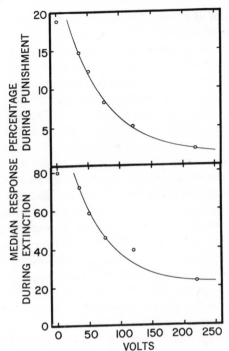

Figure 12.2   Median response percentage during the 15-min. punishment period (upper panel) and during nine extinction sessions (lower panel) as a function of punishment intensity (voltage). (The formulas for the exponential function fit to the observed values are $R = 23.01e^{-.015V} + 1.25$, and $R = 96.40e^{-.018V} + 21.30$, respectively, where R represents response percentage and V represents voltage.)

fitted to the observed values. The observed value for the unpunished control group was not included in the curve-fitting procedure because the threshold for the punishing effect of an electric shock obviously lies somewhere above zero voltage. Extrapolation of the curve upward to the control group's level of response percentage suggests that the punishment threshold is approximately 17 v. under the conditions of this experiment. A Kruskal-Wallis analysis of variance test of the six observed medians indicated that their differences were highly significant ($H = 44.9$, $df = 5$, $p < .001$). In addition, individual tests showed that both the 35-v. and 50-v. groups were significantly below the control group (Mann-Whitney one-tailed U test, $p < .05$ in both cases).

The effect of variation in punishment intensity on total responses during extinction is shown in the lower section of Figure 12.2. An exponential curve similar to that shown in the upper section again fits the observed values well, and the overall effect of variation in punishment intensity was highly significant (Kruskal-Wallis analysis of variance, $H = 25.2$, $df = 5$, $p < .001$). For the reasons presented above, the value for the control group was not used in fitting the curve. Compensatory recovery obviously did not occur in the more intense punishment groups, and there are two substantial reasons for concluding that it did not occur in the 35-v. and 50-v. groups as well. The first reason is that the observed values for both groups are below the control group and fall near the exponential function. The second reason is that the differences between the control and the two mild punishment groups increased following the discontinuation of punishment instead of decreasing as required for compensatory recovery to occur. Whereas the 35-v. and 50-v. groups were 4.2 and 6.6 percentage points, respectively, lower than the control group after 15 min. of punishment, they dropped an additional 4.3 and 12.3 percentage points, respectively, lower during the subsequent 8 hr. and 40 min. of extinction.

Since punishment was programmed on a 30-sec. interval schedule, the number of punishments received was not necessarily correlated with the amount of responding, i.e., a slow but steady rate of responding would be sufficient to produce the maximum of 30 punishments in the 15-min. punishment period. Slow but steady response rates were not maintained during punishment, however, and the number of punishments delivered was also an exponential function of shock intensity. Median number of punishments delivered, beginning with the 35-v. group and in order of intensity thereafter, were 26.5, 25.0, 16.0, 9.8, and 4.2. Control Ss responded at a rate that would have produced a median of 28.8 of a possible 30.0 punishments. The effect of variation in shock intensity was again highly significant (Kruskal-Wallis analysis of variance, $H = 42.5$, $df = 5$, $p < .001$).

In an important sense, the relationship between shock intensity and response percentage reported in Figure 12.2 does not represent the full effect of increasing intensity, because punishment

frequency simultaneously diminishes. A more meaningful measure
might be the amount of response suppression produced per punishment. This measure was computed by first subtracting the response
percentage of each of the punished groups from the response percentage of the control group as reported in the upper section of Figure 12.2, and then dividing this difference by the actual number of
punishments delivered. The subtraction yields the amount of suppression as a function of punishment intensity, and the division
yields the measure of suppression per punishment. This variable is
plotted as a function of shock intensity in Figure 12.3, both in terms
of raw units and of their logarithms. The power function fit to the

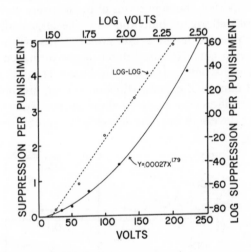

Figure 12.3 Amount of suppression per punishment in response percentage
units as a function of punishment intensity (voltage) presented in two ways.
(The solid, curved line is plotted against the scales at the left and lower margins,
while the dashed, straight line is plotted against the logarithmic transformation
of those scales located at the top and right margins.)

observed values closely resembles those found in psychophysical
experiments of the relationship between current and the subjective
estimation of shock intensity by human Ss (Kalikow, 1966; Sternbach
& Tursky, 1964; Stevens, Carton, & Shickman, 1958).

Although compensatory recovery did not occur in most of

Estes' (1944) experiments, he reported that punishment did not reduce the amount of time needed for extinction in some of these. While the present data also indicate that a time measure of extinction was much less sensitive to experimental manipulations than the response percentage measure, an effect on the time measure was detected. Most Ss (90 percent) reached the criterion of less than 2 percent within nine extinction sessions (overall median equaled about five sessions). The median sessions to this criterion for each group from control to most severely punished (220 v.) were 6.0, 7.5, 5.3, 4.5, 3.2, and 3.5 (Kruskal-Wallis analysis of variance, $H = 11.7$, $df = 5, p < .05$).

Except for Ss in the most intense (220-v.) punishment group, the results reported above in terms of medians are representative of the response patterns of individual Ss. The large individual differences that appeared in the 220-v. group are shown in Figure 12.4. Each extinction curve is based upon the performance of a single S following the discontinuation of punishment (i.e., responses during the first 20 min. of the first extinction session are not included in the figure). Differences between these curves were not related to performance levels during the immediately preceding punishment period.

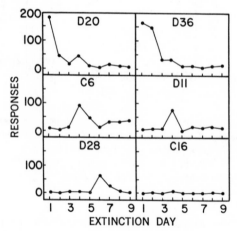

Figure 12.4   Number of lever-pressing responses as a function of extinction session for six individual Ss in the 220-v. punishment group

Two Ss in the 220-v. punishment group (D20 and D36) resumed responding almost immediately after punishment was discontinued, and they gradually diminished their response rate over the subsequent extinction sessions (Figure 12.4). This pattern was characteristic of the performance of the 49 Ss in all the other groups. Three Ss (C6, D11, and D28) had a delayed onset of extinction. After three or more sessions of almost complete suppression, these Ss increased their response rate and then reduced it. Obviously, punishment had not eliminated response strength entirely, but it apparently had reduced it. The third pattern of responding is illustrated by C16, and it was characteristic of the remaining 4 Ss in the 220-v. group. The brief period of intense punishment appears to have eliminated lever pressing (i.e., reduced it to operant level or below). At the very least, an enduring suppression was produced by intense punishment in half of the Ss exposed to it.

Differences in rate of responding during retraining as a function of punishment intensity (and total responses during extinction, too, since they are related) were also examined. Medians for each of the six groups were computed for response percentage during the first 15 min. of the first hourly session, during the first 30 min. of the first session, during the entire first session, and during all three sessions combined. None of the probability levels produced by the Kruskal-Wallis analysis of variance tests even approached conventional levels of significance. Furthermore, the 5 Ss that were almost completely suppressed by punishment in the 220-v. group were comparable to the other 5 Ss that were not. All Ss simply reconditioned rapidly. The failure of a compensatory increase in response rate during retraining to be proportional to the amount of suppression during extinction is further evidence that punishment permanently reduced response strength in direct relation to its intensity.

Experiment 2

A question of considerable theoretical importance is whether or not the permanent reduction in number of responses produced by punishment during extinction is a function of the correlation between the lever-pressing response and shock. Although Estes (1944) concluded that "The result of a period during which a disturbing stimulus is associated with the stimuli which normally act as an occasion for the occurrence of the response is a depression in strength of the response during subsequent periods of extinction very similar to that produced by a period of actual punishment of the response [p. 35]" on the basis of his Experiments I and J, he also recognized that the response contingency characteristic of punishment was relevant to its suppressing effect under some conditions. With respect to recovery from punishment, the importance of shock being contingent upon responses in comparison to its being contingent upon discriminative stimuli has been demonstrated by Hunt and Brady (1955)[2] and by Azrin (1956). However, more rapid recovery occurred after punishment than noncontingent shock in the Hunt and Brady experiment, while punishment prolonged the period of suppression in the Azrin experiment. Since experimental procedures of Estes, Hunt and Brady, and Azrin differed in many respects, it is impossible to determine the source of these widely differing results. Although the weight of more recent research clearly indicates that punishment is more suppressive than noncontingent shock during the period of its application, no new data on their relative rates of recovery have been forthcoming. Experiment 2 was designed to provide further information on the unsettled question of contingency effects on recovery from punishment.

Method

The kind and number of Ss, apparatus, and the training procedures were like those reported for Experiment 1. The experimental design (but not all procedural details) of Estes' (1944) Experiment J (Part 2) was used.

The 60 Ss were first randomly assigned in equal numbers to the six conditions of a 2 × 3 factorial experiment. The independent variable at two levels was the administration (or not) of a session with the lever removed; the variable at three levels was shock condition (punishment, noncontingent shock, unpunished control). On the day following the third hourly session of reinforced training, a 20-min. extinction session was conducted in which (a) the lever-pressing response was punished for 20 Ss in the punishment condition, (b) shocks were periodically delivered independent of re-

[2] [See Selection 14.—Eds.]

sponding for 20 Ss in the noncontingent shock condition, and (c) simple extinction was given to 20 Ss in the control condition. As in Experiment 1, all shocks (120 v. at .1 sec.) were delivered during Minutes 5–20 of the first extinction session. Under the punishment condition, lever-pressing responses were shocked on the 30-sec. intermittent schedule used in Experiment 1. Under the noncontingent shock condition, the electrical stimulus was automatically delivered every 30 sec. without regard to responding.

An hourly session in the box with the lever removed was conducted the next day for 10 Ss in each of the punishment, noncontingent shock, and control conditions. The other 10 Ss in each condition were simply removed from their living cages, handled briefly, and then returned to their cages. Hourly extinction sessions with the lever present were conducted for the remaining 9 days of the experiment.

Results

Since the session in the leverless box produced little or no effect on resistance to extinction, the two groups of 10 Ss each given punishment, the two groups given noncontingent shock, and the two groups given simple extinction were combined. The main results are therefore reported for three groups of 20 Ss each in Figure 12.5. Both

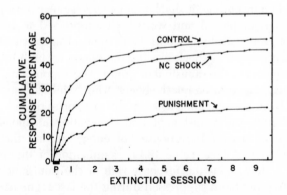

Figure 12.5 Cumulative median response percentage during extinction. (Punishment, *P*, was contingent upon lever pressing during Minutes 5–20 of the 20-min. initial extinction session.)

punishment and noncontingent shock reduced response rate during the 15-min. punishment session. During several of the subsequent extinction sessions, however, the response rate of punished Ss continued to be suppressed in comparison with the control group, while the noncontingently shocked Ss were not suppressed following the discontinuation of shock. Instead, they resumed responding almost immediately at a rate comparable to that of the control group.

Median response percentages and tests of significance at selected times during extinction are presented in Table 12.1. These

Table 12.1   Median response percentage during extinction

Session	Punish-ment	NC shock	Control
Punishment period	4.2	7.0	16.4[a]
First postpunishment extinction session	8.8[a]	19.4	21.0
All extinction sessions	36.8[a]	51.8	58.8

Note—The medians tabulated in each row differ significantly from each other at the .001 level (Kruskal-Wallis analysis of variance).

[a]Medians differ significantly ($p < .001$) from others in the row (Mann-Whitney U tests). Other pairs of medians in same row do not differ significantly from each other ($p < .05$).

data confirm the impressions given in Figure 12.5, viz., that the punishment and noncontingent shock groups were similar during the 20-min. punishment period and were both suppressed in relation to the control group, while the control and noncontingent shock groups were similar as soon as shock was discontinued and both had higher response rates than the punishment group. The suppressing effect of punishment seemed to be relatively enduring, while the suppression produced by noncontingent shock rapidly disappeared.

Although the punishment and noncontingent shock groups did not differ in overall response percentage during the 15-min. punishment period (see Table 12.1), examination of this period in Figure 12.5 shows that the response rate of the punishment group was considerably more suppressed during the last segments. Consequently, the significance of this observed difference between median response percentages was computed for each of the three 5-min. blocks during the 15-min. punishment period. The two groups were not significantly different during the first 5-min. block, but on each of the second two blocks, punishment Ss were significantly (U test, $p < .001$) more suppressed although they received only about one-third as many shocks as the noncontingent Ss (median of 8.8 shocks vs. a uniform 30 for noncontingent Ss).

Discussion

Observations that a brief period of punishment at the beginning of extinction merely depresses performance temporarily but does not reduce the total number of responses emitted during the course of extinction have provided the strongest empirical basis for rejection of Thorndike's (1913) early view (hereafter referred to as the suppression hypothesis) that punishment substracts strength from a learned connection. The results of Experiment 1, an attempt to replicate the conditions of an experiment in which compensatory recovery was reported (Estes, 1944, Experiment A), are consistent with the results of a number of other experiments (Akhtar, 1963; Boe, 1964; Estes, 1944) in suggesting that the range of conditions under which compensatory recovery can be reproduced, if at all, is very narrow. Thus a major reason for rejection of the suppression hypothesis is removed. This is not to suggest, however, that the suppression hypothesis provides a complete account of the results, e.g., the acceleration in rate shortly after the punishment was discontinued that was particularly prominent in the 75-v. and 120-v. groups. An adequate explanation of punishment effects must entail several different principles, one of which might be the suppression hypothesis.

Perhaps the discrepancy between the present results and those of Skinner (1938) and Estes (1944, Experiment A) can be reconciled on the basis of differences in intensity of the punishing stimulus. It is possible that the punishing stimulus used by Estes (a condenser discharge) was milder than the lowest intensity used in the present experiment, since he did not report that his mild shock produced statistically significant suppression; the stimuli used by Skinner (a kickback of the lever combined with a "fairly loud click") may also have been milder than the lowest intensity used in the present experiment since a moderate response rate was maintained despite the fact that each response was followed by the stimulus. Compensatory recovery may occur only when responses are followed by stimuli that serve to change the stimulus context (i.e., external inhibitors) but that are not aversive (punishing) stimuli.

Current theories of punishment may be classified into those for which a correlation between instrumental responding and punishment is necessary and those for which such a correlation is irrelevant (Church, 1963). Results of Experiment 2 indicate that the correlation between response and shock was of major importance both during punishment and following its discontinuation. Noncontingent shock suppressed responding considerably (though not as much as punishment) during the treatment period, but had no detectable effect on the course of subsequent extinction. These results, as well as others, suggest that an adequate theoretical account of punishment must entail at least two factors, one of which requires response contingency and one that does not.

Summary

The lever-pressing response by rats was punished on an intermittent schedule with brief shocks during a 15-min. period at the beginning of extinction. In Experiment 1, total responses during both the punishment period and the entire course of extinction were an exponential decreasing function of punishment intensity. In Experiment 2, punishment (response-contingent shock) suppressed response rate more than noncontingent shocks during a brief punishment period and during subsequent extinction sessions. In both experiments, punishment produced a permanent reduction in the number of responses instead of only temporarily depressing response rate.

13   The law of effect, conditioning, and the problem of punishment

O. Hobart Mowrer

I. Thorndike's Early Position Re-evaluated and Revised

Thorndike's original position was to the effect that learning is a reversible process, reward strengthening and punishment weakening it. In a grossly empirical, descriptive sense, the Law of Effect is almost certainly valid: other things being equal, an act is more

Reprinted from Chapter 2 of *Learning Theory and Behavior*, New York, Wiley, 1960, by permission of the author and the publisher.

[Mowrer's avoidance hypothesis of the suppressing effects of punishment begins with the assumption that punishment produces emotional learning (i.e., fear conditioning). Whereas Skinner and Estes attributed a great deal of punishment-produced suppression to competing emotional responses (i.e., the fear hypotheses), Mowrer merely considers the conditioning of fear to be but the first of two stages. As fear becomes conditioned to stimuli associated with punishment (particularly response-produced stimuli), it becomes an aversive drive which is reduced when alternative instrumental responses, such as withdrawal responses, are emitted. Competing skeletal responses that are reinforced by fear reduction gain ascendency and supplant the punished responses. The learning of competing instrumental responses (which constitutes the second stage of the theory) interferes with the punished responses and thereby allows the subject to avoid the punishing stimulus. For a somewhat different version of the avoidance hypothesis, see Dinsmoor (1954).—Eds.]

181

likely to recur if its prior occurrence has led to reward, and it is less likely to recur if its prior occurrence has led to punishment. Such a bifurcated principle is, to say the least, congruent with common sense; and it seems well calculated to make behavior adaptive, in the biological scheme of things.

However, at another level of interpretation, the Law of Effect has come under increasingly critical scrutiny. For at least two decades now, it has been clear that the "negative" half of the law, in its more molecular aspects, was miscast. Just as reward was said to "stamp in" bonds, associations, or connections, punishment was thought to weaken, or "stamp out," such connections. Learning, or S-R "bonding" was thus, as already noted, a reversible process. Just as reward caused it to proceed in a forward direction, punishment caused it to recede. If rewards, so to say, opened neural pathways, punishment closed them. And the one action was assumed to be just as immediate and direct as the other.

Whatever learning may be in its "forward," positive phase, it became increasingly clear that unlearning, or "punishment," is not a simple matter of obliterating, stamping out stimulus-response "bonds." But a more declarative approach to the negative side of learning could not occur until at least certain forms of that type of learning known as *conditioning* were taken into account. And here our story starts with the phenomenon of *fear* conditioning.

II. Punishment and Fear Conditioning

Punishment thus emerges, not as one of two aspects of a single (reversible) learning process, but rather as a subprinciple, or "application," of another seemingly separate type of learning. This other type of learning is fear conditioning and, in its most general form, can be conveniently depicted as shown in Figure 13.1. If fear, with its powerful motivational properties, is conditioned to stimuli which are response-produced, occurrence of that response will tend, as already indicated, to be blocked: the occurrence or continuation of the response arouses fear and its discontinuation causes the fear to abate. If, on the other hand, fear is conditioned to stimuli not specifically associated with behavior, resolution of the fear will very likely be best achieved, not by inaction, but by action—action which will eliminate the fear-producing stimulus or situation either by removing the affected organism therefrom or by changing the situation. In the one case, i.e., where the stimuli are response-produced, we are likely to speak of "punishment" and, in the other case, of "avoidance learning," although it is now evident that "avoidance," in the sense of averting painful, noxious stimulation, is achieved in *both* instances through the arousal of fear and appropriate (though different) reactions thereto.

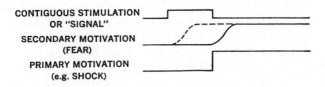

CONTIGUOUS STIMULATION OR "SIGNAL"

SECONDARY MOTIVATION (FEAR)

PRIMARY MOTIVATION (e.g. SHOCK)

Figure 13.1   Diagrammatic representation of fear conditioning. This emotion is originally elicited by some primary drive, such as electric shock; but if some other, formerly neutral stimulus immediately precedes the primary drive, the fear response, after a few pairings of signal and drive, will become attached to the signal and "move forward," as shown by the dotted line. When this occurs, the fear response is said to have become "anticipatory." The above diagram is schematic, but very similar actual records can be obtained by using the GSR (galvanic skin reaction) as an indicator of fear (Mowrer, 1938; Woodworth & Schlosberg, 1954, Ch. 6).

The term, "punishment," is usually applied to the procedure employed when an organism, prompted by some drive such as hunger, exhibits a mode of behavior which has previously satisfied this drive and an effort is then made (usually by another organism) to disrupt or eliminate this "habit" by the introduction of a competing drive or drives. Suppose, for example, that a hungry laboratory rat has learned to run to a small iron rod (or "spatula") with a bit of mash pressed on its flattened end whenever this rod is inserted up through the grill-like floor of the apparatus in which the rat is located. The rat will have received considerable training in getting food in this way, over a period of two or three days, so that, at the time of the demonstration, its response to the insertion of the food-bearing rod will be prompt and specific ("habitual"). Now suppose that we have decided to "break" the rat of the 'habit" of running to and taking the food from this rod by means of punishment in the form of an electric shock of, say, two seconds duration—administered to the rat's feet from the grill floor of the apparatus.

One can easily surmise what would happen to the rat's behavior as a result of the introduction of this sort of punishment; but let us reproduce here notes made in connection with an actual demonstration of the kind described.

1st trial: On insertion of food rod, rat dashed, quite as usual, to the rod and, taking it in his forepaws, started eating. Shock was applied. Rat dropped rod and "danced" around on the grill until shock went off.

2nd trial: After an interval of 2 minutes, food rod was again presented. Rat immediately ran to the rod, took it in forepaws, and started eating. When shock was applied, rat dropped rod, danced much as before, and squealed slightly.

3rd trial: This time rat ran toward rod and tried to grab the food off it, with teeth, without taking rod in forepaws. Probably got some food, but also got shocked. Danced and squealed.

4th trial: Very much like preceding trial.

5th trial: Rat would run toward food rod, then suddenly withdraw, pause a moment, and then repeat this performance. The "conflict," between hunger and fear of being shocked, was thus very evident. After four or five successive advances toward and retreats from the food bar (without actually touching it), the rat came briefly to rest at some distance, and the experiment was discontinued.

III. Fear Conditioning and Active Avoidance Learning

Through historical accident and carelessness, the practice has grown up of speaking of "punishment" and of "avoidance learning" as if the former were, itself, not also a form of "avoidance." As seen in the preceding section, this practice is misleading and blinds us to the commonality of the principles involved. Hence it is here proposed that so-called punishment be termed *passive* avoidance learning (learning to "avoid" by *not* doing something) and that the contrasting form of avoidance (learning *to* do something as a means of avoidance) be termed *active* avoidance learning. It is with the latter that we shall now be especially concerned.

Imagine an elongated, narrow box, about three feet in length, a foot and a half high, and five or six inches wide or "deep." Imagine also that the box is divided into two compartments, by a partition in the middle with a small hole or "doorway" in it. In order to make the two compartments easily distinguishable, one—let us say the one at the observer's right—is painted white and is illuminated by a small electric light, while the other is painted black and is unilluminated. Moreover, the floor of the black compartment is made of wood, while the floor of the white, or right-hand, compartment consists of a metal grill, through which an electric shock can be administered by the experimenter.

With a laboratory rat at hand, we are ready to start a simple demonstration of active avoidance learning. We put the rat into the apparatus and let it thoroughly explore for four or five minutes. The rat, which we can observe through a one-way mirror which acts as the front side of the apparatus, will move about sniffing, looking, and feeling with its vibrassae. It will thus explore first one of the compartments and then the other, passing back and forth between them until its "curiosity" has been satisfied. Then it will settle down, perhaps groom itself, and give the appearance of being just a bit bored with it all.

The following are notes from an actual demonstration of this kind:

1st trial: Rat soon came to rest, quite conveniently, in the white compartment. (Otherwise, after exploration, rat would have been placed in the white compartment.) When shock was applied, rat churned its feet, squealed, circled about in the compartment, and, at the end of 6 seconds, escaped the shock by running through door into black compartment. But very soon the rat came back into the white compartment and had to be driven out with a second shock. This time the escape took less than 3 seconds.

2nd trial: When, after an interval of 2 minutes, rat was removed from black compartment and placed in white compartment, it promptly ran out of the white compartment into the black one. No shock applied. A little later the rat came and *looked through the door*, into the white compartment, but it did not enter.

3rd, 4th, and *5th trials*: Fled from the white compartment into the black one within a second or two, without application of shock. Rat is now content to stay in black compartment, some distance from the door. Demonstration ended.

IV. Active and Passive Avoidance Learning Compared

The foregoing demonstration helps one to see the similarity between the principles involved in so-called punishment and what is commonly, though also too restrictively, known as avoidance learning. In both instances, there is fear conditioning; and in both instances a way of behaving is found which eliminates or controls the fear. The only important distinction, it seems, is that the *stimuli* to which the fear gets connected are different. In so-called punishment, these stimuli are produced by (correlated with) the behavior, or response, which we wish to block; whereas, in so-called avoidance learning, the fear-arousing stimuli are not response-produced—they are, so to say, extrinsic rather than intrinsic, independent rather than response-dependent. But in both cases there is *avoidance* and in both cases there is its antithesis, *punishment;* hence the impropriety of referring to the one as "punishment" and to the other as "avoidance learning." Obviously precision and clarity of understanding are better served by the alternative terms here suggested, namely, *passive* avoidance learning and *active* avoidance learning, respectively.

Perhaps the relationship, and also the distinction, between these two forms of learning is best expressed by noting that in active avoidance learning, there is first fear (produced by some external stimulus, or danger signal) and then overt response (which the fear produces), whereas in passive avoidance learning, there is first a response (produced by some other drive, such as hunger) and then fear produced by response-correlated stimuli. What the organism has to do, in the two cases, to reduce the fear is, of course, quite different, because of the difference in the nature of the stimuli to which the fear is conditioned: activity which eliminates (or removes the subject from) the external stimulus, in the one case, and cessation of the activity which is producing the response-correlated stimuli, in the other. But, as we have seen, the two phenomena involve exactly the same basic principles, of fear conditioning and of the reinforcement of whatever action (or inaction) eliminates the fear.

The similarity and contrast between active and passive avoidance learning can be indicated in yet another way. By means of a noxious stimulus, such as electric shock, one can teach a rat (or other organism) either to do something it does not wish to do or not to do something it wishes to do. In other words, both situations imply conflict; but this phenomenon is usually more obvious in passive avoidance, where the subject, because of hunger or some other definite drive, is set to do something, which can be blocked only if a competing motive (fear) is introduced. In active avoidance, there may at first seem to be no competing motive; but there is always some inertia against movement; and there is at least this to contend with when an attempt is being made to coerce, or drive, an organism to do something, as opposed to preventing it from doing something. Hence, although conflict is not wholly absent in active avoidance (and may be relatively intense, in a fatigued or ill organism), in passive avoidance conflict—almost by definition—is always present and of an intensity proportional to the drive underlying the behavior which is being blocked.

14   Some effects of punishment and intercurrent "anxiety" on a simple operant

Howard F. Hunt and Joseph V. Brady

In interpreting the findings of his monumental study of punishment (1944),[1] Estes drew heavily on earlier research which indicated that conditioned emotional disturbance ("anxiety") could suppress or stop completely the output of lever responses among rats that had

Reprinted from the *Journal of Comparative and Physiological Psychology*, 1955, *48*, 305–310 by permission of the senior author and the American Psychological Association. This research was supported in part by a grant from the Social Science Research Committee of the University of Chicago and in part by the Medical Research and Development Board, Office of the Surgeon General, Department of the Army, under Contract No. DA-49-007-MD-291.

[One of the main differences between the fear hypothesis of Skinner and Estes and the avoidance hypothesis of Mowrer is the importance attached to the contingency between a response and onset of aversive stimulation. As previously noted, this contingency is irrelevant to the fear hypothesis while of great significance to the avoidance hypothesis. Hunt and Brady evaluate the importance of the contingency between response and aversive stimulus by an experimental comparison of the conditioned emotional response (CER) and the signalled punishment procedures. In both cases, a signal under the control of the experimenter is periodically introduced in the lever box. Under the CER procedure, noncontingent shock occurs at some point during, or at the end of, the signal regardless of the subject's performance. Under the signalled punishment procedure, only responses emitted during the signal are punished. If no response occurs, punishment is not delivered.—Eds.]

[1] [See Selection 11.—Eds.]

acquired a stable lever-pressing habit (Estes & Skinner, 1941). He concluded that a substantial part of the initial suppressant effect of punishment on lever-pressing (with a shock to the feet) reflected conditioning of this sort (1944, p. 36). The compound of stimuli (from the apparatus, etc.) which provided the occasion for lever-pressing, together with stimuli arising out of the movements of initiating and making lever responses, occurred prior to and contiguously with the punishing shocks. Through conditioning, these stimuli could acquire the power to evoke an "emotional state" which would disrupt the normal behavior of S, including lever-pressing, as in the earlier anxiety study. In support of this, Estes found that a substantial part of the suppressant effect of punishment tended to dissipate if the Ss spend an "adaptation" period in the Skinner box, without shocks and with the lever removed.

Estes also found that punishment, particularly if intermittent, had a more specific suppressant effect which dissipated only if S actually made unpunished lever responses. He suggested that, with repeated punishment, withdrawal responses (R_w) incompatible with lever-pressing also become conditioned, particularly to stimuli arising from movements involved in pressing the lever.

Subsequent research has confirmed decisively the suppressant effect of conditioned "fear" or "anxiety" (following the Estes-Skinner model) on lever-pressing and other activity (Brady & Hunt, 1950, 1951; Hunt, Jernberg, & Brady, 1952). But preliminary observations (Brady & Hunt, 1951, exp. 3) early suggested that the effects of punishment and "anxiety" conditioning (the CER) differ in important details. The R_w or avoidant component in punishment appears to deserve greater emphasis than Estes' interpretation gave it. Similarly, recent discussions of punishment (Dinsmoor, 1954; Schoenfeld, 1950) have stressed the importance of conditioned aversive properties acquired by the stimuli arising from the movements of initiating and making lever-responses. Avoidant behavior, incompatible with the punished response, is thought to be positively reinforced by termination of these stimuli, while the punished response becomes increasingly unlikely to occur.

The present experiment compares a discrimination based on punishment with a conditioned "anxiety" discrimination or "conditioned emotional response" (the CER), which also suppresses lever-pressing. For both, the shocks appear only during the presentation of an arbitrary CS (a clicking noise). In punishment, the shocks are given only if and when S presses the lever during the duration or at the end of the CS, and no lever-response is punished. In the CER, the CS acquires the power to evoke generalized emotional disturbance, as indicated by freezing and defecation. If the suppressant effect of punishment depends primarily on the disruptive effects of emotional disturbance evoked by the CS, both groups should show an approximately equal incidence of freezing and defecation. If, on the other hand, the punishment effect depends primarily upon the development of more specific avoidant behavior, these Ss should show a lower incidence of emotional disturbance and a higher incidence of overt behavior which has an avoidant topography. Further, the punishment suppression should dissipate rapidly as the Ss make unpunished lever responses in the presence of the CS.

Method

Twenty-two naive, male albino rats, 80 to 90 days old, were trained to press the lever in a Skinner box, first for regular and then for aperiodic water reward, available to S about once per minute on the average. After lever-pressing outputs had stabilized on the aperiodic schedule, the Ss were divided into four groups, roughly equated for rate and regularity of lever-pressing, and treated as follows:

The *CER I* group ($N = 6$) received a total of nine conditioning trials during Skinner-box runs, in accordance with the standard procedure (see Hunt, Jernberg, & Brady, 1952). Each trial consisted of the presentation of the CS (a clicking noise) during the fourth through the sixth minutes of a 12-min. lever-pressing run. The CS was terminated approximately contiguously with two momentary shocks to the feet (of approximately 1.5 ma. intensity), one just before and one just after the clicker went off.

The *CER II* group ($N = 5$) received a total of nine conditioning trials as above except that the shocks were introduced at the end of the first 1½ min. of the 3-min. CS in each conditioning trial. For both CER groups every effort was made, and successfully as far as could be determined, to avoid accidental coincidence of a shock and a lever response.

The *punishment I* group (P I) ($N = 6$) received a total of nine conditioning trials during Skinner-box runs. Each trial consisted of a 3-min. presentation of the clicker CS, from the fourth through the sixth minutes of the run, during which all lever responses produced a shock to the feet (approximately 1.5 ma.) through the grill floor. The shock was keyed by a micro-switch on the lever and continued as long as the lever was depressed sufficiently to throw the switch.

The *punishment II* group (P II) ($N = 5$) received nine conditioning trials as given to the P I group except that only those lever responses made during the last 1½ min. of the 3-min. CS were punished.

The conditioning schedule was the same for all groups. Adaptation runs (A 1, A 2, etc.) in the apparatus, with the lever in but without CS or shocks were interspersed among the conditioning trials (C 1, C 2, etc.) as follows: C 1, C 2, A 1, C 3, C 4, A 2, A 3, A 4, A 5, C 5, A 6, C 6, A 7, A 8, C 7, A 9, C 8, and A 10. Following A 10, the Ss rested in the home cages for five days. Then all Ss had two more adaptation runs followed by the last conditioning trial C 9, all with the top of the Skinner box open to permit direct observation of behavior.

On the day following C 9, all Ss were tested for their reaction to the CS alone in the grill box. This apparatus consisted of a chamber with a grill floor, one transparent wall to permit observation of behavior, and an earphone for administration of the auditory CS (Brady & Hunt, 1951). Afterward, on the same day, all Ss received an adaptation run in the Skinner box with the top closed.

Finally, starting on the day following the grill box test, all Ss received a total of ten test-extinction trials (T 1, T 2, etc.) in the Skinner box with the top closed, one trial per day for ten consecutive days. Each trial consisted of the presentation of the CS, without shock reinforcement, for 3 min. at the usual time during the run.

Except during the rest period, all Ss had a daily 12-min. run in the Skinner box, with the standard aperiodic water reinforcement schedule maintained throughout. All Ss were on a 23-hr. water deprivation schedule during the entire experiment.

The P II procedure, with lever responses unpunished for the first 1½ min. of the CS, was included to permit the observation of the effect of the conditioning, independently of any direct suppressant effect the punishing shocks themselves might have. The CER II procedure was included partly as a rough control for P II and partly to find out whether the Ss would discriminate the shocks as a signal that the CS no longer presaged a future shock in that trial. Not unexpectedly, it actually turned out that the I and II conditions for both punishment and CER produced neither appreciable nor statistically significant differences in behavior, with one trivial exception. The P II Ss showed less suppression of lever-pressing than the P I Ss during the CS on the first conditioning trial, a result to be expected as the first 1½ min. of lever-pressing was unpunished for P II but punished for P I. Accordingly, in the discussion here, the I and II P groups will be combined into a single punishment group (PUN) for comparison with a single CER group, similarly combined.

Results

Figure 14.1 shows the effect of the punishment and CER procedures on the output of lever responses during the 3-min. period from the fourth through the sixth minute of the Skinner-box runs—the critical segment of the run during which the CS appeared.

The top panel, A, shows the mean outputs of the combined PUN and combined CER groups during the critical segment of the last preconditioning and the first ten adaptation trials. These curves indicate the generalization of the suppressant effects to periods in the apparatus in which the CS and shocks did not appear. At least 9 of the 11 Ss in each group made fewer lever responses in each adaptation trial than in the last preconditioning trial ($p < .05$, for each group separately, assuming a null $p = .50$). Both procedures produced a generalized suppression of lever-pressing—generalized in that it appeared in the absence of CS and shocks. The CER produced the greater generalized suppression, however. For example, the mean output for the CER group was significantly below that for the PUN group on A 1 ($t = 2.35$, $p < .05$) as well as on A 10 ($t = 2.51$, $p < .05$).

Panel B shows the mean outputs for these groups during presentation of the CS for conditioning trials C 1 through C 8 and for the extinction trials T 1 through T 10 in which the CS but no shock

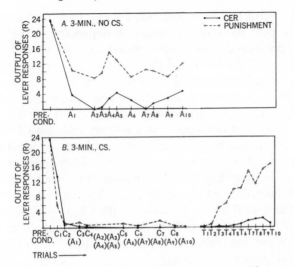

Figure 14.1   The effect of CER and punishment on output of lever responses

appeared. The preconditioning output appears, again, for comparison. On trial C 2, all Ss made fewer lever responses during the CS than they made during the equivalent segment of the last preconditioning trial. The suppressant effects of PUN and CER conditioning are obvious. But the PUN suppression was less resistant to extinction.[2] The two groups did not differ significantly in mean output during the CS on T 1. By T 5, however, 9 of the PUN and only 1 of the CER Ss made more responses during the CS than each had made on T 1 ($p < .01$) (Finney, 1948).

In trial 9, in the open Skinner box, all CER Ss showed the usual crouching or freezing behavior during presentation of the CS. But only three PUN Ss responded thus; the remaining eight showed at least some "abortive lever-pressing" activity. Typically, these Ss

---

[2] [This result has not been replicated in other experiments that have compared punishment with noncontingent shock without an external signal. Both Azrin (1956) and Boe and Church (1967, see Selection 12) found more enduring suppression with punishment than with noncontingent shock. Estes (1944, see Selection 11) found no differences in recovery rate between the two procedures. The explanation of these differences poses interesting problems for further research.—Eds.]

oriented toward the lever and water cup, often placing a paw or lower jaw over the lever, occasionally depressing it slightly, then usually approached the empty water cup. Sometimes S simply oriented toward the lever and then went to the cup; at other times the whole sequence appeared. If S pressed the lever too far and gave itself a shock, it showed a mild startle response, withdrawing from the lever, usually to resume abortive lever-pressing in a few seconds. No CER S showed any sign of this activity while five PUN Ss engaged in it repeatedly and continuously without any signs of freezing, a significant difference ($p < .04$). An earlier report on punishment also has described this phenomenon (Dinsmoor, 1952).

In the grill box test, on the day following C 9, most CER Ss showed the typical freezing reaction to the CS, as expected (Hunt & Brady, 1951a), while the PUN Ss did not. Table 14.1 shows how the groups differed. Interestingly enough, six CER Ss but no PUN S, defecated during this test ($p < .02$).

Table 14.1   Incidence of crouching and immobility in response to the CS during grill box test *

| | Group | |
Behavior	CER	PUN
Crouch, no movement	9	0
Mixed crouching and movement	2	5
Normal movement, no crouching	0	6
Total	11	11

* $\chi^2 = 16.28$, $p < .01$.

The CER group characteristically showed a higher incidence of defecation during conditioning and early in extinction. Originally the groups did not differ in this regard; on first receiving shocks in C 1, 7 CER and 6 PUN Ss defecated. But during C 8, for example, 9 CER and 2 PUN Ss defecated ($p < .01$). And during T 1, when no shocks were given, 11 CER and no PUN Ss defecated. Together with the observations of C 9 and the grill box test, these data indicate that the CS evoked more general emotional disturbance among CER than among PUN Ss (Hunt & Otis, 1953).

In summary, both the punishment (PUN) and "anxiety" (CER) procedures endowed an ordinarily neutral stimulus, the clicker CS, with the power to suppress lever-pressing. Both produced generalized suppression (in the absence of CS or shock) as well, with the CER procedure producing the greater generalized suppression even though no lever response had ever been punished. The PUN Ss showed fewer signs of general emotional disturbance— they showed a lower incidence of freezing and defecation in both Skinner box and grill box. A number of them developed a characteristic abortive lever-pressing behavior not seen in any CER Ss—an activity appearing to have clear-cut avoidant or escape components. And the suppressant power acquired by the CS was more stable for CER than for PUN in that the CER proved more resistant to extinction, as arbitrarily defined by the repeated presentation of the CS without shocks.

Discussion

The relatively strong shocks so effectively suppressed lever-pressing that the PUN Ss actually received less than half as many shocks on the average as were received by all CER Ss (8.36 as compared with 18). Voltage control lamps in parallel with S blinked when S received each shock, permitting such a count. Perhaps the PUN Ss showed less emotional disturbance and more rapid extinction simply because they had received fewer shocks in the presence of the CS.

But some of the major effects of the procedures appeared before the groups differed so greatly in amount of shock. By the end of C 2, all CER Ss had received 4 shocks. By then, the PUN Ss had received from 2 to 5 shocks, with a mean of 3.3, and 5 PUN Ss had received 4 or more. During C 2, 9 CER and 2 PUN Ss defecated; on the next day, during A 1, 8 CER Ss but no PUN S defecated (both $p < .01$). If only those PUN Ss which received 4 or more shocks are compared with the CER Ss, the difference in defecation on A 1 is still significant ($p < .03$). Also, the characteristic similarities and differences in lever-pressing had appeared by C 2 and A 1.

Data already available from an earlier experiment argue more convincingly, however (Hunt & Brady, 1951b). This earlier study compared the effects of the CER I and PUN I procedures on lever-pressing, using 0.6-ma. shocks given over 6 conditioning trials. Here the PUN Ss received from 9 to 22 shocks in the presence of the CS (with a mean of 14.25) while the CER Ss received 12. Both procedures suppressed lever-pressing during the CS and produced some generalized suppression during adaptation runs. As in the present experiment, the CER produced the greater generalized suppression and endowed the CS with suppressant effects more resistant to extinction. The CER Ss showed much the higher incidence of defecation. Only the PUN Ss developed abortive lever-pressing. Each of these differences or effects was significant ($p < .05$, or better). The characteristic differences between PUN and CER conditioning appeared here even though the PUN Ss received, on the average, *more* shocks than the CER Ss. The results of the present experiment should not be attributed simply to the difference between the groups in the amount of shock received.

The data from the present and earlier experiments indicate that punishment can suppress lever-pressing in the absence of a general emotional disturbance sufficiently severe to produce defecation and crouching. Conditioned emotional response conditioning sufficient to have the same suppressant effects, usually entails the development of such a degree of emotional disturbance. However, the generalized suppression of lever-pressing in the adaptation trials could be interpreted to indicate that the apparatus had acquired at least some power to evoke an emotional disturbance among PUN Ss. And the progressive increase in output during the consecutive adaptation trials A 2 through A 5 could be interpreted as showing the extinction of this effect. Also, subsequent observations in the open Skinner box have indicated that most Ss show some crouching or freezing in response to the first few instances of punishment. Thus, some general emotional disturbance probably was evoked by the apparatus and CS in punishment, to contribute to the suppression of lever-pressing. But general emotional disturbance developed to a lesser degree than in CER conditioning and probably was not the major factor in suppressing the punished behavior. And had the CS acquired the power to evoke, by itself, a substantial emotional disturbance in the PUN Ss, they should have showed a higher incidence of freezing and defecation in the grill box test.

Some speculative comments

The more rapid extinction of the punishment discrimination is not inconsistent with the emphasis by Schoenfeld (1950) and Dinsmoor (1952, 1954) on the role in punishment of the conditioned aversive properties acquired by stimuli arising from the lever response. In the present experiment, the aversive stimulus governing the suppression of lever pressing among PUN Ss might be a compound—the CS plus those stimuli arising from a complete depression of the lever. During extinction, the PUN Ss would receive their full aversive compound without reinforcement each time they pressed the lever during a single presentation of the CS. For the CER Ss, the full aversive compound—the CS plus stimuli arising from the apparatus—could be presented without shock reinforcement only once during each extinction trial. Thus a PUN S could have had several functional "extinction trials" while a CER S was having only one. Similarly, the PUN Ss could have showed less emotional disturbance in the grill box simply because they were receiving only that part of their full conditioned aversive compound not associated with shock in the absence of lever pressing. The same argument could account also for their lower incidence of crouching and defecation in the Skinner box.

This formulation hinges upon the acquisition of aversive properties by stimuli arising out of lever pressing. In a situation employing a free operant as an indicator (Ferster, 1953), these stimuli could not be manipulated independently of the lever response itself. Accordingly, the present interpretation must be considered tentative.

Conclusions

1. Both intercurrent "anxiety" (the CER) and punishment suppressed the output of lever responses significantly. The suppression appeared not only during presentation of the signal (the CS) but also was generalized to appear during periods in the apparatus when

this stimulus was absent. This generalized suppression was significantly less severe among punished Ss, however.

2. The suppression produced by punishment disappeared more rapidly than that produced in the CER, as a function of the repeated presentation of the CS without reinforcement by shock.

3. The punished Ss consistently showed a lower incidence of signs of general emotional disturbance (defecation and immobility) than CER Ss. Further, in the presence of the CS, the punished Ss tended to show abortive lever-pressing activity, with withdrawal or avoidant components, while no signs of such behavior appeared among CER Ss.

4. The suppressant effect of punishment here did not appear to depend exclusively, or even largely, upon the evocation of a general emotional state or disturbance by the CS, as exemplified in the CER, though such an emotional reaction may have been present in a degree to contribute somewhat to the total suppressant effect.

5. Rather, the results were interpreted as consistent with the view that the effects of punishment depend heavily upon specific aversive conditioning in which stimuli arising from the punished response itself became a significant and critical part of the compound conditioned aversive stimulus which governs the suppression.

15   Discriminative properties of punishment

William C. Holz and Nathan H. Azrin

Some stimuli, such as light and sound, may function either as discriminative or as aversive stimuli. The lower-intensity range of such stimuli is generally used to investigate the discriminative property, whereas the higher-intensity range is used to study the aversive property and little attention has been given to its discriminative property. However, one experimenter (Azrin, 1958) has shown that

✕   Reprinted from the *Journal of the Experimental Analysis of Behavior*, 1961, *4*, 225–232 by permission of the senior author and the Society for the Experimental Analysis of Behavior. This report is in part based upon a dissertation submitted by the senior author to the Graduate School of the Southern Illinois University in partial fulfillment of the requirements for the Ph.D. degree. The investigation was supported by a grant from the Psychiatric Training and Research Fund of the Illinois Department of Public Welfare and from NSF grant G16357. The authors acknowledge the assistance of I. Goldiamond and R. Hutchinson.

[Holz and Azrin maintain that not all of the response suppression produced by punishment is due to its aversive property. Punishing stimulation functions as a cue as well as a means of eliciting pain, fear, and other unconditioned responses. Some of the reduction in response strength observed when punishment is introduced might be attributed to its alteration of the complex of stimuli guiding learned responses. Holz and Azrin clearly demonstrate that punishing stimuli can serve as cues or discriminative stimuli. This interpretation of punishment may be called the discrimination hypothesis. For further research corroborating the results shown here as well as showing that punishment also has aversive properties, see Holz and Azrin's (1962) later article.—Eds.]

stimuli of such intensity as to be aversive can also function as discriminative stimuli. Azrin presented intense noise continuously during selected portions of a fixed-interval reinforcement schedule; and he found that if the noise had been temporally associated with reinforcement, responding increased during the noise. Conversely, if the noise had been associated with extinction, responding decreased.

This experiment considers the discriminative property of an aversive stimulus in a somewhat different situation. Instead of being presented continuously for a period of time, the aversive stimulus is presented only after a response has occurred. This procedure is the typical punishment paradigm. The occurrence or nonoccurrence of punishment is then selectively related to reinforcement.

Method

Subjects

Three male, White Carneaux pigeons were used as subjects. They were deprived of food until their weights were 75 to 80 percent of their free-feeding levels. Controlled feeding maintained the weights of the individual subjects within a 15-gram range during the experiment.

Apparatus

The experimental chamber is essentially the same as that described elsewhere (Ferster, 1953). The experimental space is 13 by 14 by 15 inches, and it is enclosed within a lightproof, sound-attenuating compartment. The floor of the chamber is an electrically insulated wire grid. The response was a peck on a plastic disc with a force of at least 10 grams, and reinforcement consisted of a 3-second presentation of grain from a feed magazine. All experimental conditions were programmed by standard electrical timing and switching devices located in a separate room. Responses were recorded by electrical impulse counters and a Gerbrands cumulative recorder.

Punishment consisted of an electric shock delivered through electrodes implanted in the tail region of the pigeon (Azrin, 1959). Daily recordings show that the subject's resistance was approximately 900 ohms (measured with a 50-millivolt input) with a range of approximately ± 100 ohms. Alternating current was delivered to the subject through a 10,000-ohm resistor for 65 ± 3 milliseconds. When shock was not being delivered, the leads were shorted together to avoid shock inductance.

Results and Procedure

The usual procedure for establishing a discrimination is to reinforce all responses in the presence of a given stimulus and to extinguish all responses in its absence. In order to establish punishment as a discriminative stimulus, the occurrence of punishment must be differentially related to reinforcement. For differential pairing, two types of experimental sessions were given each day. One type of session provided both punishment and reinforcement, and the other type provided neither punishment nor reinforcement. Otherwise, the stimulus conditions of these sessions were the same. The order of presentation of the sessions was varied irregularly.

Two subjects were first conditioned to respond on a 2-minute, variable-interval schedule of food reinforcement. Daily 30-minute sessions were given until the response rate stabilized. The cumulative-response record labeled C in Figure 15.1 illustrates the high, uniform response rate that characterized performance under this reinforcement schedule. Although the records in this figure are for

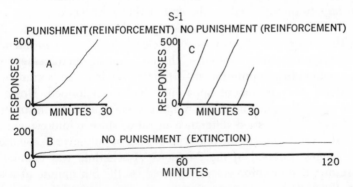

Figure 15.1 Response patterns under these conditions: A, punishment and reinforcement; B, no punishment and extinction; C, no punishment and reinforcement

one subject, the results were essentially the same for both subjects. With responding thus established, punishment was administered to each response in these food-reinforcement sessions. The intensity of the shock was adjusted until a consistent, moderate suppression resulted. A shock intensity of 60 volts A. C. effectively reduced the responding to one-half of the unpunished response level. Record A in Figure 15.1 illustrates the suppression of response rate that resulted when the punishment was combined with reinforcement. After responding was established in these sessions that paired punishment and reinforcement, the additional sessions were introduced. The new sessions were 2 hours long, and, as stated above, provided neither punishment nor reinforcement for the subject's response.

After these sessions had been provided for approximately 3 weeks, a consistent response pattern developed in each type of session. Responding in the punishment and reinforcement session maintained the pattern illustrated in Record A of Figure 15.1. Responding started slowly and then increased until a moderate rate was reached. This rate then continued throughout the rest of the session. Responding in the absence of punishment and reinforcement reached the pattern illustrated in Record B of this figure. Under this condition, responding was negatively accelerated and invariably reached a near-zero rate after the first half-hour. The rate in these no-punishment sessions continued to fall throughout the experiment; and in one instance, only 11 responses were made in a 2-hour session. The flurries of rapid responding that are often characteristic of extinction had largely disappeared by the end of the third week.

After the 3-week stabilization period, the response rates during the two types of sessions were clearly different. Considerably more responses were emitted in the punishment-reinforcement sessions than in the no-punishment–extinction sessions. A discrimination based on the punishment apparently had been formed. However, there was still a possibility that reinforcement—and not punishment—produced the observed difference in rates, since reinforcement occurred several times in the one type of session but never in the other. The longest interval in the 2-minute VI schedule was 5 minutes; therefore, if no reinforcement occurred by the 5th minute of a session, the probability of further reinforcement was zero. If a reinforcement did occur within the first 5 minutes of a session, the probability of additional reinforcement was 1.00. Because of the differential oc-

currence of reinforcement, the subjects conceivably could have
formed a discrimination on this basis rather than on the basis of the
presence or absence of punishment.

We tried to determine the role of punishment in controlling
the responding by temporarily excluding reinforcement from the
punishment sessions. Before reinforcement occurs, the only difference in the two types of sessions is the presence or absence of punishment. If reinforcement alone controls the rate, the level of responding should be low in both sessions. On the other hand, if the
punishment controls the higher rate, the rate of responding should
be higher under punishment. Figure 15.2 shows that the responding

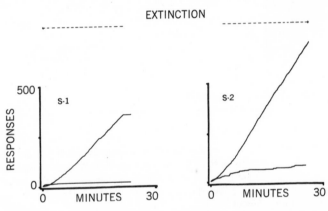

Figure 15.2   The effect of punishment on responding after the punishment had
been paired with reinforcement. A cumulative record from a punishment session is superimposed upon a cumulative record for a no-punishment session for
each subject. Reinforcement was not provided in either session.

increased when the responses were punished, even though reinforcement was withheld. The pattern of responding was essentially
the same as when reinforcement was provided; i.e., the responding
was positively accelerated. The same increase in responding under
the punishment was observed on all five occasions of this procedure.
Therefore, because of its differential pairing with reinforcement, the
punishment in and of itself clearly had come to increase responding.

As a further assessment of the discriminative property of the punishment, 10-minute periods of punishment were introduced into the middle of the sessions that normally did not provide punishment. Punishment was administered to the first response after the end of the first hour of the session, and then to all subsequent responses during the next 10 minutes. No reinforcement was given at any time during these sessions. Figure 15.3 shows that the responding was at

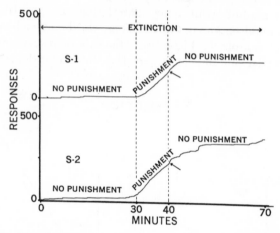

Figure 15.3 Cumulative-response records of sessions in which a 10-minute punishment period was introduced. The records include a 30-minute period before the introduction of punishment and a 30-minute period after the punishment. The arrows point out the increase in rate that occurred immediately upon the termination of punishment.

a near-zero rate before the introduction of punishment. The introduction of punishment produced a positive acceleration of responding, and was maintained at a moderate level throughout the remainder of the 10-minute period. When punishment was discontinued, responding decreased to the usual no-punishment level. A noteworthy aspect of the performance was the sudden, though short-lived, increase in rate when the punishment was discontinued (arrows, Figure 15.3). This increase was observed the first two times that punishment was discontinued with this procedure, but was not clearly present on the subsequent trials.

These 10-minute punishment periods were introduced into five of the no-punishment, no-reinforcement sessions. Figure 15.4

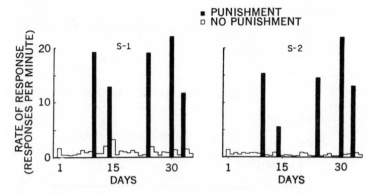

Figure 15.4 The bar graph contrasts the response rate during the 10-minute punishment period that was introduced into the no-punishment session with the usual response rate in these sessions.

contrasts the response rate during the 10-minute punishment periods with the rate (unpunished and unreinforced) that normally occurred in these sessions. This figure also provides an over-all view of the consistent low rate prevailing in the sessions which did not provide punishment.

In the results reported thus far, the electric shock always followed the response. Additional experiments demonstrated that the shock would increase responding even when presented independently of the responses. Unavoidable shocks were scheduled to occur at various times in the sessions that did not ordinarily provide punishment. Figure 15.5 shows the effect of these unavoidable shocks. When these shocks were administered only occasionally, they typically elicited a slight flurry of responding shortly after their delivery. Similarly, when the shocks were delivered in fairly rapid succession, a moderate amount of responding resulted. This responding did not reach the magnitude observed when the shocks were response-produced, but was considerably greater than otherwise occurred during the no-punishment sessions. It may be noted that the responses elicited by the unavoidable shock were not punished and hence produced the condition associated with extinction. Therefore, the responding produced by unavoidable shocks could not be expected to be so high as that produced by punishment.

The present results demonstrate that punishment will increase

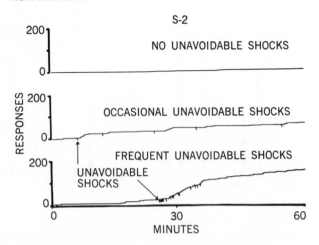

Figure 15.5   Cumulative-response records of sessions in which A, no shocks were administered; B, unavoidable shocks were occasionally presented independently of the subject response; and C, unavoidable shocks were administered frequently during a 10-minute period

response rate when it has been paired with reinforcement. A third subject was studied to determine whether punishment would also *decrease* the response rate when it was paired with *extinction*. In pairing punishment with extinction, certain ambiguities arise. A stimulus that has been associated with extinction decreases response rate when that stimulus is presented. An aversive stimulus that follows a response ordinarily has this same effect. If punishment is paired with extinction and the rate decreases, it is difficult to determine whether the discriminative or the aversive property of the punishment produced the decrement. Because of this, a very low-intensity shock was used in order to minimize the aversive property of the punishment. Figure 15.6 (upper section) shows that a 20-volt A. C. shock has little or no aversive effect. The stable rate that developed when each response was punished was essentially the same as the rate when the responses were not punished.

This subject was placed under conditions similar to those of the first two subjects, except that the punishment was paired with extinction. Two sessions were administered daily. One session, 30 minutes long, paired the absence of punishment with the 2-minute

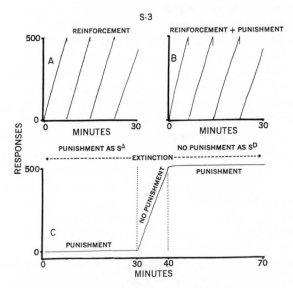

Figure 15.6   Records of A, responding on a 2-minute VI reinforcement sched-ule without punishment; B, responding on a 2-minute VI reinforcement schedule with mild punishment for each response; and C, the effect of removing the mild punishment for a 10-minute period after the mild punishment had been paired with extinction and the absence of punishment had been paired with re-inforcement

VI reinforcement. The other session, 2 hours long, paired the 20-volt punishment with the absence of reinforcement. After several weeks, the response rate dropped to a low level in the sessions that paired punishment and extinction, but remained high in the sessions that paired the absence of punishment and reinforcement. When punish-ment was temporarily eliminated from the 2-hour sessions that pro-vided punishment and extinction, the response rate increased (lower section of Figure 15.6). The punishment had come to control a low response rate simply because of its discriminative property.

Discussion

These experiments demonstrate that a relatively severe punishment can increase responding, and a nonaversive punishment can greatly reduce responding. Such results are contrary to what would be expected from the aversive property of the punishing stimulus. However, the anomalous results are clarified if one considers the other consequences of the responding. The severe punishment came to increase responding only after it had been selectively paired with reinforcement. The nonaversive punishment came to reduce responding only after it had been selectively paired with extinction. This procedure of selectively pairing a stimulus (in this case, the presence or absence of punishment) with reinforcement is the usual procedure for establishing a discrimination. This discriminative property that the punishment acquired produced the apparent anomaly. Indeed, the discriminative property came to exert an even greater effect on responding than did the aversive property.

● The fact that punishment does not always suppress responding is often taken as evidence that punishment is an ineffective method of controlling behavior. However, in such cases the discriminative properties the punishment may have acquired should be considered. For example, experiments by Muenzinger (1934)[1] have shown that correct maze responses (i.e., those responses that are reinforced) are learned more quickly if they are punished. The punishment in this case is explicitly paired with reinforcement. Faster learning can be expected because the stimulus (punishment) is delivered immediately upon completion of the correct response. Another example of the alleged ineffectiveness of punishment is the finding (Estes, 1944)[2] that punishment does not reduce the number of responses required for extinction. In these experiments, punishment was initiated at the same time that extinction was begun, so that the punishment is associated with extinction. The termination of punishment reinstated the stimulus situation associated with reinforcement. The discriminative property of this absence of punishment is sufficient to account for the increase of responding that was observed.

—   These discriminative properties of punishment may also account for some of the anomalous effects of punishment that are observed outside the laboratory. In situations where the consequences of behavior are not explicitly arranged, accidental contingencies may occur. These accidental contingencies may be inadvertently over-

[1] [See Selection 2.—Eds.]
[2] [See Selection 11.—Eds.]

looked, and yet they may play an important part in determining behavior. For example, one might be *more* disposed to supply reinforcement to an individual following administration of punishment,
in a sense to try to "make up" for the punishment. If so, the punishment would be (inadvertently) paired with reinforcement and it
could be expected to acquire a discriminative property. Thus, the
severe punishment would be ineffective as a deterrent. On the other
hand, one might be *less* disposed to supply reinforcement after punishing. A slap on the wrist, a frown, or a shout would appear to be
only mildly adversive—if at all. However, if one were less inclined to
reinforce after such mild punishment, then these events would become associated with extinction. In this instance, a trivial degree of
punishment would be quite effective as a deterrent of behavior.

Summary

This experiment investigated the discriminative properties of punishment. It was found that when a severe punishment was differentially paired with reinforcement, punishment served to increase
responding. Conversely, when an otherwise ineffective punishment
was paired with extinction, punishment came to decrease responding. These discriminative properties of punishment are an explanation for a number of ambiguous findings in experiments on punishment.

III

Prior Aversive Stimulation

Behavior is a function not only of the current stimulus situation but also of the previous experiences of the subject. In the case of punishment, the subject's history of prior exposure to aversive stimulation is an important consideration in predicting the effect of later punishment. For example, a given level of punishment may become progressively less effective in suppressing an unwanted response in a child as his experience with punishment increases. The experimental analogue of this phenomenon is frequently observed in the laboratory (e.g., Azrin, 1960b; Camp, Raymond, & Church, 1967). Miller (1960) demonstrated that the suppression produced by a given level of punishment can be minimized by gradually increasing punishment intensity over trials. Prior exposure of this nature attenuates the effect of later punishment. However, the opposite result has also been observed. Among others, Walters and Rogers (1963) have found that prior exposure to electric shock enhances the suppressing effect of subsequent punishing shock.

Many interesting experimental and theoretical problems arise from findings showing that approximately the same sequence of events can produce reliable results in opposite directions. For example, what variable or variables interact with amount of prior exposure to produce a diminution or an enhancement in suppression produced by punishment? One possible answer to this question is found in an experiment by Karsh (1963) who demonstrated that prior exposure to a weak shock reduced the effect of subsequent punishment while prior exposure to a strong shock increased the effect of subsequent punishment.

The experiments reproduced in this part are all similar to the experiments of Part II in that a strong response was first established by positive reinforcement before punishment was made contingent upon it. Thus, the expected effect of punishment would be to reduce the strength of the learned response. As the experiments will show, the amount of this reduction depends upon the type of experience with prior aversive stimulation.

16 Learning resistance to pain and fear: effects of overlearning, exposure, and rewarded exposure in context

Neal E. Miller

This study grows out of theoretical applications of learning principles to mental health by Dollard and Miller (1950) and to fear in combat by Miller (1954). It is a first step toward systematic experi-

Reprinted from the *Journal of Experimental Psychology,* 1960, *60,* 137–145 by permission of the author and the American Psychological Association. The author was responsible for the ideas, design, and write-up. James A. Faust performed Exp. I; Nariyuki Agarie and Libby Michel, supervised by Arlo K. Myers, performed Exp. II; Russell Tousley and Hanna Weston, supervised by Gordon Bower, performed Exp. III. This work was supported by a research grant, M647, from the National Institute of Mental Health of the National Institutes of Health, Public Health Service, Department of Health, Education, and Welfare, Bethesda, Maryland. We thank the Harkness Bursary Fund of Yale University for the support of Faust and Tousley.

[Miller's results clearly show that prior exposure to punishment that gradually increases in intensity diminishes its suppressive effect in comparison with the procedure of suddenly introducing punishment at its final level of intensity. This outcome can be described as an adaptation-like phenomenon. The use of this term, however, should not rule out other possible interpretations. Prior exposure to punishment that is (1) mild, (2) of short duration, (3) infrequent, or (4) long delayed after a response apparently attenuates the magnitude of suppression to a punishment that is more intense, of longer duration, more frequent, or temporally 'closer to a response (Banks, 1966; Church, 1969; Feirstein & Miller, 1963; Karsh, 1966).—Eds.]

mental investigation of the general problem of whether resistance to stressful situations, especially fear-evoking ones, can be learned. If such learning is possible, what are the laws determining its effectiveness and generality?

One common type of stress situation is that in which S is in conflict because he has motivations to approach and also to avoid the same goal. Examples are the person who wants to come forward and express his ideas but is restrained by stage fright or the person who wants to approach and have normal relations with the opposite sex but is restrained by fear. Similarly, a soldier may be in conflict because he is motivated both to advance to complete his mission and to retreat to escape intense fear. Severe conflicts of this kind play an important role in neurotic behavior (Dollard & Miller, 1950).

Since the approach-avoidance conflict seems to be such an important source of stress and also has been extensively analyzed theoretically and studied experimentally (Miller, 1959), it was selected for this study. Hungry albino rats were trained to approach the goal end of an alley to receive food. Then they were placed into conflict by receiving painful electric shocks at the goal. We investigated different ways of training the rats to persist in going to the goal in spite of the fear aroused by the painful shocks.

Experiment I

The first experiment compared the effect on ultimate performance of gradual habituation to increasingly strong electric shocks at the goal with that of the sudden introduction of shock at full strength. A subsidiary purpose was to investigate a problem posed by Miller (1959, p. 225), namely, whether the first noticeable effects of weak electric shocks at the goal will be a reduction in the speed of running as would be expected from simple algebraic summation of approach and avoidance throughout the range, or whether there will be an initial period of dynamogenic effect which facilitates running.

Returning to the main problem, two factors should cause the gradual introduction to shock to help the animals to learn to resist its disruptive effects, while another factor might work in the opposite direction: (a) During the weaker shocks S will be rewarded for continuing in spite of fear, so that increasingly strong fear will become a cue for approaching. By contrast, when the strong shock is suddenly introduced, the strong fear will change the stimulus situation drastically and produce a stimulus-generalization decrement in the strength of approach in addition to eliciting the competing response of avoidance. (b) If Pavlov's (1927, p. 30) observations are correct, the reward occurring after the mild shocks should suppress by counterconditioning some of the fear-evoking effects of pain, and thus help S to continue in the face of increasingly strong shocks. (c) But, during the process of habituation to increasingly strong shocks, Ss will receive a greater number of painful shocks, which may tend to make them more fearful that Ss receiving only a single suddenly introduced strong shock. Perhaps the foregoing opposing factors are behind the two schools of thought among laymen—those who would deal with fear of water by gradual familiarization and those who would throw the victim in to sink or swim.

During the first trials of criterion testing with strong electric shock, we do not have any way of evaluating the strength of Factor c, the total number of shocks, relative to those it opposes. Therefore we cannot make any firm prediction. On the other hand, if the criterion tests extend over enough trials, Ss with suddenly introduced strong shocks will have time to approach their asymptote of learning to avoid. As these Ss approach their asymptote, the difference in total number of shocks received will become irrelevant. Since we know that learning to avoid occurs rapidly, we may tentatively assume that it occurs faster than the learning to advance to the cue of fear and the counter-conditioning. On the basis of this somewhat shaky assumption, we can predict that, during the latter part of an extensive series of test trials, a group gradually habituated to increasingly strong shocks will perform better than one suddenly exposed to strong shocks.

Method

Subjects

The Ss were 28 male Sprague-Dawley rats approximately 90 days old at the outset.

Apparatus

An enclosed alley 8 ft. long, 3½ in. wide, and 5¼ in. high was painted flat white inside and had a hinged transparent top. Its floor was a grid of stainless steel bar $\frac{1}{16}$ in. in diameter spaced $\frac{1}{4}$ in. apart, supported by strips of wood which had been boiled in paraffin.

The first 7 in. of the alley was a startbox which opened by means of a guillotine door released by a catch, pulled down by a spring, and activating a microswitch which started an electric timer. The goal was a wet pellet of Purina mash about the size of a pea placed on an insulated aluminum plate at the end of the alley, and illuminated from above by a 6-w. bulb which was the sole source of light in the alley. When the animal touched the moist pellet, a sub-threshold current operated an electronic relay which stopped the electric timer, and, on appropriate trials, turned on the shock.

The electric shock was administered to the animal's feet via the grid floor. The output of a radio transformer was regulated by a 25,000 ohm potentiometer used as a voltage divider. The output of this voltage divider was applied to the grid with a 250,000 ohm resistor in series with the rat. The output of the voltage divider was calibrated with an ac voltmeter and the duration of shock was controlled at 0.1 sec. by an electronic timer.

The rats in this experiment wore a rubber-band harness connected by a snap on the end of a T bar to a cord running along the top of the alley, going around two pulleys at either end of the alley, and back outside to form an endless loop. One of these large pulleys contained a smaller reducing one which operated a recording pen on a polygraph. The setup was like that described by Brown (1948). Since no graphic records were made in this experiment, this part of the apparatus is relevant only as part of the stimulus situation for the rat.

Feeding Schedule and Approach Training

The Ss were on ad lib. water and were fed each day after the end of the experiment 10 gm. of ground Purina Lab Chow mixed with 10 gm. of water. After two days on this feeding schedule they were given three training trials, at the rate of one per day, without the starting door or harness. Then the starting door was introduced and the number of trials increased so that by Day 7, which began with Trial 11, the Ss were running five trials a day. These trials were quasidistributed by completing a given trial on all Ss before starting the first S on its next trial. On Trial 16 the harness was introduced. By approximately 50 trials, the Ss seemed to reach their asymptote of speed, but they were continued on for a total of 75 approach-training trials.

Habituation to Electric Shock

After Ss had clearly reached their asymptote, they were divided into two groups of 14, matched on the basis of average speed on the last 10 trials and randomly assigned as the Sudden and the Gradual groups which were given the following treatments during Trials 76–150: (*a*) The Sudden group continued the rewarded non-shock training of five trials a day. (*b*) The Gradual group began with a shock of 125 v. for the first day and had the level of shock increased in 15 percent steps. On the first day there was no noticeable effect during the five trials. On the second day with a shock of 144 v., the first flinching reactions were observed. This level was continued for five days to determine the effect of low-level punishment. From then on the daily voltages of shock were 166, 191, 220, 253, 253, 291, 335, 335, 335. If S failed to reach the goal and eat within 3 min., he was removed from the alley but started on subsequent trials as usual.

Test for Resistance to Electric Shock

After the Gradual group had the foregoing 15 days of habituation to increasing shock and the Sudden group merely 15 days of additional training, both groups were given 20 test trials (5 per day) with the 335-v. shock at the goal.

Results and discussion

The results are presented in Figure 16.1. The part to the left of the dotted line presents the average speed (for daily groups of five trials) on the last three nonshock training days and on all of the days when the Gradual group received habituation training. The part to the right of the dotted line presents the average speed for each of the individual test trials during which both groups received the 335-v. shock at the goal.

It can be seen that the groups were reasonably well equated during the last three days of training. The first day of five shocks at the 125-v. level produced little, if any, effect. The first noticeable effect of the shock was a slight decrement produced by the days

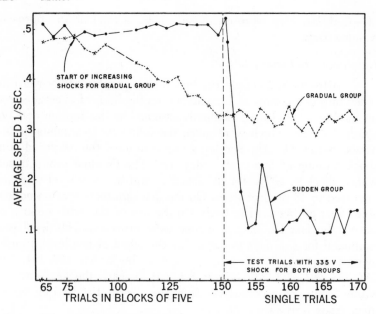

Figure 16.1   Effect on speed of approach of gradual vs. sudden introduction of electric shock at the goal

with 144 v.[1] From then on, increasingly stronger shocks produced greater decrements until the speed of the Gradual group was reduced ($P < .01$) approximately 30 percent by the 335-v. shocks.[2]

The foregoing results show no evidence of an initial dynamogenic effect of weak shocks, but rather show algebraic summation as soon as any effects appear. Through an unfortunate misunderstanding, however, the initial levels of shock were higher than had originally been planned. Thus there is some possibility that the

[1] Scores for the last two of these four days were distorted by apparatus trouble and have been omitted. To compensate for a change in the apparatus, a correction constant of .07 has been added to the average scores of both groups on all trials before these days.

[2] All reliabilities in this paper are two-tailed and, unless otherwise indicated, based on t tests. When a number of trials are combined, each S is given the sum of speeds on these trials as a single score; when trials are compared, a difference-score is computed for each S. The foregoing probability is for Trials 71–75 minus Trials 146–150. The next probability is for independent groups of Trials 166–170, and the final one is for Trial 156 minus Trial 155.

125-v. shock, which showed no effect, is at just the level where a dynamogenic effect (which might have showed up with weaker shocks) and the interfering effect of a stronger shock, are cancelling each other out.

Looking at the right side of the figure, it can be seen that on the first test trial the Ss in the Sudden group, not yet having experienced what is in store for them at the goal, continue to run much faster than those in the Gradual group. After one shock, their performance is reduced to approximately that of the Gradual group, and with subsequent shocks, their performance drops considerably below that of the Gradual group ($P < .001$). On the first trial of the second day the Sudden group makes a temporary partial recovery ($P < .01$)—perhaps because the overnight rest introduced new cues that had less association with shock—followed by a rapid decline without any recovery on the first trials of the third or fourth days.

To present the results in a different way, on the last day of testing the 14 Ss in each group received 5 trials for a total of 70 tests to a group. On only three such tests were there failures to achieve the goal within the 3-min. limit in the Gradual group, while there were 14 times as many (i.e., 43) such failures in the Sudden group.

Further differences were apparent from watching the characteristic reactions of the two groups to the shocks. The Ss in the Gradual group flinched and sometimes squealed but remained at the goal and continued to eat. Those in the Sudden group seemed much more disturbed, lurching violently back, running away and crouching a distance from the goal. Theoretically (Miller, 1959, p. 268) Ss should learn the type of response they make to the shock and the responses of the Sudden group should interfere with running more than those of the Gradual group.

The results were in accord with our theoretical expectations in that a superiority of the Gradual group emerged during the later test trials. According to our theoretical analysis, the factors favoring the Gradual group were (*a*) learning to advance to the cue of fear instead of suffering a stimulus-generalization decrement, and (*b*) counter-conditioning. According to our analysis both of these effects depended on reward in the fear-evoking training situation. It is conceivable, however, that mere exposure to a sequence of increasingly strong shocks will help S to adjust irrespective of whether these shocks are associated with reward or administered in the training situation. The following experiments investigate this and other possibilities.

Experiment II

The main purpose of this experiment was to determine whether exposure to a series of gradually increasing shocks would be as beneficial when given outside of the test apparatus as when given as part of the rewarded training in it. A subsidiary purpose was to get a first approximation of the function relating the length of the habituation series to its effectiveness.

Method

The general procedure was the same as that in the preceding experiment with the following exceptions:

The apparatus was an alley 60 in. long, the last 12 in. of which were grid floor. At the goal Ss pushed back a little transparent plastic door hinged at the top until an iron strip on it came within range of a small permanent magnet which snapped the door open, exposing a food tray containing 10 P. J. Noyes Co. pellets weighing .045 gm. each, and actuating a microswitch which stopped a clock and, on appropriate trials, tiggered the electric shock. For further details see Bower and Miller (1960).

The Ss did not wear harnesses. The initial training consisted of 70 trials after which Ss were divided into four matched groups. In order to cover a wider range of values and to fit into available schedules, E_M (Michel) increased the shocks in her groups twice as fast as did E_A (Agarie). The resultant groups were:

(*a*) *Gradual in alley.* For Ss run by E_A, shocks began at 50 v. and were increased 13 percent on each day (i.e., 5 trials), to the eventual test level of 353 v. on Day 17. For Ss run by E_M, the sequence started and ended at the same levels, but included only every other step of E_A's sequence, except that both the 11th and 12th values were included.

(*b*) *Gradual outside alley.* The Ss run by each E received exactly the same sequence of shocks as their partners in the foregoing group, but all of the shocks below the test level of 353 v. were given outside of the alley approximately 30 min. after the end of the daily trials in the alley. These shocks were given in a distinctive box 10 in. × 14 in. × 10½ in. deep with aluminum sides, a grid floor and a hinged Plexiglas lid. The Ss were put into this box for each of their five daily trials which were distributed like the trials in the alley.

(*c*) *Faster in alley*. As with Group *a*, Ss received shocks in the alley, but the series was shorter and increased at a faster rate. With E_A the increases were approximately 63 percent, generating the following sequence of voltages: 50, 82, 133, 217, 353. For E_M the sequence of voltages was 50, 133, and 353.

(*d*) *Sudden in alley*. For both Es this group received a 353-v. shock in the alley on the same day that the other groups first reached this voltage level.

There were 5 rats in each group for each *E*, making a total of 40 Ss. For each *E* trials with shock were started so that the final test level was reached on the same day by all groups and so that all groups had received the same number of trials in the alley by that day.

Results

The average speeds for the 20 test trials with a 353-v. shock at the goal are presented in Table 16.1. It can be seen that there is a large

Table 16.1 Average speed during 20 test trials with 353-V. shock

Previous Treatment	Experimenter A	M
Gradual in alley	.48	.61
Faster in alley	.37	.55
Sudden in alley	.35	.53
Gradual outside alley	.33	.47

difference between the speeds of Ss run by the two Es, but that for each *E* the rank order of the groups is exactly the same. The Ss given the gradually increasing series of shocks in the alley were better in the test series than those given the faster series of shocks in the alley, which in turn were better than those suddenly introduced to the shock for the first time. These differences are in the same direction as those secured in Exp. I. In both cases Ss exposed to shocks outside of the alley showed the poorest performance. There was so much variability among Ss, however, that only the difference between Es (which was confounded with a difference in the weight of Ss in the two batches of Ss) was statistically reliable. Therefore, an additional experiment was run.

Experiment III

The purpose of Exp. III was to compare the effect of three procedures on subsequent resistance to stress in the conflict test situation. The three procedures were gradual increase of shock in the rewarded conflict-training situation, gradual increase of shock outside of the conflict situation, and sudden introduction of shock for the first time in the test situation. In addition a control was added for the effects of the number of rewarded training trials.

In the preceding experiments Ss in the Sudden group received rewarded training trials in the alley while their partners received increasing shock and regular rewards in the alley. This procedure equated the number of training trials before the test with strong shock was introduced, but meant that the Gradual group received its first experience with shocks after fewer training trials than did the Sudden group. Since all groups had reached the asymptote of speed, any effects of this difference in the number of rewarded training trials was expected to be minor. Furthermore, any such minor effect of the fewer trials was expected to work against the Gradual Group, and hence to be in the opposite direction to our experimental results.

In the meantime, Karsh (1959) secured evidence in our laboratory suggesting that additional training trials beyond the asymptote may decrease (rather than increase) the resistance of a rat's performance to disruption by shock. To control for this surprising possibility, the present experiment used an additional Sudden group which started to receive its test with strong shocks in the alley as soon as the habituation series was started for the two Gradual groups.

Method

The Ss were 32 male albino Sprague-Dawley rats, approximately 90 days old at the beginning of the experiment. They were on ad lib. water and were fed 13 gm. of Purina Lab Chow approximately 15 min. after the experimental session each day. This feeding cycle started 7 days before the experiment proper.

The apparatus was the same as in the previous experiment.

For each trial in the alley the reward was 5 P. J. Noyes pellets. First each S was trained to push open the door over the food cup and eat pellets by being placed directly into the goalbox until it started to eat within 15 sec. on three consecutive trials. Then Ss were trained to run down the alley by being given two trials each day, separated by approximately 45 min. in the home cage with water. This training was continued for a total of 42 trials. It was started by Tousley, but four of the last trials were run by Weston, who also did the testing. After this training Ss were assigned to four groups of 8 Ss each. These groups were matched for mean speed on the last 10 trials and randomly assigned to the following conditions:

(a) *Gradual in alley.* The Ss were given a 60-v. shock of 0.1 sec. duration at the goal on both of their trials on Day 22 and given shock increased by 20 v. each day until they received a 380-v. shock on Day 38. The shock sequence was changed from a percentage increment (power series) to a constant increment (linear series) because the first part of the former series seemed to be too weak while its final steps seemed to be too large.

(b) *Gradual outside alley.* The Ss were given exactly the same sequence of shocks outside of the alley in the distinctive box. They were taken out of the home cage and given this shock approximately 15 min. after a run in the alley and immediately returned to the home cage.

(c) *Early sudden in alley.* The Ss received their first shock, which was a 400-v. test trial, on the same day (Day 22) that the foregoing groups received their first weak shocks.

(d) *Late sudden in alley.* The Ss received their first shock, which was a 400-v. test trial, on the same day (Day 39) that the first two groups received their first test trial.

Throughout the part of the experiment during which shock

trials were given, any S failing to open the food door within 60 sec. after the start was returned to the home cage, given a speed score of zero, and run as usual on all subsequent trials.

Test trials were the same as training trials, except that all groups were given a 400-v. shock at the goal. Groups *a, b,* and *d* had 28 such trials, distributed over 14 days, Ss in Group *c* had 62 trials distributed over 31 days.

Results

The results are shown in Figure 16.2. It can be seen that all groups were approximately equal by the end of training. As in Exp. II, the group given gradually increasing shocks during rewarded training

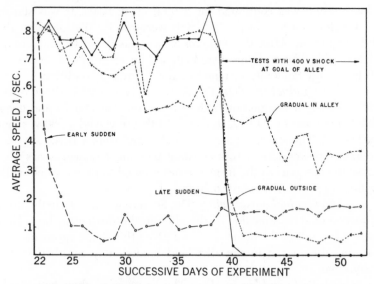

Figure 16.2   How speed of approach in a conflict situation is affected by following treatments: Early Sudden group given 400-v. test shocks at goal after 21 days of approach training; Late Sudden group given similar test shocks after 38 days of approach training; Gradual in Alley group habituated to series of increasingly strong shocks at goal before test shocks; Gradual Outside group habituated to similar series of shocks in distinctive box outside of alley. Each point is average of the two trials given each day, but on the day shock is suddenly introduced producing a sharp drop, each trial is plotted separately.

in the alley performs the best during the test series of strong shocks at the goal. In order to test for the statistical reliability of this superiority, the speed scores for each S were summed for the 25 test trials following the first shock. Since the distributions of total speed scores were not normal, the difference between each pair of groups was tested by tabulating the proportion of scores above and below the median of the combined pair. The differences between the gradual group and each of the other three were reliable ($P < .01$). The differences among the other groups did not approach statistical reliability except that the Mann-Whitney U test yielded a P of less than .02 for the difference between the speeds of the Early Sudden and the Late Sudden groups during the first 25 shocks received. This difference confirms Karsh's (1959) suggestive results and shows that overtraining with additional rewarded trials can paradoxically *decrease* the resistance of the habit to disruption by painful electric shocks.[3]

Finally, one unusual feature of the results should be mentioned. One of the animals in the Early Sudden group which had failed to run on 11 successive trials, gradually resumed running and by the 60th shock trial was the second fastest rat in the experiment. The fastest rat of all happened to be also in this same group in which all of the rest of the rats eventually stopped running.

Discussion

The results of these experiments show that rats can be trained to resist stresses such as pain and fear. It should be profitable to study the laws governing such learning and also to study learning to resist other stresses such as frustration, fatigue, noise, nausea, and extremes of temperature. Studies of partial reinforcement are relevant, of course, to the problem of learning to resist frustration.

Parallel studies could be designed at the human level to investigate the laws governing the way people learn to resist various stresses known to be important in civilian and military activity. Human studies should investigate especially the effect of mediating,

[3] Other experimenters such as Estes (1944, see Experiment F of Selection 11) and Boe (1964) have found that punishment has less of a suppressing effect when additional training is given.

symbolic factors, the importance of which in neurosis, psychotherapy, and problem solving I have emphasized elsewhere (Dollard & Miller, 1950; Miller, 1959).

Summary

In three experiments a total of 100 hungry rats were trained to run an alley for food reward and then given electric shocks at the goal to induce an approach-avoidance conflict. These experiments yielded the following results and conclusions:

1. During all but the first one or two trials of an extended test series with strong electric shocks at the goal, Ss which previously had been habituated to a gradually increasing series of shocks at the goal performed markedly better than those suddenly exposed to the test shocks for the first time. Under the conditions of these experiments we were able to teach rats considerable resistance to the stress of quite strong electric shocks at the goal.

2. A similar gradually increasing series of shocks given outside of the rewarded conflict situation produced little, if any, effect; Ss receiving this treatment were similar to the nonshock controls and reliably poorer than those habituated to the shocks in the rewarded training situation. Apparently, mere exposure to tough treatment will not necessarily improve resistance to stress in a different criterion situation.

3. Contrary to original expectation, additional rewarded training trials given to Ss which had reached the asymptote of speed reduced, rather than increased, the resistance of their running habit to disruption by shocks at the goal. Although widely advocated, mere overtraining may not always be helpful preparation for subsequent stress.

4. The results of these experiments suggest that it should be feasible and profitable to analyze further at both the animal and human level the laws governing the learning of resistance to stresses such as pain, fear, fatigue, frustration, noise, nausea, and extremes of temperature.

17 Aversive stimulation of the rat: long term effects on subsequent behavior

Gary C. Walters and Judith V. Rogers

Abstract. *One year after exposure to intense electric shock, rats were punished with shocks of lesser intensity. The previous exposure increased the suppressive effects of the punishment during both the initial encounter with punishment and over the course of a 7-day test period. Rats that had not been previously exposed to shock recovered during continued shock punishment.*

When a mature animal is exposed for a brief period to experiences of intense aversive stimulation, its reactions to fear-producing

Reprinted from *Science*, October 4, 1963, *142*, 70–71 by permission of the senior author and the American Association for the Advancement of Science. Copyright 1963 by the American Association for the Advancement of Science.
[In the previous article, Miller reported that aversive stimulation applied in a different situation had little effect on the action of subsequent punishment. Walters and Rogers show that (1) under some conditions aversive stimulation applied in such a manner will strongly affect the action of punishment, and (2) the effect can be to render subsequent punishments even more effective. This outcome can be described as a sensitization-like phenomenon. The use of this term, however, should not rule out other possible interpretations. In addition to other research cited by Walters and Rogers, see also Pearl, Walters, and Anderson (1964).—Eds.]

stimuli in subsequent test situations are drastically modified.[1] The results of a number of recent studies have been consistent with the hypothesis, originally proposed by Kurtz and Pearl (1960), that prior experiences of intense fear serve to sensitize an organism, predisposing it to react with "increased fearfulness" during later encounters with aversive stimulation. For example, such prior treatment results in increased resistance to extinction of an acquired-fear response (Kurtz & Pearl, 1960), greater disruptive effects during an approach-avoidance conflict task (Kurtz & Walters, 1962; Walters, 1963), and an increase in the suppressive effects of punishment on both conditioned (Pearl, 1961) and unconditioned (Pearl, 1963) activity. One of the major questions which remained unanswered in these studies was whether such treatment merely produces a transient change in the organism's fear reactions or results in a more enduring modification.

We confined 14 albino rats, approximately 50 days old, individually in small compartments with grid floors through which shock could be delivered. The animals were divided into two groups. Group A (seven animals) received ten unavoidable shocks of approximately 1.50 ma intensity, as measured with the rat in series with a constant-current source. Each shock lasted 5 seconds and was given, without warning and at irregular intervals, on the average of one shock every 2 minutes. After this treatment, each animal was returned to its regular cage and was reared under normal laboratory conditions. The remaining seven animals (group B) received no shocks, but in all other respects they received the same treatment.

One year after the original treatment, all animals were placed on a 23-hour schedule of food deprivation and trained to press a lever to receive a pellet of food weighing 0.45 mg. Upon completion of preliminary training, each animal was given a daily 10-minute session in the apparatus for five consecutive days. During this period the animal procured a food pellet each time it pressed a lever. The chamber used during training and testing was different from the one in which shock had been administered.

On the day after the last training session, each animal was placed in the test chamber as before; but now, each time the lever

[1] There is reason to believe that prior treatment does not always result in unidirectional changes in emotionality (for example, Brookshire, Littman, & Stewart, 1961).

was pressed, the animal received punishment in the form of a 0.20-ma shock of 0.20-second duration. The metal lever served as one pole and the grid floor as the other. The shock source was triggered automatically by the animal at the same time the food magazine was activated; hence the animal did not receive a shock unless the magazine was activated. The animal was rewarded by a food pellet each time it pressed the lever. Each experimental session lasted 10 minutes, and a total of seven daily sessions was given.

As shown in Figure 17.1, there was no appreciable difference between the two groups in the rates at which they pressed the lever until after they were subjected to punishment. This result confirms previous findings (Kurtz & Walters, 1962; Pearl, 1961; Walters, 1963).

While the lever-pressing activity on the first day of punishment was low in both groups, the rate was significantly higher in group B (U of 0; $p < .01$).[2] There was no overlap in the response rates of the two groups on this day; the ranges were: group A, 3 to 9; group B, 12 to 32. An overall comparison of the distributions of response rates shown in Figure 17.1 during the seven test days showed that the rate in group A remained significantly lower than that in group B (U of 5; $p = .01$). This finding was confirmed by separate analyses of results from the two groups, for each of the seven test days (U's ranged from 0 to 7; p's from $< .01$ to .03). By the last day of testing, group B had attained rates of lever pressing approximately equal to those they had attained before they were punished.

These results are consistent with the results of previous studies in which the intervals between the shocks and the punishments were much shorter (Kurtz & Pearl, 1960; Kurtz & Walters, 1962; Pearl, 1961; Walters, 1963). Our work indicates that prior exposure to intense electric shock has an enduring effect upon the organism.[3] By contrast, the control group (B) demonstrated recovery from the disruptive effects of shock punishment. The recovery during punishment of a previously suppressed response is not a unique finding, having been reported by other investigators who used special train-

[2] Mann-Whitney test in Siegel (1956, pp. 116–127). All probabilities reported in this paper are two-sided.

[3] Other workers (Hoffman, Flesher, & Jensen, 1962) have reported the long-term retention of a conditioned emotional response where a discrete stimulus complex is repeatedly paired with aversive stimulation.

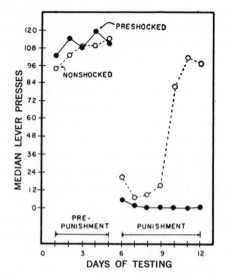

Figure 17.1 Rates of response (median number of lever presses during each 10-minute session) in tests before punishment (left) and tests accompanied by punishment (right). Animals in group A (solid lines) had received shock 1 year before; animals in group B (broken lines) had not received those shocks.

ing conditions. Azrin (1960a) studied the effects of shock after each response during a variable-interval schedule of food reinforcement in pigeons. Although the initial introduction of punishment produced a marked depression in the rate of response, the pigeons often displayed complete recovery even though punishment was maintained. Azrin also reported that the intensity of shock was an important variable, with little or no recovery at very high intensities. Preliminary studies in our laboratory, with test conditions identical with those described here, support Azrin's finding that recovery of a punished response is dependent on the intensity of the shock.[4]

[4] Partially supported by the Alumni Foundation for Faculty Research, University of Portland.

18   Changes in intensity of punishment: effect on running behavior of rats

Eileen B. Karsh

Abstract. *Changing the strength of punishment produced only minor changes in rats' speed of running to food and shock at the goal of an alley. The persistence of running behavior after increased or decreased shock intensity is attributed to a stereotyped withdrawal response conditioned at the goal during initial punishment training.*

Reprinted from *Science*, June 7, 1963, *140*, 1084–1085 by permission of the author and the American Association for the Advancement of Science. Copyright 1963 by the American Association for the Advancement of Science.
[Miller (Selection 16) found an adaptation-like phenomenon when he changed shock intensity over time from "low" to "high." In contrast Walters and Rogers (Selection 17) found a sensitization-like phenomenon when they changed shock intensity over time from "high" to "low." In this article, Karsh demonstrates both phenomena by experimentally manipulating the intensity of punishment during the first phase, and then switching intensities during a second phase. These results suggest that prior exposure to punishment of low intensity attenuates the effect of subsequent punishment, but punishment of high intensity increases the effect of subsequent punishment. Alternatively, the suppression produced by punishment may be intermediate between the amount that would ordinarily occur to that punishment and the amount produced by the prior exposure. For more recent research that confirms and extends Karsh's findings, see Church (1969).— Eds.]

Earlier research concerning the effects of punishment of a learned response showed that electric shock given late in training had a more disruptive effect upon that response than shock introduced earlier in the learning process (Karsh, 1962[1]; Miller, 1960). These results seemed paradoxical, since increased training theoretically adds to habit strength and thus is expected to reduce the effect of the punishment. However, it appeared that because the stimulus situation became better established with more trials, the introduction of shock caused a greater change, which in turn weakened the strength of the goal-approaching response. If the disruptive effect of strong punishment is thus partly due to the novelty which it brings into the situation, persistence of running behavior during strong punishment should be increased by prior training with weak punishment and reward, as opposed to training with reward alone. Miller found that a series of shocks which gradually increased from weak to strong was less disruptive than a suddenly introduced strong shock (Miller, 1960). The first experiment in the present study investigated the effectiveness of training with mild shock (which causes only a small decrease in responding) in preserving the learned response when it was later strongly punished.

Adult male rats were trained to run down an 8-foot straight alley to get a food pellet (0.3 g of wet mash) at the goal. Running time from start-box to food cup was automatically recorded, and a reciprocal transformation provided speed scores. On punished trials, a 0.1-second, 60-cy, a-c shock was delivered to the animal's feet through the grid floor (with a 250-k ohm, current-limiting resistor in series with the rat) as the rat touched the moist pellet in the food cup (Karsh, 1962). Subjects were given one trial daily, after 23½ hours' food deprivation, throughout the experiment. The experimental group (36 rats) received an average of 40 training trials with food, followed by 100 trials with food and a weak shock (120 volts). This caused them to slow down and then stabilize their approach at a speed about 15 percent lower than that of the control group. The 12 control animals were given 140 trials with food and no shock. After this, both groups received food and strong shock (200 volts) for 30 trials. Figure 18.1 shows that the speed of the control group

[1] This paper includes a description of the apparatus used in the present study.

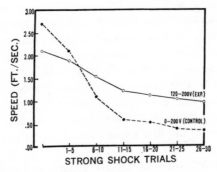

Figure 18.1   Effect of strong shock (200 volts) on the running speed of rats after training with weak shock (120 volts) or no shock

dropped sharply for the first 15 trials and then leveled off at a very low rate. The experimental group started at a speed reliably lower than that of the control group, but the experimental group's speed decreased more gradually and remained well above that of the control group after the first five trials with strong shock. An analysis of variance showed that the differential decline was significant ($F = 18.41$; $df = 6,276$; $p < .001$). Some of the animals stopped running, that is, failed to reach the goal within a 5-minute period. These animals were removed without being shocked and were given speed scores of zero. During the last five strong-shock trials, more than half of the control animals but only one-third of the experimental rats had stopped running. Thus, training with relatively mild punishment, which slightly depressed responding, resulted in persistence of running behavior when stronger punishment was applied. This persistent running was not due to adaptation to the punishing effects of mild shock, since the experimental group did not increase their running speed to the level of the control group during the trials with weak shock.

The slow, gradual decrease in responding shown when the subjects were changed from weak to strong shock contrasts with previous data showing rapid shifts in performance with both increases and decreases in amount of reinforcement. These earlier studies showed complete shifts within 15 trials when the amount of food at the goal was changed (Crespi, 1942; Zeaman, 1949) and also when the amount of shock reduction was changed for animals running to escape shock (Bower, Fowler, & Trapold, 1959).[2]

To complete the comparison between changes in amount of reinforcement and changes in amount of punishment, it was necessary to determine the effect of *decreasing* shock intensity. Consequently, the second experiment varied shock intensity in both directions (strong to weak and weak to strong). Sixty rats, randomly divided into five groups of 12 each, were trained to run down the alley for food, as in the first experiment. Five to ten training trials were given.

After training, three of the five groups received 50 trials with food and strong shock (200 volts). A final shock period consisting of 30 additional trials was given to these three groups as follows: one group was maintained at the same intensity, the second group was shifted to a weaker shock (120 volts), and the third group was changed to no shock.

The other two of the five groups received 50 trials with food and mild shock (120 volts). During the final shock period, one of these groups received the 30 additional trials at the same shock level, while the second group had these last 30 trials at a stronger shock level (200 volts).

During the first 50 trials, all five groups reached and maintained stable levels of speed commensurate with the amount of shock given. The two weak-shock groups were running at about 3½ feet per second, significantly faster than the three strong-shock groups, which all averaged about 2 feet per second. ($F = 25.93$; $df = 1, 55$; $p < .001$). Animals given strong shock did not stop running, as did the rats in the first experiment. Instead, they ran slowly down the alley and hesitated in the goal area before touching the food cup.[3]

During the final shock period of 30 trials, shown in Figure 18.2, the two control groups—those that received the *same* shock as on

[2] Both shock *reduction* and food presentation are reinforcing events which strengthen responses associated with them. However, the *presentation* of a noxious stimulus like shock is a punishing circumstance which may inhibit the response producing the punishment.

[3] Rats in the second experiment ran faster both in training and in shock conditions than rats in the first experiment, because of an apparatus improvement which made the food more accessible and reduced the delay in obtaining reward.

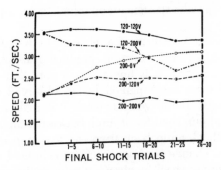

Figure 18.2 Effect of strong shock, weak shock, or no shock on the running speed of rats after training with the same or a different shock intensity. Figures before the hyphens indicate shock voltage given in 50 preliminary trials. Figures after the hyphens show voltage in 30 subsequent trials.

the first 50 trials (120 or 200 volts, respectively)—maintained fairly stable speeds, as expected. The group that was changed from weak to strong shock (from 120 to 200 volts) decreased its speed gradually below its control group (shock maintained at 120 volts), but still ran much faster than the group that received 200-volt shock in both sets of trials. Similarly, the rats shifted from strong to weak shock gradually increased their speed, but did not reach the speed of the rats that received a weak shock in the first 50 trials. The change from strong to no shock caused a greater increase during the final 30 shock trials than the shift from strong to weak shock ($F = 3.95$; $df = 6, 132$; $p < .005$).

An analysis of variance performed on the scores for the final 10 shock trials showed that both groups which received changes in shock intensity (120 to 200 volts, or vice versa) altered their speed reliably compared to their respective control groups maintained at constant shock intensity ($F = 4.49$; $df = 1, 44$; $p < .01$). However, the group that was switched from 120 to 200 volts still ran significantly faster than the group that had been maintained at 200 volts; and the group switched from 200 to 120 volts, significantly slower than the group maintained at 120 volts ($F = 8.99$; $df = 1, 44$; $p < .001$). In fact, the change in shock caused these two groups to approach a level midway between the speeds of the two unchanged controls ($F < 1$). Thus, running speed after a change in shock intensity was determined by both present and previous shock experi-

ence, with the initial experience appearing to be the more potent
factor.

The results clearly indicate that changes in the intensity of punishment, regardless of the direction, produce gradual, "incomplete"
shifts in running speed. It is important to note that these gradual
shifts in speed were accompanied by an observed response stereotypy after shock at the goal. Typically, animals receiving weak
shock at the food cup shudder or lurch backward slightly, while rats
getting strong shock jump back from the food cup more violently.
Animals given a change in shock intensity exhibited approximately
the same response to shock as observed prior to the change. That is,
rats getting a weak shock after experience with a stronger one continued to jump back after the weak shock just as they had jumped
after the strong one. However, rats getting strong shock after weak
shock never jumped very hard. The amount of change in running
speed when shock intensity is shifted appears to be strongly influenced by the response stereotypy developed during initial shock
training.

The withdrawing response to shock is associated with two
reinforcing events, shock termination and eating, and thus apparently becomes strongly conditioned to the goal cues. Changing the
strength of shock does not produce an immediate change in the
strongly conditioned withdrawal response and this could account for
the gradual, incomplete shift in running speed. During the first punished trials the withdrawal response tends to become anticipatory,
that is, incipient withdrawal responses occur progressively nearer to
the beginning of the alley, with the result that the rats run more
slowly when punished than before. Running speed during punished trials depends on the strength of the withdrawal response—the
stronger the initial punishment, the stronger the withdrawal response
and the slower the speed. However, when intensity of punishment is
changed, the withdrawal response does not change and running
speed also resists change because it reflects the strength of the withdrawal response. The development of such a persistent withdrawal
response at the goal is characteristic of the punishment situation and
distinguishes it from learning with reward alone.[4]

[4] I thank Dr. Frank A. Logan and Dr. Neal E. Miller for advice. The work
was supported in part by grant M647 and preparation of the report was aided by
grant MH 06951-01, both from the National Institute of Mental Health.

IV

Punishment of Learned
Aversive Responses

Most of the previous selections have described the effects of punishment on appetitive responses, instrumental responses that typically resulted in food. This part contains several experiments on the punishment of aversive responses, instrumental responses that terminate, prevent, or postpone the occurrence of a noxious stimulus. Mowrer (1947) described, and attempted to explain, a phenomenon he termed a "vicious circle." A rat that has been trained to avoid an electric shock may, if punished during extinction, persist in the response for a greater number of trials than if it is not punished. The first extensive examination of this phenomenon (Gwinn, 1949) corroborated the original analysis, but others (e.g., Seward & Raskin, 1960) found a decrease rather than an increase in resistance to extinction attributable to punishment during extinction trials. The study of Kamin (1959), in which rats were punished during the extinction of an avoidance response, also serves to limit the generality of the paradoxical "vicious circle" phenomenon. Nonetheless, self-punitive behavior has been observed in a variety of experimental conditions (e.g., Brown, Martin, & Morrow, 1964), and these authors have developed a theoretical basis for the phenomenon. At the present time, it is not possible to integrate all the apparently discrepant findings, and the effects of punishment on aversive behavior are less predictable than the effects of punishment on appetitive behavior.

19   A "vicious circle" explained

O. Hobart Mowrer

Another puzzling phenomenon which was brought to the writer's attention a few years ago (by Dr. Judson S. Brown) is the following. If a rat is put at one end of a straight alley about 4 feet long and if, after a period of 10 seconds, the floor of the alley (consisting of a metal grill) is electrified, the rat will soon scamper to the opposite end of the alley and, if a small nonelectrified compartment is available, escape into it. After a few repetitions of this procedure, the subject, as might be expected, will run to the opposite end as soon as placed in the alley, without receiving the shock. What obviously happens is that the rat's fear becomes conditioned to the "danger situation" and, since the running response carries the rat out of that situation, with an attendant reduction in fear, this response is quickly fixated.

Once this response is well established, it will persist for many trials; but the rat will tend to become more and more leisurely in making the run and will eventually delay beyond the ten-second period. If the shock is not applied under these circumstances, the

Reprinted from pages 133–134 of Mowrer, O. H., On the dual nature of learning—a reinterpretation of "conditioning" and "problem-solving." *Harvard Educational Review*, 1947, 17(2) by permission of the author and the publisher. Copyright 1947 by the *Harvard Educational Review*.

tendency on the part of the rat to flee from the end of the maze where it is introduced deteriorates still further; and ultimately the flight response will disappear completely.

This behavior is, of course, in no way surprising, since it conforms perfectly to what is well known concerning the extinction of avoidance reactions. What is surprising, however, is this: If, after a "conditioned" response of the kind just described is well established, a small section of the floor-grill, at the far end of the alley, is permanently electrified so that in the process of getting from the starting point to the safety compartment, the rat must always receive at least a momentary shock, the running response does not extinguish! Even though shock is never again experienced in the part of the alley where the animal is introduced, flight from this area continues to occur indefinitely.

When subjected to the first procedure described above, rats behave in a perfectly "normal" and understandable manner. But in the case of the second procedure, their behavior is very surprising, strange, "abnormal"—for they seem to be manifesting a "masochistic trend," a "need for punishment," "pleasure in pain." They continue to cross the electrified segment of the floor-grill and get shocked, whereas if they merely "sat tight" in the first part of the alley, nothing would happen to them. Under these circumstances, the running response obviously gets "punished," and yet, instead of being inhibited by this punishment, it is apparently strengthened by it.[1]

How can this paradox be resolved? The answer seems to be relatively simple on the basis of a two-factor theory of reinforcement. Each time the rat is placed in the experimental apparatus and gets a brief shock on the way to the safety compartment, the part of the alley where the rat is introduced gets "reinforced" as a danger situation (or "conditioned stimulus"), since it continues to be temporally associated with pain. This means that the fear continues to be aroused each time the animal is placed in the alley and this fear is most effectively reduced by the running response, which carries the animal to the safety compartment. The running response, as skeletal behavior, is thereby reinforced (through effect learning); but this

---

[1] Although the experiment just described is not strictly comparable to the situations employed by Muenzinger and Wood (1935) and others in studying the facilitation of learning by means of punishing "right" responses, there is at least an oblique similarity. Perhaps the latter studies can be usefully reexamined with the assumptions underlying the present analysis in mind.

behavior is of such a nature that it also provides the kind of reinforcement whereby the fear, or motivation for running, is kept alive.

It is always hazardous to interpret clinical phenomena on the human level in terms of animal experiments, yet there seems to be more than a superficial resemblance between the behavior just described and "compulsive," "self-defeating," "masochistic" behavior which Horney (1937) and others (Mowrer & Ullman, 1945) have discussed under the concept of the "vicious circle." Perhaps the two-factor theory of learning will turn out to have important clinical significance.

By thus sharply differentiating between two types of learning process, or "reinforcement," one is able to resolve the paradox involved in the experiment just described (and possibly also in at least certain types of "vicious circles" found at the human level). Yet a question remains as to what happens to the inhibitory tendency which is undoubtedly created by the fact that the response of running is consistently punished, i.e., regularly followed by electric shock. As a tentative hypothesis, one may assume that this tendency is present but that it is overridden by the reinforcement processes just described.[2]

[2] Since the above was written, experimental results obtained by Mr. U. E. Whiteis indicate that this hypothesis is well founded. Once the shock on the right side of the grill is removed, the running response quickly deteriorates, reflecting a conflict on the part of the subject between a fear of not running and a fear of running. [A report of this experiment was subsequently published (Whiteis, 1956).—Eds.]

20 The effects of punishment on acts motivated by fear

Gordon T. Gwinn

Introduction

Individuals often tend to stop performing punished acts and to avoid punishing situations. In accounting for this fact some psychologists assume that punishment weakens or depresses the S-R connections involved. Others hold that it produces expectancies or negative valences resulting in avoidance of the punishing stimulus. These theoretical propositions are in essential agreement with Hilgard and Marquis' empirical principle of "inhibition by punishment." They hold that *"if a response is followed by a noxious stimulus it will tend*

This selection is reprinted from the *Journal of Experimental Psychology,* 1949, 39, 260–269 by permission of the author and the American Psychological Association.

This report is based on a dissertation presented in 1948 to the Faculty of Yale University in partial fulfillment of the requirements for the Ph.D. degree. I am indebted to Dr. Neal E. Miller, under whose direction the research was conducted, and to the other members of the Psychology Department for many helpful criticisms and suggestions, and to my wife, Adelaide S. Gwinn, for assistance in conducting the experiments and for drawing the figures.

[This is the first extensive examination of the "vicious circle" phenomenon described by Mowrer in Selection 19.—Eds.]

to be weakened in strength and less likely to occur on the next presentation of the situation" (1940, p. 125). It should be noted that the term "inhibition," as used by these authors and in this paper, refers to a decrease in response *performance* rather than to any hypothetical mechanism.[1]

On the other hand, according to S-R contiguity and drive-reduction theories of learning, punishment does not necessarily have any inhibitory effects. The only learning resulting from punishment is the learning of the responses, especially escape responses, evoked by the punishing stimulus and conditioned to the cues for the punished act. Whether or not a given punishment will be inhibitory depends on whether or not these "anticipatory" responses are incompatible and so interfere with the punished act. It also depends, according to the fear hypothesis of Miller and Dollard (1941, especially p. 61), and Mowrer (1947),[2] on whether or not the dominant response to fear is incompatible with the punished act. This is because anticipatory fear-responses produce stimuli tending to elicit, innately or as a result of learning, responses which may or may not interfere with the act.[3]

It follows from these "interference" theories that, if the response to the punishing stimulus is compatible with the punished act, *punishment will facilitate rather than inhibit an act motivated by fear.* The fear produced by the punishment will strengthen the fear-drive motivating the punished act. The act will be facilitated because response performance is a positive function of drive-strength. Furthermore, the fear-drive, and hence the facilitation, will increase with the intensity and frequency of the punishment. There will be no interference and hence no inhibition, because the dominant response to fear *is* the punished act and it is not incompatible with the response to the punishing stimulus.

The experiment reported below was designed to test this facilitation hypothesis as against the view that punishment necessarily has inhibitory effects.

---

[1] Similarly, McGeoch (1946) proposes as a valid "empirical law" the view that punishment "eliminates" the punished act whatever may be the underlying mechanisms.

[2] [See Selection 19.—Eds.]

[3] For summaries of the divergent views concerning the mechanisms mediating the effects of punishment see McGeoch (1946), Postman (1947), and Hilgard (1948).

Method

Subjects

A group of 24 experimentally naive male albino rats from three to four months old were used after three days during which they were handled in order to tame them.

Apparatus

The circular alley diagrammed in Figure 20.1 was used. Raised three feet from the floor, it was three in. wide and four in. high, and had an inside diameter of 19 in. The runway consisted of a wire grill to which alternating electric current could be delivered by means of a telegraph key. A potentiometer was used to control voltage, and a one-fourth megohm resistance in series with the grill helped to minimize the effects of fluctuations in the animals' resistance.

Four gauze-covered glass panes, individually removable from a wooden frame, constituted a one-way vision cover for the sheet-metal alley walls. Eight sections of the alley were labeled for purposes of reference.

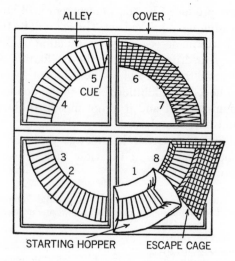

Figure 20.1   Diagram of the alley

Placed in a darkroom, the alley was illuminated through the grill by a 200-watt bulb and reflector placed 18 in. below the center. Attached under sections 6 and 7 was a black cardboard shield making the floor black, in contrast to the bright floor of the rest of the alley, and casting a sharp shadow upon the walls of the alley. Thus sections 6–7, where the punishing shock occurred during the test trials, was visually distinct from the rest of the alley. The line between the bright section 5 and the dark section 6 will be called the "cue," since it provided a "danger signal" at the point where the shock area began.

The Ss were placed in the alley through a removable hopper with flared sides placed over section 1 (replacing the glass cover for that section). A barrier attached to the hopper prevented movement from section 1 directly into section 8. A wooden block, made to fit flush with the top of the alley walls, was used to ensure the Ss' entrance into the alley and to prevent exit by way of the hopper. The only exit possible was by way of an escape cage which replaced glass over any desired section. A barrier attached to the escape cage prevented movement beyond the cage.

Two electric timers were manually operated by an assistant who also made the required recordings.

Preliminary training

The Ss were given preliminary training which was designed to produce a fear-drive in the alley and a tendency to run forward and escape from the alley as a consequence of this fear.

Each animal received 18 trials during which he started at section 1 and received 60-volt shocks throughout the alley until he jumped into the escape cage. To facilitate the training, the escape cage was placed over section 2 for 4 trials, then moved successively to sections 4 and 6 for 3 trials each, and finally to section 8 for 8 trials.[4] Upon escape from the alley, the animal was removed to a neutral restraining cage for 10 sec. before the next trial.

On the first few trials all the animals reacted to the shock with a variety of responses other than running forward. These responses

---

[4] During the first few trials, occasionally an S stood motionless on his hind legs, apparently reducing the effectiveness of the shock. When this happened, the experimenter prodded the animal's feet and movement was resumed.

soon disappeared, however, and rapid running forward and jumping into the escape cage occurred consistently by the end of the training session. Furthermore, on the first test trial following this training, although no shocks were received from start to "cue" (i.e., the line between section 5 and the darkened section 6), the Ss promptly ran that distance (the mean running time being less than two sec.). By the fear hypothesis, these facts indicate that the training sessions effectively established fear in the alley and also established running as the dominant response to fear as well as to shock. This was the response which was to be punished during the test trials.

Test trials

One min. after completion of the preliminary training, each animal was tested under one of the following randomly selected conditions:

(a) *Shock vs. non-shock*. To determine whether shock administered only as a "punishment" for running to the "cue" would facilitate or inhibit that response, 16 of the animals received shock only if they ran past the cue and entered the dark area of the alley (sections 6–7). The remaining eight animals received no shocks and thus provided an experimental "control" of factors other than the punishing shock which influenced the running tendency.

(b) *Weak shock vs. strong shock*. To determine the effects of different intensities of shock, eight of the shocked animals received shocks of 60 volts (the same as in the preliminary training) while the remaining eight received 120-volt shocks (double the training voltage).

(c) *Shock-100 percent vs. shock-33 percent*. To determine the effects of different frequencies of shock, half of each of the above shock groups received shocks on every trial; the other half received shocks on the first trial but only on every third trial thereafter. The shock-33 percent condition also provided a basis for comparing the effects of shock trials as against non-shock trials for the same animals.

Under all conditions the animals were started at section 1, and the escape cage remained at section 8. On all shock trials the shock went "on" as soon as the animals passed the cue. Once the shock was on, it remained on throughout the alley until they ran into section 8, which was not electrified during test trials. It is important, for theoretical reasons to be discussed later, to note that all the animals were observed to respond to the shock by dashing forward into section 8. Since no returning to section 5 occurred, none of the animals received shocks anywhere except in the dark sections 6–7, and for all of them the response accompanied by termination of the shock was invariably the response of running forward.

Upon escape from the alley, the animals were removed to the restraining cage for an interval of 10 sec. before the next trial.[5] Trials were repeated until the running time from start to cue exceeded a "stopping" criterion of 10 sec.

Measures

On each trial the time required to run from start to cue, and also the time from cue to escape, were measured to the nearest tenth of a sec. These scores were converted to speed, i.e., the number of sections run per sec., and the mean of each individual's speed on all trials was computed. Then the group mean of these individual mean speeds was computed for each experimental condition. The mean number of trials required to reach the 10-sec. stopping criterion was also computed for each condition.

The speed of running and the number of trials run before reaching the stopping criterion were used to measure any facilitation or inhibition of the punished act of running to the cue. In addition, since the effects of punishment whether facilitatory or inhibitory were expected to influence the frequency and location of any tendencies to stop running, the location of every instance of stopping was recorded.

Results

Evidence of facilitation by punishment

(*a*) *Effects of shock vs. non-shock.* It may be seen in Table 20.1 that the animals that received the punishing shock at the cue

[5] Occasionally Ss of the non-shock group turned around and started to return to section 5. Such movement was blocked by the insertion of a metal gate through the grill in section 5. Also, occasionally, animals of this group remained in sections 6–8 longer than 10 sec. and, when tapping the apparatus failed to result in jumping into the escape cage, they were removed directly from the alley. This was unnecessary for shocked animals because they never returned to section 5 and always jumped into the escape cage.

Table 20.1   Analysis of effects of varying intensity and relative frequency of shock upon mean speed (number of sections per second) of running from start to cue *

A. Group means

Test condition	Strong shock (SS)	Weak shock (WS)	Non–shock (NS)	Shock–100% (S100)	Shock–33% (S33)
Number	8	7	7	7	8
Mean	2.70	2.06	1.43	2.46	2.34

B. Differences between means

Means compared	Effect of intensity			Effect of frequency		
	SS–WS	SS–NS	WS–NS	S100–S33	S100–NS	S33–NS
Difference	.64	1.27	.63	.12	1.03	.92
Level sig.**	1%	1%	1%	35%	1%	1%

*Analysis of the effects of varying intensity is based on the same data as those used for frequency, but the data were recombined.

One weak–shock–100 percent and one non–shock animal were excluded from their respective groups in computing mean speeds. This was done because each ran only one trial. A "mean" of a single score is unreliable on a priori grounds and, furthermore, these scores deviated from their group means by 4.88 and 3.66 sigmas respectively.

** The t-tests of statistical significance described by Lindquist (1940) were used in all the analyses in this paper. In all instances the "levels of significance" stated refer to the percent of cases in which differences in the same direction as large or larger than those obtained would be expected to occur by chance; all percentages smaller than one are reported as 1 percent.

ran to the cue faster than the animals that were not shocked. The differences between the mean speeds for all trials run by the non-shock as against the shock groups, whether the shock was strong or weak, every trial or every third trial, are statistically highly significant in all cases.

The fact that the punishing shock at the cue produced faster running to the cue than non-shock is shown graphically in Figure 20.2. The curve for shocked animals in this figure also shows that the initial running tendency was increased by the punishment during the first half of the test trials. All but one of the 16 shocked animals ran faster, on at least one of the first half of trials, than they did on the initial trial. This contrast with the curve for non-shock groups which reflects the fact that all eight of these animals tended to slow

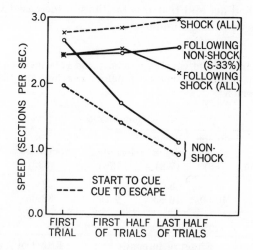

Figure 20.2   Mean speeds on the first test trial and on the first and last halves of test trials. The curves show the speed of running to the cue on trials following shocks for all shocked animals, on trials following the non-shock trials in the shock-33 percent condition, and on all trials in the non-shock condition. They also show the speed of running from cue to escape on all shock trials and on all trials in the non-shock condition.

down immediately, and at no time did any of them ever run faster than on the first trial.

Animals shocked at the cue not only ran to the cue faster than those not shocked, but also they tended to perform this act for more trials. Table 20.2 shows that shocked animals ran more trials before reaching the stopping criterion than non-shocked. The differences in the mean for the non-shock group as compared with the means for the various conditions of shock are all in the direction of longer running for shocked animals and are highly reliable for strong shock and shock every third trial.

(*b*) *Effects of strong shock vs. weak shock*. Referring again to Tables 20.1 and 20.2, it may be seen that running to the cue was faster and continued for more trials when it was punished by strong shock than when punished by weak shock. For both measures, the means for strong shock were reliably greater than those for weak shock.

These facts indicate that punishment facilitated performance of the punished act and that this facilitation increased with the intensity of the punishing stimulus.

Table 20.2   Analysis of varying intensity and relative frequency of shock upon the number of trials run before reaching the 10-second stopping criterion*

A. Group means

Test condition	Strong shock (SS)	Weak shock (WS)	Non-shock (NS)	Shock–33% (S33)	Shock–100% (S100)
Number	8	8	8	8	8
Mean	40.50	16.63	9.25	32.00	25.13

B. Differences between means

Means compared	Effect of intensity			Effect of frequency		
	SS–WS	SS–NS	WS–NS	S33–S100	S33–NS	S100–NS
Difference	23.87	31.25	7.38	6.87	22.75	15.88
Level sig.	2%	1%	10%	30%	1%	5%

*Analysis of the effects of varying intensity is based on the same data as those used for frequency, but the data were recombined.

Evidence of inhibition by punishment

Despite the above facts, there was evidence in the behavior of the shocked animals which indicated that the shock not only facilitated the running tendency but also produced a conflicting tendency *not* to run into the shock area.

(a) *Effects of shock in shock-33 percent condition.* Running to the cue, in animals shocked at the cue on every third trial only, slowed down immediately following shock trials and speeded up during the intervening non-shock trials. The mean speed for all trials following shock is very reliably less (significant beyond the 1 percent level) than for trials immediately preceding shock.[6] This decrease in speed following the occasional shock trials, by comparison

[6] The analyses of the mean differences here and in the following paragraphs are based on distributions of the differences for individuals.

with speed following the non-shock, shows that the shock had inhibitory effects upon the act of running to the cue. It has already been shown (cf. Tables 20.1 and 20.2) that, by comparison with no shock at all, the occasional shock facilitated that act. It may be said, therefore, that the shock had both facilitatory and inhibitory effects at least in the shock-33 percent condition.

(*b*) *Effects of repetition of trials.* Despite the facilitatory effects of the punishing shock, all the animals in all the shock groups as well as the non-shock eventually slowed down and stopped running to the cue long enough to meet the 10-sec. stopping criterion. Referring again to Figure 20.2, it may be seen that the speed of running to the cue on trials following the punishing shock was less for the second half of trials run than it was for the first half. The mean difference in speed for the two halves is statistically significant beyond the 3 percent level. That this eventual slowing down after repeated shocks was an inhibitory consequence of the shock is suggested by the fact that the speed of running following the *non-shock* trials of animals shocked only on every third trial did *not* decrease with repetition of trials (cf. Figure 20.2).

It is important to note, in consideration of "interference" interpretations of the inhibitory effects of punishment, that for shocked animals the slowing down from start to cue accompanied a progressive increase in speed of running forward from cue to escape in response to the shock (cf. Figure 20.2). The mean speed from cue to escape was significantly greater on the second half than on the first half of the shock trials (significant beyond the 5 percent level).

(*c*) *Location of stopping and conflict behavior.* The eventual decrease in the measured speed of running to the cue was due more to an increase in the occurrence and duration of stopping than to slower running. In shocked animals this tendency to stop was stronger, i.e., was more frequent, *just in front of the cue* than anywhere else in the alley. The greater frequency of stopping in front of the cue (sections 4–5) than near the start (sections 1–2) is significant beyond the 1 percent level. Stopping in the area from cue to escape was extremely rare in shocked animals even when shock was omitted in the shock-33 percent condition; for all individuals in the shock groups it was less frequent than stopping in front of the cue. All non-shock animals, on the other hand, stopped most frequently near the escape cage.

It was observed that the stopping of shocked animals in front of the cue was almost always accompanied by either "freezing" or slight but obvious vacillatory movements followed by dashing forward to the escape cage. Stopping and then spurting past the cue eventually became so pronounced that visitors in the laboratory were inclined to believe that the experimenter shocked the animals by mistake on non-shock trials in the shock-33 percent condition. Such behavior did not occur in the non-shocked animals.

It should be noted that, in terms of sign-gestalt theories, stopping in front of the cue but running from cue to escape even when shock was omitted shows that the animals "knew" the shock was located at the cue and were avoiding it; yet running into the shock area tended to continue for many trials after they acquired this knowledge.

These facts indicate that the punishment both facilitated and inhibited the punished act, i.e., it produced a conflict between tendencies to run to the escape cage and not to run to the cue.

The influence of frequency of punishment

In Tables 20.1 and 20.2 it may be seen that the running tendency of animals shocked on every trial did not differ significantly, nor in any consistent direction for the two measures, from that of animals shocked on every third trial only. It is possible that the different frequencies of shock did not have a differential influence. It has already been shown, however, that the inhibitory effects of the shock eventually increased with its repetition despite the facilitatory effects. This suggests that both inhibition and facilitation may have increased with the frequency of shock and that the counterbalancing of these opposing effects minimized measurable differences between shock every trial and shock every third trial.

Interpretation

On the basis of theories consistent with the general principle of inhibition by punishment it was expected that the punishment at the cue would inhibit rather than facilitate running to the cue. The fact is that the most powerful effect of the punishment was, for many trials at least, facilitation rather than inhibition of that act, and the facilitation increased with the intensity of the punishment. This suggests that punishment does not necessarily inhibit punished acts and that these theories need to be extended or stated more precisely to account for the experimental facts. It is possible to "explain" the results in terms of sign-gestalt-expectancies by inferring from the observed behavior which of several possible expectancies must have operated to produce responses appropriate to them; but it is difficult, if not impossible, to derive these expectancies from expectancy theories as presently formulated.

On the other hand, the fact of facilitation by punishment was predicted in terms of S-R contiguity and drive-reduction theories including the fear hypothesis. This prediction, however, involved the assumption that the punishment would have no inhibitory effects. The fact that inhibition was observed suggests that a modification of these theories is required before they can provide an adequate account of the present results.

It is proposed that interpretation of the apparently "inconsistent" effects of punishment in this and other experiments (Postman, 1947) can be furthered by elaborating Mowrer's (1947) most recent version of the fear hypothesis as follows:

1. Fear is a *central* rather than peripheral reaction[7] to noxious stimuli such as shock and is learned in accordance with Pavlovian (1927) principles of conditioning by contiguity; whereas *sequences of locomotor responses* such as running are learned in accordance with principles of reinforcement by drive-reduction.

2. As a central process, fear directly mediates those S-R events usually regarded as indicative of fear, e.g., startle responses to sudden intense stimulation. Therefore, *a sudden increase in fear tends to elicit a startle response,* the strength of the startle being a positive function of the rate of increase. This response is an innate, short-latency "reflex" of very short duration and is not subject to "extinction" (Hunt & Landis, 1936). While fear *per se* may evoke any of the possible locomotor responses in accordance with learning principles, an *increase* in fear always tends to evoke a startle.

It may be deduced from general S-R theory and the fear hypothesis, as modified above, that the various effects of punishment on

[7] See Morgan (1943) for various physiological theories of emotion, especially the Cannon-Bard thalamic theory.

punished acts are mediated by conditioned fear. The nature and amount of the effects depend upon the strength of the fear and upon the responses it tends to evoke. The effects of punishment are not mediated by the learning of "anticipatory" locomotor responses to the punishing stimulus, because, unlike fear, such responses cannot be conditioned (and can generalize little, if at all) to the cues for the punished act.

An analysis in these terms of the present experimental results is suggested in the following paragraphs.

Facilitation by punishment

On the initial test trials, the fear conditioned to the alley during pre-liminary training motivated the animals to run and escape from the alley. On all test trials under all the test conditions this running response to fear continued to be rewarded by fear-reduction upon escape into the escape cage. But the punishing shock strengthened the conditioned fear throughout the alley, while fear was extinguished in the absence of shock. These changes in the strength of the fear-drive motivating the running response produced the observed speeding up of running for several trials in shocked animals in contrast with the slowing down in non-shocked.

Running was facilitated more by strong shock than by weak shock because the strength of the fear-drive increased with the intensity of the shock.

Inhibition by punishment

After many repetitions of shock at the cue, the strength of fear became greater just in front of the cue than near the start, i.e., fear increased upon approach to the cue. This increase in fear eventually became rapid enough to evoke an effective startle and momentarily stop the running. The *rate* of increase in fear, and hence the observed inhibition of running, increased with repetition of shocks and was greatest just in front of the cue.[8] It did not increase with the

---

[8] Statements concerning differences in the strength of conditioned fear in various parts of the alley are derived from Hull's (1943) quantitative assumptions concerning the strength of S-R connections.

intensity of the shock,[9] so the strong shock was no more inhibitory than the weak shock. The reason there were no significant differences between the observed behavior of animals shocked every trial and those shocked on a third of the trials only is that *both* the fear-drive strength and the effectiveness of the startle response increased with the frequency of shock; these opposing influences counterbalanced each other and minimized measurable differences between the two conditions.

There was no inhibition by punishment until after many trials. This was because, during the 18 preliminary training trials, the fear conditioned by shock was of approximately equal strength throughout the alley; but a tendency to *stop* being afraid in the escape cage, i.e., a non-fear response, was conditioned more strongly near the escape than near the start. Therefore, on the first test trials, as the animals ran from start to escape (via the cue) their fear decreased. In support of this proposition is the fact that, on the first test trials, non-shocked animals ran more slowly near the escape than near the start of the alley (cf. Figure 20.2). Because of the counteracting effect of this initial decrease in fear as the animals ran toward the escape, many shocks at the cue were needed before an increase in fear accompanied approach to the cue. There could be no inhibition until such an increase occurred and became rapid enough to evoke an effective startle response.

Whenever a startle stopped the running, a tendency to remain immobile, i.e., to "freeze," was reinforced by fear-reduction to the pattern of visual, proprioceptive and other stimuli resulting from not running. The fear-reduction was due to the cessation of many of the fear-producing stimuli, i.e., the stimuli involved in running to the cue. The conflict behavior in front of the cue was due to the development of the tendency to freeze in opposition to the initially dominant tendency to run in response to fear. Through the process of discrimination, freezing eventually outcompeted running in front of the cue so that all animals reached the 10-sec. "stopping" criterion.

[9] A study by Brown (1948) of spatial gradients of avoidance, here assumed to be based on the strength of conditioned fear, showed that the height (strength of fear) but not the steepness (rate of increase in strength of fear) of the gradients increased with the intensity of the shock being avoided.

Summary

It is implied by "interference" theories in general and the fear hypothesis in particular that acts motivated by fear will not be inhibited but rather will be facilitated by punishment, when they are compatible with the responses to the punishing stimulus. Furthermore, the facilitation will increase with the intensity and frequency of occurrence of the punishing stimulus. The present experiment established conditions designed to test this proposition as against the view that punishment necessarily tends to inhibit punished acts. The results showed that:

1. The punishment facilitated the punished act, and the facilitation increased with the intensity of the punishing stimulus. There was no evidence of inhibition until after many repetitions of the punishment.

2. Despite its facilitatory effects, the punishment eventually inhibited the punished act, and the inhibition increased with continued repetitions of the punishment.

3. The observed effects of punishment did not differ significantly for subjects punished on every trial as compared with those punished on every third trial only.

An interpretation of the results in terms of a modification of the fear hypothesis was suggested.

21   The role of fear in aversive behavior

John P. Seward and David C. Raskin

A complete theory of avoidance behavior must explain how it origi-
nates and how it is maintained. Hull (1937) answered the first question by assuming that an escape response was conditioned to traces
of preceding stimuli, thus appearing earlier in the sequence. But this
failed to answer the second question and left unresolved the "dilemma of the conditioned defense reaction" (Hull, 1929).

Mowrer resolved the dilemma (Mowrer & Lamoreaux, 1942)
by supposing that the internal response to punishment contained a
fraction, *anxiety* or *fear*, that could be conditioned to preceding stimuli and serve as a learned drive; any response that removed these
stimuli would therefore be reinforced by secondary-drive reduction.
Miller (1951) gave the theory strong support. Schoenfeld (1950)
and Dinsmoor (1955) have argued that the construct of "anxiety"
is unnecessary, since we need assume only that the CSs themselves

Reprinted from the *Journal of Comparative and Physiological Psychology*,
1960, 53, 328–335 by permission of the senior author and the American Psychological Association. Aided by a grant (G4419) from the National Science
Foundation.
    [These studies of punishment on aversive behavior (escape and avoid-
ance) serve to limit the generality of the "vicious circle" phenomenon. The results of a later study by Seward, King, Chow, and Shiflett (1965) are consistent
with those reported here.—Eds.]

become aversive for their termination to be reinforcing. No useful distinction appears, however, between "anxiety-arousing" and "aversive."

By combining these processes—the conditioning and bringing-forward of an escape response and a fear drive—we have a mechanism for the origin and maintenance of avoidance behavior. The theory will work as long as the response that terminates punishment is incompatible with the response that produced it. In this case the antedating escape response will prevent the punished response from being made. Fortunately, in everyday life the requirement is usually met. But what if conditions were so arranged that punishment was escaped by the same response that produced it? We should then have to predict that the punished response would be repeated more and more readily.

Hilgard (1948) pointed out this implication and denied its validity in the following passage:

> If an animal runs down an alley, meets a charged grid, and leaps ahead from it to safety, the leap is associated with need-reduction (pain-alleviation) so that, by strict reinforcement theory, the animal should do what it last did, only perhaps more intensely. It should run down the alley faster, touch the grid and make a jump ahead to safety. (This, by the way, should be Guthrie's prediction also, since leaping from the grid prevented any unlearning of the last bit of behavior to the grid.) Rats do not do this. They slow up in the alley, and try not to approach the grid. That is the difference between escape and avoidance behavior (p. 108).

Sheffield (1949) challenged Hilgard's statement on empirical grounds, citing occasions when rats showed just the type of behavior predicted by S-R theory.

The following experiments were therefore devised to find out what rats would do in the situation Hilgard described.

Experiment 1

Method

Apparatus

We used a straight, enclosed, gray runway consisting of three sections, each 24 by ¾ by 2½ in., separated by sliding doors and with grid floors. The middle section was wired to a shock stimulator set to deliver 190 volts ac through 150,000 ohms of external resistance. A manually operated microswitch started a 1-rps timer and turned *off* the shock; breaking the beam of a photocell at the mid-point of the runway stopped the timer and turned *on* the shock. By this arrangement S received the shock when it was halfway across the middle section; it could escape by either going ahead or retreating an equal distance.

Subjects

Eighteen naive male albino rats were used, 9 to 10 weeks old at the start. Fourteen Ss were assigned at random to Group E, four to Group C.

Procedure

On the first day Ss were given 15 min. to explore the runway in groups of three with doors open and shock off. Next day they were given a maximum of 10 massed trials as follows: Group E—Starting the timer at the same moment, E put S at the start of the runway facing the end wall. After S had reached the photocell, shocked itself, and left the middle section, E closed the door to prevent retracing and recorded which section S had entered and the time from start to photocell. Thirty seconds after entering either section S was removed and the next trial started. If S failed to break the photocell beam in 60 sec., it was removed and started again at once; if it failed three times in succession its trials were stopped. From two to five days later all Ss were retested under the same conditions. Group C—The procedure was the same except that there was no shock. The retest was omitted.

Results

On Trial 1, 13 of the 14 Ss in Group E escaped shock by running ahead to the end section; 1 ran back. On Trial 2, 7 of the 13 escaped by retreating to the start section, 3 refused to leave the start section within 60 sec., and 3 kept going as before. The single S that had previously gone back to the start stayed there. On Trial 3 only one experimental S left the start section, and thereafter no S did so.

To test the significance of shift in Group E from Trial 1 to 2 we combined retreats with refusals and applied McNemar's test (1947). The obtained χ^2 of 8.1 is significant at the .01 level.

To compare shocked with unshocked rats we added to Group C the two control Ss from Experiment 3 below, tested under the same conditions. All six controls entered the end section on both Trials 1 and 2. The difference between Groups E and C in number of Ss re-entering and not re-entering the end section on the second trial was significant at the .006 level by Fisher's exact test (two-tailed).

Times from start to photocell in Group E were much longer on the second trial than the first. The median time on Trial 1 was 3.12 sec.; on Trial 2, 23.66. All 14 Ss took longer on the second trial.

On retest one trial was given all experimental Ss; only one left the start section and none reached the photocell in 60 sec.

On the qualitative side, most Ss responded to the onset of shock by vigorous activity. After two or three trials, however, both escape from shock and replacement in the runway were followed immediately by "freezing," characterized by immobility and altered breathing. The six control Ss, on the other hand, showed normal exploratory behavior. All but one ran on every trial; the exception refused on the last three. Total refusals and returns to the start section in 10 trials ranged from 0 to 5. Times showed a gradually increasing trend.

Discussion

The results clearly supported Hilgard's conjecture about the avoidance behavior of rats. It seemed possible, however, that their generality was limited. They might be explained by a high degree of generalization between the start and end sections of the runway. A rat that escaped shock by running into the end section might, on the next trial, react to the almost identical start section as a "safe place" and be loathe to leave it. We therefore repeated the experiment with the end section so modified as to reduce generalization.

Experiment 2

Method

Apparatus

The only change was to line completely the walls and floor of the end section with black cardboard.

Subjects

Ten naive male albino rats, 10 to 11 weeks old, were assigned at random, eight to Group E, two to Group C.

Procedure

Only two changes were made: (*a*) The criterion for stopping trials was reduced to two successive trials of over 60 sec.; (*b*) experimental Ss were retested on the following day, when they were started in the *end* section.

Results

The chief effect of differentiating the end section was to diminish the number of times it was entered. After receiving shock on Trial 1, three Ss escaped by running ahead while five returned to the start. On Trial 2 all three of the former and one of the latter withdrew to the start section on being shocked; the other four failed to leave it. All eight experimental Ss reached the stopping criterion by Trial 5. Combining the results for Trials 1 and 2 with those of Experiment 1 and applying McNemar's test, we obtained a χ^2 of 11.08, $p = .001$.

As in Experiment 1, times on the second trial were severely retarded. The median time on Trial 1 was 4.25 sec.; on Trial 2 it was indeterminate, since four Ss refused to run, but the shortest time was 16.8 sec. All eight Ss increased their times.

The two control Ss also showed increased reluctance to enter the demarcated end section, returning instead to the start on six and eight trials, respectively.

On the 24-hr. retest, although it was run in the opposite direction, none of the eight Ss reached the photocell within 60 sec.

Discussion

Experiment 2 did not bear out the reasoning that prompted it. Making the end section distinct from the rest of the runway was intended to reduce two forms of generalization: that of "anxiety" from shock section to end section and that of "security" from end section to start. In other words, we hoped to enhance secondary reinforcement in the end section and reduce it in the start section; either effect should have produced more crossings. Any such tendency was more than offset by the enhanced negative valence of the end section itself. It is noteworthy, however, that preference for the start section was not strong enough to pull the Ss across the grid on retest.

To test our interpretation we need a way of distinguishing the end section without setting up a barrier. Perhaps giving the Ss more preliminary exploration would do it.

Experiment 3

The tendency of our shocked rats to freeze suggested that our findings might be a function of strength of shock. We therefore decided to try a lower intensity.

Method

Apparatus

The runway was the same as in Experiment 1, with the end section unlined. Shock voltage was reduced to 125.

Subjects

Ten naive male albino rats, 10 to 11 weeks old, were used. Eight were assigned at random to Group E, two to Group C.

Procedure

Procedure was the same as in the first experiment. The original stopping criterion of three successive failures to reach the photo-cell in 60 sec. was restored. There was no retest.

Results

On Trial 1 six experimental Ss escaped to the end section. On Trial 2 three of these did so again and three went back to the start. On Trial 3 one S entered the end section for the last time; the other seven either returned to the start or refused to run.

Both control Ss entered the end section on the first four trials. By combining them with the four controls of Experiment 1 it was possible to compare the six experimental Ss with six controls in number of entrances into the end section before shifting. The median for the pooled groups was 2.5. Five Ss in Group E fell below that number and five Ss in Group C fell above it. The chance probability of such a split by Fisher's test is .08 (two-tailed).

Median times for Group E on Trials 1 to 3 were 3.04, 5.30, and 28.66 sec., respectively.

Discussion

Comparing Experiments 1 and 3 we see that lowering the shock level retarded the tendency to fixate on the start section but did not reverse it. Even a relatively mild punishment seemed to weaken an approach response that, continued, led to escape.

The three experiments together lend weight to Hilgard's critique of the S-R theory of avoidance.

Experiment 4

It is possible that if the escape response in our Ss had been better established it would have persisted. Gwinn's (1949) experiment, confirmed by Brown and by Whiteis (Mowrer, 1950, pp. 258 ff.), points in this direction.[1] Gwinn trained 24 rats to escape shock by running to a goal box. After 18 trials he extinguished three groups under the following conditions: (*a*) without shock; (*b*) with a section of grid between start and goal charged on all trials; (*c*) with the section charged on one-third of the trials. He found no difference between (*b*) and (*c*), but both groups took about three times as many trials to extinguish as (*a*) and ran almost twice as fast before reaching the shock point.

In view of its apparent inconsistency with our own results, the next task was to see if we could duplicate Gwinn's finding under our conditions.

Method

Apparatus

The same runway and circuits were used as in Experiment 2. Since intensive escape training should overcome any initial aversion

[1] [See Selection 20.—Eds.]

to the end section, its black cardboard lining was restored. One change in construction was made: the first 8 in. of the start section was converted into a shaft 3¾ in. wide and 7¾ in. deep through which a rat could be dropped on a "hot" grid. A second shock stimulator, wired to the first two sections and controlled by E, was introduced for use in training; the original stimulator was used only during extinction. As before, a 1-rps timer was started manually and stopped by a photocell at the mid-point of the runway.

Subjects

Forty-five naive male albino rats about 3 mo. old served as Ss.

Procedure

Subjects were assigned at random to three groups and run three a day, one from each group.

Training for all Ss consisted of 20 massed trials conducted as follows: With the training shock stimulator turned on at 190 v., E lowered S through the starting shaft to the grid, at the same time starting the timer. When S entered the end section, E closed the door, left S there for 30 sec., then carried it directly to the start shaft for the next trial.

After 20 trials the stimulator was turned off and extinction trials followed without interruption until S either took more than 10 sec. to reach the photocell on 2 trials in succession or reached a limit of 60 trials. The intertrial interval was 30 sec., spent in the end section. Retracing from any section was prevented. If on any trial S failed to leave the grid in 10 sec., it was removed and placed in the end section for 30 sec.

Group C received no shocks during extinction. On every extinction trial Group E100 turned on a shock of 190 v. by breaking the beam of the photocell. On half the extinction trials in irregular order Group E50 received a shock in the same manner.

Results

Two Ss in Group E100 and one in Group C met the extinction criterion on the first two trials; i.e., they refused to run at all. They were therefore eliminated from group comparisons.

Mean running speeds (10 × reciprocal of running time) for

the last 10 training trials were: Group E100, 17.5; Group E50, 18.5; Group C, 15.9. The *F* ratio of 2.2 for 2 and 39 *df* is insignificant, giving no evidence that the groups were unequal at the end of training.

Figure 21.1 shows the percentage of Ss in each group that reached the extinction criterion in a given number of trials or less. The median numbers of trials to criterion were as follows: E100, 5; E50, 18; C, 27.

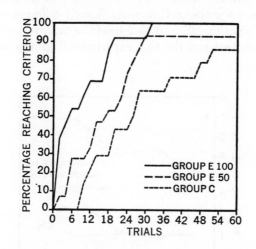

Figure 21.1   Cumulative percentile distributions of Ss reaching the criterion of extinction in a given number of trials (Experiment 4)

Since two Ss in Group C and one in E50 ran 60 trials without meeting the criterion, the choice of significance tests was restricted. The median test applied to all three groups gave a χ^2 of 6.48, $p =$ .05. For comparisons involving Group E100 the Mann-Whitney *U* test could be used. This group extinguished significantly faster than Group C at the .002 level and faster than Group E50 at the .05 level (both by two-tailed tests). Groups E50 and C, however, were not significantly different by the median test.

Inspection of running times on extinction trials suggested a difference between the experimental groups and the control. The shocked rats appeared to meet the criterion suddenly; i.e., they ran fast or not at all. Control Ss, on the other hand, slowed down progressively. To verify this impression, we tabulated the times of the last five trials, exclusive of 10-sec. trials, before the criterion was met. All Ss were included that ran at least five times and met the criterion in less than 60 trials. Seven Ss in Group E100, 13 in E50, and 12 in C met these requirements.

Figure 21.2 shows the median times of the three groups. To test for significance, individual medians for the five trials were ranked. The Kruskal-Wallis test gave $p = .001$ for all groups. By the Mann-Whitney test Group C was significantly different from Groups E100 and E50 at the .02 and .002 levels, respectively (two-tailed); the difference between the two experimental groups was not significant.

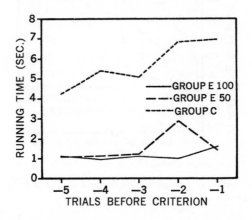

Figure 21.2   Median running times on the last five trials before meeting the criterion of extinction (Experiment 4)

To check a finding of Gwinn we compared the running times in Group E50 on trials immediately following a shock trial with those following a no-shock trial. There were no consistent differences, even within individuals.

Discussion

Contrary to Gwinn's results, our group shocked on every trial extinguished first; the trend was toward earlier extinction with increased frequency of punishment. The most likely cause of this discrepancy was not at first clear. To counteract the exceedingly rapid extinction in Group E100, we looked for more favorable training conditions.

Sheffield and Temmer (1950), using a similar runway, found that avoidance training produced higher resistance to extinction than escape training. They attributed their finding to the same factor as in other types of partial reinforcement, viz., conditioning of the response to nonreinforcement cues. But avoidance training also involves conditioning the response to *delayed shock*, which is precisely what our experimental Ss experienced during extinction. These groups, as well as Group C, should therefore extinguish more slowly after avoidance than after escape training. Group E50, moreover, might well extinguish last of all, since both training and extinction would involve shock on only part of the trials.

To test these predictions we decided to study the effect of shock on extinction after avoidance training. Further interpretation of Experiment 4 is postponed until the results of this investigation are before us.

Experiment 5

Method

Apparatus

The only change from Experiment 4 was the introduction of a second electric timer used during training to time the interval between putting S in the runway and turning on the shock.

Subjects

Forty-five naive male albino rats were used, 11 to 12 weeks old.

Procedure

Experiment 4 was repeated in every detail except for the conduct of training trials. This time E lowered S on a cold grid and started both timers.

After a fixed interval E turned on the shock. The interval was 5 sec. on the first 10 trials and 2½ sec. on the last 10. If S entered the end section within the delay interval, it avoided shock. A record was kept of shocks received.

Results

One S in Group E100 and two in C were eliminated from group comparisons for refusing to run on the first two extinction trials. Mean speeds (time reciprocals $\times$ 10) for the last 10 training trials fell between 6.2 and 7.0, giving an F ratio less than 1.

Median numbers of trials to extinction were: for Group E100, 22.5; E50, 22; C, 17.5. None of the differences approached significance.

As in the previous experiment, we compared running times on the last five trials before meeting the criterion. The median for 11 Ss in Group E100 was 1.55 sec.; for 10 Ss in E50, 1.40 sec.; and for 8 Ss in C, 3.49 sec. These differences, too, proved insignificant.

In Group E50 median times on trials immediately following a shock trial were not consistently different from those following a no-shock trial. There seemed, however, to be more exceptionally long times after shock. We therefore counted the number of times over 2½ sec. (the delay interval in the last half of training) for each S after each type of trial. (Two Ss were omitted: 1 with only two times to be compared; the other with five times, all over 2½ sec.) Of 13 Ss 9 had more long times after shock than no shock, 2 had less, and 2 had the same number. The data just missed significance at the .05 level (two-tailed) by the sign test and Wilcoxon's T test; a t test, however, was significant at that level.

The results of Experiments 4 and 5 were compared to test the prediction that extinction would be slower for all three conditions after avoidance training than after escape training. For this purpose all 15 Ss in each group were available. Median trials to extinction after escape and avoidance training, respectively, were as follows: Group E100, 3 and 17; Group E50, 18 and 22; Group C, 26 and 18. For Group E100 the Mann-Whitney U test reached a confidence level of .10 (two-tailed); the other differences, with only median tests permissible, were even less significant.

To evaluate these largely insignificant differences between escape and avoidance, some indication of the range of individual extinction scores would help. Although for statistical treatment the three escape groups could not be pooled, for this purpose we combined the 45 Ss of each experiment in a single distribution. The two sets of frequencies are shown in Figure 21.3. The figure reveals a slight tendency toward higher resistance to extinction after avoidance, but it also brings out two features of both distributions likely to obscure any average difference: a wide range of scores and a pronounced positive skewness.

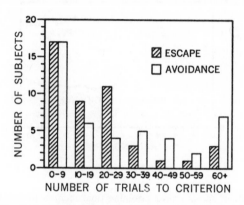

Figure 21.3   Number of Ss reaching the criterion of extinction in a given number of trials after escape training (Experiment 4) and avoidance training (Experiment 5)

Sheffield and Temmer's rats ran faster during training to escape a charged grid than to avoid a delayed shock. For a similar comparison individual time scores were converted into their reciprocals $\times$ 10, and the mean was obtained for each training trial of the 45 Ss in Experiment 4 and in Experiment 5. These appear in Figure 21.4; the greater speed of escape than avoidance is beyond doubt.

A point of special interest in Figure 21.4 is the slight dip in the avoidance curve from the first trial to the second and third. These points correspond to median times of 3.0, 5.8, and 7.2 sec. (It will be recalled that the shock was delayed 5 sec. on these trials.) Compared with Trial 1, Trial 2 was slower for 37 of 45 Ss and Trial 3 for 40, with chance probabilities beyond .0002. Twenty-nine Ss took longer on Trial 3 than Trial 2; by the normal approximation to the binomial, $p = .075$ (two-tailed). The data reflect a marked tendency in these animals, for a few trials after their first shock, to freeze in the start section until the shock came on. Since all Ss escaped their first shock by running forward to the end section, their behavior on the next two trials confirmed Experiments 1, 2, and 3 in showing that a response that removes punishment is not necessarily strengthened thereby.

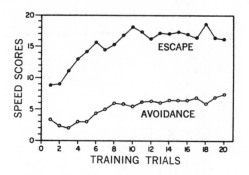

Figure 21.4   Mean speed scores (running-time reciprocals × 10) of 45 Ss in escape training (Experiment 4) and 45 Ss in avoidance training (Experiment 5)

Discussion

Neither Experiment 4 nor 5 confirmed Gwinn's finding that punishment retarded extinction of a fear-motivated response. After escape training the opposite trend appeared, while after avoidance training there was no trend at all.

The most likely explanation of this discrepancy is the difference in intensity of shock. Gwinn's training shock was 60 v. through 250,000 ohms of external resistance; in extinction he used two shock levels, 60 and 120 v. Our shock was 190 v. through 150,000 ohms. The argument, which applies to the first three experiments as well, runs as follows:

Let us assume with Mowrer (1950) and Miller (1951) that shock produces two effects in an organism: a sensory component, *pain,* and an emotional component, *fear,* readily conditioned to accompanying stimuli. Assume further that running is an innately preferred response to the pain of shock to the feet, quickly learned if it leads to escape, but that fear arouses an opposing tendency to motor inhibition, or "freezing." After mild shock this tendency is weak and easily overridden, but at high levels it may become dominant. We may infer that in Gwinn's experiment the escape response was conditioned to fear with little opposition and the prolonged running of the groups shocked in extinction could be attributed to their slower loss of fear. In the present experiments conditioned running was quickly displaced by the tendency to freeze in the start section as a result of the punishing shock encountered in the middle. The abruptness with which the shocked groups met the criterion as compared with the control in Experiment 4 suggests a punishment effect.

Gwinn (1949) reported evidence of inhibitory as well as facilitative effects of punishment in extinction (pp. 265 f.). One such finding—slower speed after shock trials than after no-shock trials—was confirmed only weakly in Experiment 5. The stronger shock may have made our Ss less discriminating.

In Experiment 4, with shock on from the beginning, there was no chance to strengthen the running response to fear apart from pain. In Experiment 5, with delayed, avoidable shock, this presumably happened to some extent. If so, the added fear in the experimental groups could have retarded extinction somewhat, but not necessarily enough to outlast the controls. This would explain the negative results.

Several factors may be responsible for our failure to confirm Sheffield and Temmer on the greater resistance to extinction after avoidance than escape training: (*a*) We gave only 20 training trials to their 40. (*b*) We delayed shock longer—5 and 2½ sec. to their 1½ sec.—, possibly accounting for our Ss' slower running speeds. (*c*) We used a stronger shock (Sheffield and Temmer used 90 v. through 250,000 ohms). This factor may explain the extreme variability of our Ss (see Figure 21.3). If the preceding argument is correct, anticipation of strong shock aroused two competing impulses, to run and to freeze; the first may well have been dominant in some Ss, the second in others. There was much qualitative evidence of conflict in the rats' behavior both in training and extinction.

Conclusion

One positive finding emerges from this series of experiments: the overt conditioned response based on severe shock was quite different from the overt unconditioned response. The unconditioned response to shock was to run ahead; the response most readily conditioned to preceding stimuli was to stop forward movement. This was strikingly demonstrated in the first two experiments, to a less degree in the third with milder shock. It could be inferred from the relative abruptness with which the punished groups stopped running in Experiment 4. It appeared again in the lengthened times on the second and third training trials of Experiment 5.

This finding has implications for the mechanism of avoidance learning. It can be explained on two assumptions: (*a*) shock conditions a mediating (emotional) process, *fear*, to accompanying stimuli; (*b*) above a certain level fear innately inhibits activity in progress, at high levels blocking all movement. The first assumption is already embodied in the Mowrer-Miller theory. The second is introduced as a necessary supplement.

As previously suggested, our use of a stronger shock probably played a large part in the disagreement between earlier results and ours. This interpretation must, of course, be confirmed by direct comparison of different strengths of shock. Meanwhile, the intensity we used, though chosen for other reasons, has this much in its favor: it led to further evidence of the usefulness, perhaps even the necessity, of the fear hypothesis.

Summary

The experiments of this series were aimed to answer the question: What will a rat do when the response that escapes punishment is the same response that produced it?

In Experiment 1 most rats shocked while moving down a runway escaped by running forward. On the next trial the majority retreated. By Trial 4 all refused to leave the starting place.

Experiment 2 tested inconclusively the role of stimulus generalization in this effect.

Experiment 3 revealed the same tendency, but less marked, under weaker shock.

Experiment 4 tested the effect of shock on the extinction of a response previously used to escape shock. Contrary to Gwinn's results, our finding was that shocked rats extinguished sooner and more abruptly than those extinguished without shock.

Experiment 5 made the same test after avoidance training. Here there was no effect of shock during extinction. Nor did Experiments 4 and 5 verify Sheffield and Temmer's finding that avoidance training produced slower extinction than escape training.

The results are thought to be mainly due to a relatively high intensity of shock. By providing clear evidence of an inhibitory factor they support the usefulness of the fear construct in the theory of avoidance behavior.

22   The delay-of-punishment gradient

Leon J. Kamin

Peculiarly, the effects of varying the interval between a response and
a subsequent punishment have been studied much less intensively
than the effects of delayed reward. There is an early and complicated study (Warden & Diamond, 1931) which offers evidence for
a gradient effect of delayed punishment on maze learning; more recently, Sidman (1953) has attributed to a delay-of-punishment gradient part of a complex function relating rate of response to the
minimum interval between responding and shock, and Azrin (1956)

Reprinted from the *Journal of Comparative and Physiological Psychology,*
1959, 52, 434–437 by permission of the author and the American Psychological
Association. This study was supported by a grant from the Associate Committee
on Applied Psychology of the National Research Council of Canada, and facilitated by a University College grant-in-aid from McMaster University. Thanks
are due to C. Hockman, F. Van Fleet, and J. Walker for experimental assistance.

[As in the experiment by Seward and Raskin (Selection 21) there is no
evidence for increased resistance to extinction by rats that are punished during
extinction trials of an avoidance response. In this experiment the inhibitory effect of punishment is a declining monotonic function of delay between response
and punishment. This result supports those theories of punishment that emphasize
the relevance of the temporal contiguity between response and punishment. The
fact that the group with the longest temporal interval between response and
punishment (40 sec.) made fewer responses during extinction than the two unpunished control groups supports those theories of punishment that emphasize the
general fear-arousing properties of a noxious stimulus. (See Part II).—Eds.]

has shown response-contingent punishment to be more effective than arbitrarily scheduled punishment. The very well known work of Estes (1944), however, seems largely to have diverted attention from the temporal factors involved in punishment.[1]

The Estes data demonstrated that punishment not correlated with responding, but merely administered within the experimental situation, inhibits performance. The random delivery of punishment, under the conditions of Estes' experiment, in fact inhibited bar pressing as much as did punishment immediately following the response. This fact led Estes and others to regard the effects of punishment as relatively nonspecific, and primarily "emotional." The Estes study, however, did not vary in a controlled fashion the time interval between the response and punishment.

The interval between response and reinforcement is of course critical for positive reinforcement; and an interpretation of the action of punishment as fundamentally different from that of reward implies that the two effects are not controlled by the same factors. The present study was designed to test whether varying the interval between performance of a learned response and a subsequent punishing shock would yield a gradient effect on resistance to extinction of the response. The response had been learned on the basis of instrumental avoidance training.

Method

There were two closely related but independent experiments, which differed in procedural details. The method for each experiment is presented under separate headings in the following paragraphs.

Subjects and apparatus

Experiment I

The surviving Ss were 48 experimentally naive hooded rats, ranging in age from 80 to 100 days and maintained on an ad lib. feeding schedule. The apparatus, a modified Mowrer-Miller shuttle-box, has been described in an earlier paper (Kamin, 1957). The CS was a 74-db. buzzer. The US (current flow to the average S of 1.1

[1] [See Selection 11.—Eds.]

ma.) was administered through a grid floor. The grid of each half of the box could be separately charged. There was no barrier between the two halves of the box at any time.

Experiment II

The surviving Ss were 60 naive rats of the same age from the same colony. The apparatus was changed in only one respect: There was now a guillotine gate between the two halves of the box which could be raised and lowered by E by means of a pedal. Thus S could be confined to one side of the apparatus.

Procedure

Training

Experiment I. The Ss were first given standard avoidance training (Kamin, 1957) with each trial ending either in escape or avoidance. The CS-US interval was 10 sec. (delayed conditioning), and the CS was response terminated. The intertrial intervals, following a fixed, irregular schedule, were 50, 60, and 70 sec., with a mean of 1 min. Training was continued in a single session until S met a criterion of 11 consecutive avoidances. When, however, S failed to meet the criterion within 75 trials, it was discarded. There were 23 such discards. The frequency of escapes and avoidances, and of intertrial responses, was tabulated.

Experiment II. The training procedure in this study was essentially similar to that employed in the first. The guillotine gate, however, was employed to prevent intertrial responses. Thus, passage between the two halves of the box was blocked by the gate at all times except during presentation of the CS and/or US. The CS in this study was therefore a compound of buzzer presentation plus lifting of the gate. The procedure in all other details duplicated that of Experiment I. There were 26 discards for failing to meet the avoidance criterion.

Punishment

Experiment I. The punishment trials began 1 min. after S met the avoidance criterion. The inauguration of punishment coincided with the introduction of an extinction procedure so far as the avoidance response is concerned. That is, S would no longer be shocked should it fail to respond to the CS. When S did respond to the CS by running, the response was followed by delivery of a punishing shock. The punishment might occur immediately with S's response, or as much as 40 sec. after the response. This was contingent upon the experimental group to which S had been assigned.

Thus, during punishment trials, when S failed to run within 10 sec. after onset of the CS, the CS was terminated and S was credited with a failure to respond. When S did respond to the CS, the CS was at once terminated, but S was then shocked at the appropriate interval following its response. The punishing shocks were, in Experiment I, terminated by S's shuttling to the opposite half of the box. The duration of punishment was thus not strictly controlled, though invariably brief. The intertrial intervals and shock intensity during the punishment trials matched those employed during training. The punishment trials were continued until S met a criterion of 10 consecutive failures to respond, or to a maximum of 50 trials.

Experiment II. The differences between experiments during punishment trials revolved about the guillotine gate. Within Experiment II, lifting the gate continued to be part of the CS. When S did not respond to the CS within 10 sec., the buzzer was terminated and gate lowered simultaneously. When S did respond to the CS, the buzzer was terminated and gate lowered at once, and the punishing shock was delivered after the appropriate interval. Within Experiment II the punishing shock was of controlled duration, 1 sec. The S was confined in the compartment in which punishment occurred until beginning of the next trial. The punishment procedure in all other respects duplicated that of Experiment I.

Design

There were, within each experiment, six experimental groups, with 8 Ss per group in Experiment I and 10 per group in Experiment II. The Ss were randomly assigned to groups. The training procedure was identical for all groups within experiments, but the groups differed with regard to the interval between responding and punishment during the punishment trials. The intervals studied were, in each experiment, 0, 10, 20, 30, and 40 sec. The sixth group in each study was a control group which, after training, was subjected to extinction of the avoidance response *without* punishment. The control group performance provides a base line against which to measure the effects of punishment.

Results

The effects of punishment on the acquired avoidance response were evaluated in terms of the total number of responses made during the punishment trials. These data are presented in Table 22.1. There is,

Table 22.1   Number of responses made in extinction, in two experiments, as a function of delay of punishment

Measure	0	10″	20″	30″	40″	Control
			Delay of punishment			
Experiment I						
Median	2.0	3.0	3.0	5.0	5.0	16.5
Mean	2.0	2.9	4.5	5.4	6.1	18.3
Range	1–5	1–6	2–14	2–14	1–19	4–50
Experiment II						
Median	3.0	5.5	10.5	9.5	9.5	46.5
Mean	3.2	6.6	9.6	12.9	10.6	44.3
Range	1–7	2–15	4–14	4–46	2–18	24–50

within each experiment, a clear tendency for responding to persist longer as delay of punishment is increased; but even with the longest delays of punishment, responding is inhibited. Within Experiment I, all animals but one control S did extinguish within 50 punishment trials; within Experiment II, one 30-sec. S and nine control Ss failed to extinguish.

The data of Table 22.1, excluding the control groups, were submitted to a 2 × 5 analysis of variance, with experiments and delay intervals as effects. The tendency for variances to be proportional to means, and heterogeneity of variance, were corrected by a log transformation.

The effect of delay of punishment was highly significant,

($F = 9.66$, 4 and 80 df, $p < .001$), as was the effect of experiments ($F = 25.30$, 1 and 80 df, $p < .001$). There are more responses made as delay of punishment increases, and more responses occur in Experiment II than in Experiment I. The F for interaction between delay of punishment and experiments was less than 1, and separate analyses of each experiment indicated effects of delay of punishment at somewhat lower significance levels.

Within each experiment, the control group performance was compared with that of the longest (40-sec.) delayed punishment group by the Mann-Whitney U test. The controls in each study far surpass the 40-sec. Ss ($p < .01$ in Experiment I, $< .001$ in Experiment II). The control Ss of Experiment II make more total responses than those of Experiment I ($p < .01$).

The delay of punishment gradient, in terms of median number of responses made during punishment, is portrayed, for each experiment, in Figure 22.1.

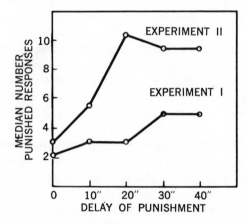

Figure 22.1   Median number of extinction responses as a function of delay of punishment

Discussion

The data, with control group performance considered as a base line, demonstrate, first, that resistance to extinction of the avoidance response is a monotonic function of the interval between the response and punishment, but, second, that punishment delayed as long as 30 or 40 sec. exerts a marked inhibitory effect on responding. The asymptote approached with delays of 30 or 40 sec.—and the fact that this asymptote is very much lower than the level of responding observed under the control procedure—supports Estes by suggesting that the effect of punishment is *in part* independent of any specific association between the response and punishment. The first finding, however, may be described as an empirical delay of punishment gradient, formally analogous to the delay-of-reward gradient. The gradient, of course, is superimposed over the nonspecific, "emotional" effects of punishment. The general form of the gradient suggests that, so far as these data are concerned, punishment may be described as "subtracting" responses in a manner similar to that in which reward "adds" responses.

The intertrial interval in these experiments was measured between onsets of consecutive CSs. Thus, groups given long delays of punishment had, as well, relatively short time intervals between the punishing shock and the CS for the following trial. The possibility then exists, if one assumes a shock-induced drive or emotional state dissipating in time, that the reported gradient might be attributable to this effect, rather than to delay of punishment. The fact, however, that the gradient reaches an asymptotic level with a time interval of 40 sec. between the punishing shock and the subsequent CS suggests very strongly that a shock-induced drive state played no significant part in the obtained gradient.

While the conclusions with regard to the effects of punishment are the same for both experiments, the differences between the studies are of some interest. The base-line resistance to extinction in Experiment II is very much higher than that in Experiment I. This finding closely parallels observations (Brush, Brush, & Solomon, 1955; Church, Brush, & Solomon, 1956; Kamin, 1954) that the use of a guillotine gate during shuttlebox avoidance training of dogs markedly increases resistance to extinction. The present data in no way indicate whether this is due to enhancement of secondary reinforcing properties of the CS, to prevention of intertrial response, or to some other factor, but the replication across species suggests that a fundamental aspect of shuttlebox avoidance training is involved. The prompt cessation of responding accomplished by immediate punishment in this study, on the other hand, contrasts with the failure of punishment as an extinction technique reported by Solomon, Kamin, and Wynne (1953).

We have, unfortunately, no data on the permanence of the extinction accomplished by punishment. Thus it is possible that, as in Estes' study, the inhibitory effect of punishment might dissipate with time. Whether, in keeping with Estes, the effect of punishment should be regarded in terms of its association with the *stimuli* correlated with responding, rather than with the response itself, is moot. The reported gradient, however, indicates that so far as the gradient effect is concerned, there is no more reason to do this in the case of punishment than in the case of reward.

Summary

This study reports two experiments concerned with the effects of varying the interval between a learned response and punishment. The Ss were 108 hooded rats given shuttlebox avoidance training to a criterion. The Ss were divided into groups, and resistance to extinction of the avoidance response was tested with punishment (shock) after no delay, or after 10, 20, 30, or 40 sec. of delay, or without punishment. The inhibitory effect of punishment was in each study a declining monotonic function of delay, suggesting that punishment acts in a manner formally analogous but opposite to reward. The no-punishment groups, however, made significantly more responses than did groups with the longest delays of punishment, supporting Estes' conclusion that punishment has nonspecific, "emotional" effects.

23 Self-punitive behavior in the rat: facilitative effects of punishment on resistance to extinction

Judson S. Brown, R. C. Martin, and Mitchell W. Morrow

Broadly conceived, the experiments reported below bear on the question of why organisms sometimes behave so as to expose themselves repeatedly to aversive stimuli even when less punishing alternatives might be chosen. That such behavior does occur is attested to by Masserman's (1946) studies of experimental masochism, by demonstrations of the facilitative effects of punishment upon resistance to extinction (Gwinn, 1949; Solomon, Kamin, & Wynne, 1953; Whiteis, 1956)[1] and by such experiments as those of Pavlov (1927)

Reprinted from the *Journal of Comparative and Physiological Psychology*, 1964, 57, 127–133 by permission of the author and the American Psychological Association. These studies were carried out in the Department of Psychology at the University of Florida and were supported by Grants M-4952 and MH-06900 from the National Institutes of Health. The authors are indebted to Robert D. Fitzgerald for a critical reading of the manuscript.

[If punishment of responses during extinction prolongs extinction, the behavior may be called self-punitive or masochistic. These experiments are designed to determine conditions under which such behavior is particularly pronounced, and to examine possible theoretical explanations for such paradoxical behavior. Additional research by Brown and others on this phenomenon is described by Brown (1969).—Eds.]

[1] [See Selection 20.—Eds.]

and of Miller (1960)[2] in which aversive stimuli appear to lose their negative properties.

Nevertheless, some investigators (e.g., Imada, 1959; Moyer, 1955, 1957; Seward & Raskin, 1960)[3] have not obtained confirmatory results in similar situations and the reasons for the discrepancies remain to be identified. Further experimentation is needed, therefore, to determine whether punishment indeed increases resistance to extinction and especially to provide more adequate information concerning variables necessary for the development and maintenance of seemingly maladaptive, self-punitive behavior.

Experiment 1

Method

Subjects

Fifty-four male hooded rats of the Long-Evans strain served as Ss. These were purchased from a commercial supplier and were 90–110 days old when first introduced into the experimental apparatus.

Apparatus

The main components of the equipment were a start box and a straight runway, both of which had grid floors and glass lids, plus a goal box that was fitted with a wooden floor and a Masonite lid. The start box (18 in. long × 5 in. wide × 11.5 in. high, inside) was divided into an upper and a lower compartment by a trap-door-like floor hinged along one edge 7 in. above the grid floor. A door at the end of the start box provided the means whereby Ss could be introduced into the upper compartment, and a 4.5 × 5 in. barrier at the alley end of that compartment prevented Ss from prematurely escaping into the alley. When the trap-door floor was automatically released S fell to the grid floor below where it was then free to run through the alley to the goal box.

The runway (6 ft. long × 3.5 in. wide × 11.5 in. high, inside) was uniform throughout save for narrow wooden strips across the

---

[2] [See Selection 16.—Eds.]
[3] [See Selection 21.—Eds.]

top at the 2- and 4-ft. positions. These strips served to support cadmium sulphide photocells which pointed downward and were energized by infrared light sources below the grid floor. Additional vertically oriented light beams and photocells were situated at the juncture of the start box and alley and at the entrance to the goal box. By means of these devices and associated electronic equipment, measurements (to the nearest ⅟₁₀₀ sec.) could be made of starting time (the interval between the release of the floor flap and the occlusion of the first light beam), the time consumed in traversing each of three 2-ft. alley segments, and total time (starting time plus the sum of the three segment times).

The goal box (18 in. long × 10 in. wide × 11.5 in. high, inside) was painted black, in contrast to the start box and runway which were light gray. A guillotine door at the entrance to the goal box prevented Ss from attempting to retrace once the goal box had been entered completely.

The grid floors were fashioned of ³⁄₃₂-in. stainless steel rods set into plastic side rails at .5-in. intervals. The six 1-ft. grid sections comprising the runway floor and the 18-in. section under the start box could be selectively energized by 60-cycle current from a variable-voltage autotransformer fed through a series resistor of 10,000 ohms. The open circuit voltage across all grid sections was monitored by means of a vacuum tube ac voltmeter. The shock intensities specified below were the open circuit voltages read from this meter.

A 60-w. lamp, suspended about 8 in. above the center of the start box served as a CS. A motor-driven circuit breaker in series with the lamp provided two .25-sec. "on" and two .25-sec. "off" periods per second.

Procedure

The general procedure involved shock-escape training for all Ss followed by "extinction" trials during which shock was interposed betweeen the start and goal boxes for two groups of Ss but not for a third.

In detail, when Ss were received from the supplier they were given unrestricted access to food and water for 2–3 days and were then placed on a regular feeding schedule calling for 14–16 gm. of Purina laboratory chow per day for 7 days. During this period water was constantly available and all Ss were handled for a few minutes each day. The food deprivation regimen was instituted in the hope that variability might be reduced and fear increased, since the results of one study (Meryman, 1952) had indicated that hungry rats were more fearful than nonhungry ones. All experimental trials were administered when Ss were approximately 22 hr. hungry.

The next 4-day period was devoted to preliminary habituation training, each S being permitted to explore all sections of the apparatus for 10 min. per day. On the first of these days, each S was carried directly from its home cage to the maze; on the second day, a short waiting period in a carrying cage preceded the 10-min. familiarization period; and on the third and fourth days, the experience of being dropped from the upper compartment of the start box to the grid floor beneath was added to the sequence.

Shock-escape training was administered at the rate of 10 trials per day for the next 4 days. Trials 1 and 2 were run with the 6-ft. alley removed and the start box connected directly to the goal box. The shock was set at 50 v. for all 10 trials of the first day. Three trials were then given with a temporary 2-ft. long alley inserted between the start and goal boxes, followed by three trials in traversing a temporary 4-ft. alley. On Trials 9 and 10 of the first acquisition day Ss were required to traverse the entire 6-ft. runway to escape shock. The shock voltage was raised to 60, 70, and 75 v. on Days 2, 3, and 4, respectively, to offset possible adaptation effects.

On every trial S was put into the starting compartment through the end door, after which the guillotine door at the entrance to the goal box was immediately raised. This latter event, accompanied by some uncontrolled and unspecifiable auditory cues, initiated the following automatically timed sequence of events: (a) after a 3-sec. delay the blinking light began to flash, followed 3 sec. later by (b) the whirring sound of the trap-door release motor, and finally, in about 2 more sec. by the release and fall of the floor itself. After S was started in this manner, the light continued to blink until the infrared beam at the entrance to the goal box was intercepted. This latter event automatically cut off the blinking light and stopped the third-segment and total-time clocks. The S was permitted to remain in the dark goal box with the guillotine door closed for about 20 sec. before being removed to an individual chamber in the carrying cage to await the next trial. The Ss were run in squads of six, two members of the squad being randomly assigned to each of three groups. The daily food ration was allotted to each S aproximately 15 min. after it had been returned to its home cage.

Extinction trials were begun on the fifth day following the initiation of escape training. At this time the six members of each squad were randomly assigned in equal numbers to three groups differing with respect to whether shock was present in the runway during extinction and with respect to its spatial location and extent. One group, the *short-shock group,* encountered shock only in the final 2-ft. segment of the alley. A second group, designated the *long-shock group,* was shocked throughout the entire 6-ft. runway, but not in the start box. The third group, termed the *no-shock group,* was never shocked during extinction, and no S, of course, was ever shocked in the goal box. On all these trials shock intensity was fixed at 60 v.

Extinction trials were continued under these conditions for 6 days (provided Ss continued to run) at the rate of 10 trials per day with approximately the same intertrial interval (i.e., 5–7 min.) as that employed during acquisition. If S failed to reach and enter the goal box within a criterional time of 60 sec., extinction trials were discontinued and arbitrary time scores of 60 sec. were entered in the protocols for that S. Exploratory studies had shown that a single failure to leave the start box within 1 min. was highly predictive of complete extinction in this situation.

Results

While starting and running times were recorded throughout the escape training phase, these data, because of their lack of direct relevance to the purposes of this study, have not been included in this report. It is worth noting, however, that the training procedures described above led to remarkably fast escape learning. Typically, asymptotic performance level was reached in 5–10 trials with the full length runway. Moreover, none of the Ss had to be discarded for failing to learn or for acquiring successful shock-escape responses other than running.

The extinction data plotted in Figure 23.1 may be taken as representative of the major results of Experiment 1. This figure shows the speed with which the entire 6-ft. alley was traversed by each of the three groups on each of the 6 extinction days. Each point rep-

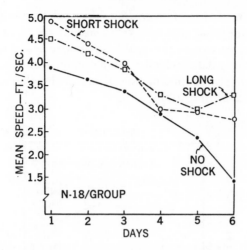

Figure 23.1 Showing the mean speeds with which short-shock, long-shock, and no-shock groups traversed the 6-ft. straight runway during each of the 6 extinction days in Experiment 1

resents a mean of 18 reciprocals which has been multiplied by 6 to yield ft/sec, each of the reciprocals, in turn, being based on an individual S's median running time for 10 daily trials. It is clear from this figure and from statistical analyses of these data that extinction took place in all groups; and, although the shocked Ss ran somewhat faster than the nonshocked Ss, the main "groups" effect was not significant ($F < 1.0$). Thus these data provide no support for the expectation that punishment prolongs the extinction process. This conclusion is further buttressed by the observation that the groups did not differ markedly with respect to the number of Ss that had met the extinction criterion by the end of the sixth day. At that time, five of the no-shock, six of the long-shock, and seven of the short-shock Ss had quit running.

By and large, the data obtained from measurements of starting speed and of running speed in the individual 2-ft. segments of the alley were consistent with the above conclusions. However, one effect approaching statistical significance was that of groups in the case of last-segment running speeds ($F = 3.08$, $df = 2/51$, $p > .05$).

Running speeds in the three alley sections averaged over 6 days are shown in Figure 23.2. From this it is evident that the no-shock group tended to slow down as the goal box was neared, the long-shock group ran at a relatively constant speed, and the short-shock Ss accelerated as the goal was approached. An analysis of variance of these data yielded the only highly significant finding of the study, namely, the interaction of groups by alley segments ($F = 12.2$, $df = 2/51$, $p < .001$).

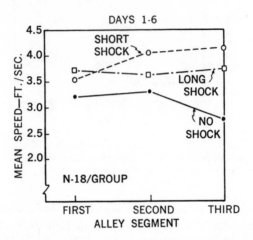

Figure 23.2   Comparative running speeds exhibited by the three groups of Ss in each of the 2-ft. segments of the alley. (Each point represents a mean based upon all 60 extinction trials in Experiment 1.)

In summary, Experiment 1 provided no substantial evidence indicating that punishment prolonged extinction. But neither did the study show that extinction was accelerated by shock, as might be expected on the basis of traditional conceptions of punishment as a behavior deterrent. This latter finding encouraged the authors in the belief that even relatively minor changes in experimental conditions might result in the prolongation of extinction by shock. The second experiment reported below confirmed this expectation.

Experiment 2

An examination of the conditions prevalent during Experiment 1 and an analysis of the behavior exhibited by Ss tested therein suggested the need for the changes introduced in Experiment 2. For one thing, shock intensity may have been high enough during extinction to evoke responses incompatible with running. Moreover, our acquisition data, supported by Martin's (1962) study of resistance to extinction as a function of number of escape training trials, suggested that the strength of the escape might actually be increased if escape trials were reduced from 40 to 20. It had also been observed during Experiment 1 that, generally speaking, running speeds were slowest at the start of each day, a warm-up-like increment appearing with additional trials. This indicated the desirability of changing the procedure so that the first no-shock trials of extinction would not coincide with the first trials of a day. Finally, it was felt that a more gradual transition from shock during acquisition to no-shock during extinction might diminish the contrast between the two procedures and thereby prolong extinction.

Method

Subjects

The Ss were 48 male hooded rats (Long-Evans strain) ranging in age from 100–140 days at the beginning of experimentation.

Apparatus

With the exception of one modification, the apparatus used in Experiment 2 was the same as that in Experiment 1. The sole change involved the substitution of an intermittently sounding buzzer for the blinking light. This modification was dictated by the observation that Ss in Experiment 1 seemed to become more excited by the whir of the trap-door release motor than by the onset of the blinking light. The buzzer, constructed of a dc relay energized by a 60-cycle source, was mounted on the side of the start box and produced not only a clearly audible sound but also tactually detectible (by Es) vibrations of the start box and of its grid floor. The sound level in the start box, as measured by a General Radio sound level meter ("C"-scale weighting) was about 53 db. above a reference level of 0.0002 dynes/cm^2 without the buzzer turned on. It increased to 67 db. when the buzzer was added and to 70 db. when the floor-release motor began to whir. With respect to duration of on-off periods, relation to floor-drop time, etc., the parameters of the buzzer variable were identical with those of the blinking light in the first experiment.

Procedure

The pre-experimental handling, feeding, and habituation procedures were the same as those followed in Experiment 1. The number of escape-training trials was reduced from 40 to 20, though the rate (10 trials per day) was not altered. The shock voltages were modified in several ways. During the escape trials of Day 1, 45 v. was applied to all grid sections. This was raised to 50 v. during the second day's training session. The shock used for the short-shock Ss in the third segment and for the long-shock Ss in the alley was 50 v. for the first trial of the first extinction day and 45 v. for all subsequent trials. The no-shock Ss received 50, 45, 40, 30, and 20 v. in the start box and in the alley during Trials 1–5, respectively, of the first extinction day and no shock anywhere thereafter. The same series of progressively declining voltages was applied to the start-box grid for the long-shock group and to the start-box grid and the grid of the adjacent 4-ft. alley segment for the short-shock group. On the sixth trial of the first extinction day, and on all subsequent extinction trials, the shock conditions for the short-shock and the long-shock groups were precisely like those holding throughout extinction in Experiment 1 save that the voltage in the electrified sections was maintained at 45 rather than at 60.

With respect to number of extinction trials, extinction criterion, intertrial intervals, etc., both experiments were identical. Starting times were not recorded, however, in Experiment 2, since this measure appeared to be the least stable in Experiment 1 and since a temporary shortage of timing devices made it mandatory to reduce the number of measures taken on each trial. Two Es were responsible for the training and testing of all Ss. Five replications ($N = 6$ per replication) were run by one E and three by the other.

Results

Summaries of the running-speed data derived from times recorded from the first and third 2-ft. segments of the runway are provided in Figure 23.3 and 23.4. From the curves in Figure 23.3 it is apparent that the long-shock group proved to be most resistant to extinction, followed sequentially by the short-shock and no-shock groups. Analysis of variance provided unequivocal support for the view that the differences, as revealed by Figure 23.3, were genuine, since the main treatment effect was highly significant ($F = 12.34$, $df = 2/45$, $p < .001$), as were the "days" effect ($F = 7.81$, $df = 5/225$, $p < .001$) and the interaction of days by treatments ($F = 10.62$, $df = 10/225$, $p < .001$). The conclusion that the groups differed in their tendency to resist extinction is further strengthened by the observation that of the 16 Ss in each group only 1 long-shock S had met the 60-sec. extinction criterion by the end of the sixth day whereas 6 of the short-shock and 11 of the no-shock Ss had ceased running by that time.

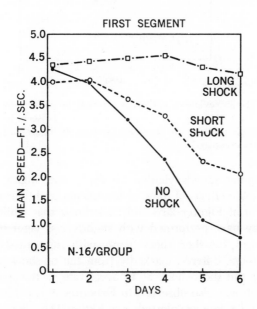

Figure 23.3 These extinction curves exhibited by the three groups of Experiment 2 were derived from measurements of running speed in the first 2-ft. segment of the alley.

The trends apparent in Figure 23.3 are paralleled by data presented in Figure 23.4 and also by plots of middle-segment running times (not shown). Analyses of variance of second- and third-

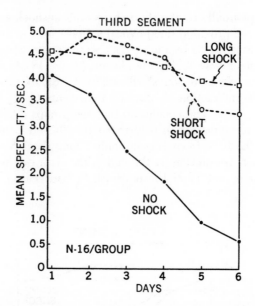

Figure 23.4   The curves shown in this figure reveal the performance of the three groups in the last 2-ft. segment of the alley, which was adjacent to the goal box. (The measures plotted here are the same as those in Figure 23.1, with which this figure may be compared.)

segment running speeds yielded, in each case, highly significant ($p < .001$) main effects of days, of treatments, and their interaction. A comparison of Figures 23.3 and 23.4 shows that while the long-shock Ss may have performed with slightly less vigor in the third (final) segment, the short-shock Ss ran with augmented speed, and that both groups differed markedly from the no-shock group. The tendency for the short-shock Ss to accelerate as the goal box was neared, which was also observed in Experiment 1, is revealed most clearly when the data are plotted as in Figure 23.5. The fact that the long-shock Ss ran faster in all segments and the short-shock Ss ran faster in the third segment than the no-shock Ss can be attributed in part, to the energizing effect of shock. But the finding that the short-shock Ss ran faster in the second than in the first segment cannot be ascribed to the energizing effects of shock and requires another interpretation.

Analysis of variance applied to the data in Figure 23.5 yielded

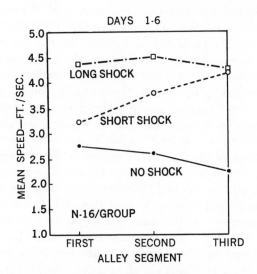

Figure 23.5   This figure, like Figure 23.2, shows that the three groups differed with respect to whether they tended to speed up or slow down in traversing the alley. (The goal-gradient-like acceleration shown by the short-shock Ss appears to be of special interest.)

a main effect ($F = 13.70$, $df = 2/45$, $p < .001$) and a segments by groups interaction that were highly significant ($F = 12.50$, $df = 4/90$, $p < .001$). In none of the analyses were replications effects found to be significant sources of variance.

Discussion

The data of our two experiments, and especially those from Experiment 2, indicate that shock in the runway not only failed to accelerate extinction, as might be predicted from the supposition that shock should act to punish approach reactions, but instead, functioned to prolong extinction. The persisting behavior involved repeated approaches toward and toleration of stimuli, which, if defined in terms of Ss' original escape reactions would have to be labeled noxious. It seems justified, therefore, to describe such behavior as "masochistic-like."

Theoretical interpretations consistent with the results of our study prove to be surprisingly numerous. Mowrer's (1950) theory of this perseverative type of behavior, which he dubbed the "vicious circle" phenomenon, has considerable appeal.[4] According to his view, the initial escape training should result in the conditioning of fear to the cues provided by the buzzer, the start box, and the alley. Then during extinction S runs because it is afraid, running produces shock which prevents (or retards) the process of fear extinction, and fear reduction perpetuates running. To this we may add the notions that shock reduction is itself a potent reinforcer for running and that shock onset may potentiate in-progress running responses.

Applied to our results, Mowrer's theory suggests that the no-shock Ss should quit running first, as they did, because their relatively long exposure to the runway cues in the absence of shock provided them with the most favorable conditions for fear to become extinguished and with no opportunity for fear to be further reinforced. The order in which the short-shock and long-shock groups extinguished would follow from the same principles.

Guthrie's (1935) concept of negative adaptation or habituation could also be applied to our data. According to this view, noxious stimuli lose their power to evoke escape reactions if they are repeatedly presented when responses that are incompatible with escape are dominant. Under such conditions, the aversive stimulus loses its negative properties to the degree that it becomes a conditioned cue for the incompatible reactions. In our studies the tactual cues provided by shock were part of the stimulus complex to which running became associated during the training series. Shock thus evoked approach reactions that interfered with responses of backing up or withdrawing; and during extinction the shocked Ss persisted in running because shock evoked and maintained forward-running behavior.

Our results are also consistent with interpretations stressing the similarity of acquisition to extinction conditions. Perhaps no-shock Ss extinguished most readily because they experienced the most marked change from acquisition to extinction, short-shock and long-shock Ss, respectively, being exposed to less drastic changes.

While the procedures used in our second study yielded un-

---

[4] [See Selection 19.—Eds.]

equivocal evidence that the aversive stimulus prolonged extinction, we are not yet able to pinpoint the crucial factor or factors. It would appear, however, that the to-be-punished response must be so well established that it will be evoked with a high degree of probability by the situational cues even when conditions are changed from acquisition to extinction plus punishment. Moreover, the intensity of the punishing stimulus should be moderate—this reduces the likelihood that competing responses will be elicited—and the shift from the acquisition to the extinction-plus-punishment phases should be gradual. Last of all, the motivational processes involved in the initiation of the response should perhaps be maintained or supported by the punishment to which the response leads. It may be worth noting that in the study by Seward and Raskin (1960)[5] in which no evidence was found for increased resistance to extinction under punishment, few of the above requirements were met. The forward-going tendency was quite weak, the punishment was intense, and the transition from acquisition to extinction was abrupt.

A final point concerns the tendency of short-shock Ss in both experiments to speed up, even before they reached the shock in the final 2-ft. section of the alley. Speed-of-locomotion gradients have been frequently observed in studies involving the use of appetitive reinforcers but the authors are unaware of prior reports of such gradients in situations where Ss are approaching a punishing stimulus. If the phenomenon is genuine, it may prove useful to assume that a short-shock S is motivated in the middle segment by a fractional anticipatory shock-approach or shock-escape reaction that is logically comparable to the Hull-Spence r_g-s_g-K mechanism.

Summary

In 2 experiments rats were trained to escape from an electrified start box and runway into a safe goal box. During subsequent "extinction" trials the start box was made safe for all Ss, but some groups could not reach the safe goal box without enduring shock in part or all of the alley. Ss shocked in this way in the 1st study failed to stop running sooner than those given no shock, and in the 2nd study, shocked

---

[5] [See Selection 21.—Eds.]

Ss resisted extinction significantly longer than nonpunished Ss. Fewer escape training trials, weaker shock, and more gradual transition from escape training to extinction characterized the 2nd study relative to the 1st. Various theories capable of explaining this masochistic-like behavior are examined.

V

Suggested Further Reading

Seven topics in punishment that were not covered in this book are introduced in the paragraphs below. For each topic, a few significant references are cited and briefly described. These references, of course, are not an exhaustive inventory of important papers; instead they are intended to serve as guides for further reading. The list of references at the end of many of these articles would be useful to the reader interested in additional research on these topics. A bibliography on punishment and an outline of experimental studies of primary punishment by independent variables and behavioral categories (Boe, 1969) can be used for further assistance in securing comprehensive coverage of the literature on a particular topic in punishment.

Review and Theoretical Articles on Punishment

The historical development of theories of punishment is closely related to the development of theories of reward. Early interest in the experimental psychology of motivation led to research on reward, punishment, and various other incentives. Diserens and Vaughn (1931) reviewed relevant experiments on punishment of animal and human subjects in the context of studies of other motives. Reward and punishment are also closely related in the early psychology of learning (e.g., the law of effect, see Selection 7). Postman (1947) described the philosophical bases for the law of effect (in associationism, hedonism, and evolution), traced its historical development, and evaluated both Thorndike's original law of effect and his modifications of it. Postman's review of experimental results clearly showed that punishment has a significant effect on learning under many conditions, that it has both general and specific effects, but that there are various mechanisms through which punishment might exert its influence on behavior. Subsequently, Postman (1962) evaluated the role of rewards and punishments in human learning, with particular emphasis on the developments from the ideas of Thorndike.

Under conditions of punishment (sometimes called "passive avoidance") a subject receives a noxious stimulus if it performs a specified response; under conditions of active avoidance a subject receives a noxious stimulus if it performs any response other than the specified response. Some theoretical treatments of punishment (e.g., Dinsmoor, 1954) have emphasized the similarity between punishment and active avoidance, and this similarity provides an interpretation for the results of many studies of punishment (Dinsmoor, 1955). Church (1963) outlined the major theories of punishment, and presented a systematic examination of the experimental studies of the varied effects of punishment on behavior. A great deal of information regarding the important variables responsible for the effects of punishment on behavior has been provided by studies of individual animals in free-responding situations. Azrin and Holz (1966) have provided an extensive summary of this research. Solomon (1964) described some of the variables contributing to the effectiveness of a punishment, further developed the similarity between active and passive avoidance, criticized some of the "legends" about the ineffectiveness of punishment for modifying instrumental responses and exaggerations regarding its unfortunate side effects, and provided some important suggestions for new lines of research on punishment. A book based on a conference on punishment at Princeton University in June, 1967, contains reviews of various research traditions and summaries of extensive empirical studies relevant to the effects of punishment on behavior (Campbell & Church, 1969).

Punishing Stimuli

By far the most frequently used stimulus as primary punishment has been electric shock. With the exception of Selection 10 by Skinner, in which the kick-back of a lever served as punishment, shock was used in all the experiments included in this book. Electric shock is particularly useful in experimental work on punishment because its intensity, duration, delay, frequency, and schedule can be precisely controlled and because it has strong behavioral effects. Although similar control can be achieved over strong auditory stimuli (e.g., Azrin, 1958; Bolles & Seelback, 1964; Tolman & Mueller, 1964) when used as punishment, they do not in general seem to be as aversive as strong electric shock. The usefulness of strong visual, olfactory, and gustatory stimuli punishment (i.e., response contingent onset) remains to be explored. Cutaneous stimuli other than electric shock such as air blasts (Masserman, 1943) and beatings (Fisher, 1955) are much more difficult to control and are rarely used experimentally. Although the effectiveness of intracranial shock (ICS) as both reward and punishment (depending upon area stimulated and the duration of the stimulus) was reported well over a decade ago (Delgado, Roberts, & Miller, 1954; Olds & Milner, 1954; Olds, 1956), it is curious that the punishing properties of ICS have not been subjected to systematic experimental research. In contrast, the rewarding properties of ICS have been extensively investigated.

Response contingent withdrawal or termination of positive reinforcement constitutes another type of primary punishment. Confinement of a child to his room or a criminal to prison are everyday examples of punishment that entail removal of positive reinforcement. A common laboratory arrangement for studying this type of punishment is to discontinue positive reinforcement for a fixed duration if a subject emits an incorrect response (Ferster & Appel, 1961; Zimmerman & Ferster, 1963). A review of literature relevant to this type of punishment has been prepared by Leitenberg (1965).

Just as secondary reinforcers can be produced by the association of neutral stimuli with primary appetitive stimuli, secondary punishers can be produced by the association of neutral stimuli with primary aversive stimuli (Mowrer & Aiken, 1954; Mowrer & Soloman, 1954). Following this association, secondary punishers tend to suppress responses upon which their onset is contingent, and the degree of suppression increases with increases in the intensity of the primary aversive stimulus (Hake & Azrin, 1965; Matsumiya, 1960). Presumably variation in parameters of secondary punishment such as duration and delay should result in different degrees of response suppression similar to variations in these parameters of primary punishment. Many experimenters have assumed that certain stimuli such as the word "wrong" (e.g., Stone, 1950), loss of money (e.g., Katz, 1964), and loss of points (e.g., Weiner, 1964) are punishing if contingent upon a response because subjects have had unpleasant experiences with these events in the past.

Parameters of Punishment

It is readily apparent from both casual observation and laboratory research that punishment varies in its severity. Perhaps the most obvious dimension of severity is intensity. However, the suppressing effect also depends upon other parameters of the punishing stimulus or the circumstances of its application. Five main parameters of punishment are (1) intensity, (2) duration, (3) delay, (4) schedule, and (5) frequency. These five variables are also major parameters of reinforcement. The behavioral effects are simply reversed.

Variation in punishment intensity has been studied in Selections 3, 4, 9, 12, 16, 18, and 20 of this book with the general result that amount of response suppression is directly related to punishment intensity. Several experimenters have reported that amount of suppression is an exponential function of punishment intensity (Appel & Peterson, 1965; Boe, 1964; Boe & Church, 1967, see Selection 12). Several factorial experiments (e.g., Boroczi, Storms, & Broen, 1964; Church, Raymond, & Beauchamp, 1967), in which intensity and duration were simultaneously varied, demonstrated that response suppression is directly related to duration of the punishing stimulus as well as its intensity. Increases in delay of punishment following the response upon which it is contingent reduces the amount of suppression (Camp, Raymond, & Church, 1967; Kamin, 1959, see Selection 22; Renner, 1964, 1966). Although few experiments on schedule of punishment have been reported, amount of suppression is inversely related to degree of intermittency of punishment (Azrin, Holz, & Hake, 1963; Estes, 1944, see Experiment E of Selection 11; Logan, 1960). The fifth and final parameter mentioned above was frequency of punishment. Although amount of suppression is directly related to the number of punishments, up to a point, many experimenters (e.g., Azrin, 1960b) have found a nonmonotonic relationship between amount of suppression and frequency for punishment of mild or moderate intensity. After response rate decreases to a minimum following several punishments, recovery occurs even though the punishment conditions remain and the frequency of punishment continues to increase.

Responses Susceptible to Punishment

Just as a variety of stimuli can be used as punishment, a variety of responses can be influenced by punishment in species over a wide range on the phylogenetic scale. The two major classes of responses that have been punished in the experiments reproduced in this book are erroneous responses during learning and previously learned responses. With few exceptions, punishment suppresses them. It also suppresses instinctive responses (Adler & Hogan, 1963), consummatory responses (Lichtenstein, 1950), exploratory responses (Fisher, 1955; Spiegel, 1957), and social responses (Fisher, 1955). A curious finding of the Fisher experiment was that dogs punished for social responses to the experimenter became more "dependent" or attached to human test subjects upon discontinuation of punishment. Punishment of consummatory responses raises the possibility that the punishing effect may be attenuated through counter conditioning since the punishment is regularly associated with an appetitive stimulus. Evidence of such counter conditioning has been found with both dogs and rats (Lichtenstein, 1950; Williams & Barry, 1966).

Approach-Avoidance Conflict

The classification of a large literature under the rubric of approach-avoidance conflict tends to obscure the fact that the punishment operation is typically used. Approach responses are first established through positive incentive; conflicting avoidance tendencies are next established by punishing the approach responses. Experiments of Part II of this book studied punishment in an approach-avoidance conflict arrangement of this nature even though they were not identified as such. The approach-avoidance conflict segment of punishment research is distinguished from other punishment research by its special concern with variables determining the height and slope of hypothetical approach and avoidance gradients, and behavioral consequences of these considerations. Miller (1959) has reviewed and systematized much of this literature while Anderson (1962) has formulated a mathematical model of Miller's theory of conflict.

Physiological Processes and Punishment

The suppressive effect of punishment on behavior is a function of physiological variables as well as the stimulus conditions and prior experiences. Research on physiological considerations relevant to punishment has centered around (1) modifications induced by drugs, (2) surgical modification of neural centers, and (3) electroconvulsive shock. Alcohol, for example, attenuates the usual effect of punishment (Conger, 1951; Masserman & Yum, 1946; Smart, 1965), as does meprobamate, phenobarbital, and pentobarbital, while promazine and d-amphetamine enhance the effect of punishment (Geller & Seifter, 1960). As might be expected, two commonly used tranquilizers, chlorpromazine and perphenazine, render punishment less effective (Grossman, 1961). Some procedural and conceptual problems in pursuing experiments such as these with drugs are discussed by Brady (1959) and Miller & Barry (1960).

Experiments with surgically modified subjects have rather consistently shown that the suppressing effect of punishment is attenuated by lesions in the septal-limbic area (Fox, Kimble, & Lickey, 1964; Kaada, Rasmussen, & Kveim, 1962; Lubar, 1964; McCleary, 1961; Zucker, 1965) and the hippocampal area of the brain (Isaacson & Wickelgren, 1962; Kimble, 1963). The magnitude of the effect of septal-limbic lesions on punishment depends upon its intensity (Harvey, Lints, Jacobson, & Hunt, 1965), while the effect of hippocampal lesions seems to be a function of the type of response, or possibly the amount of training given a response (Kimble, Kirkby, & Stein, 1966). The mechanisms that may mediate these effects are discussed in a number of these articles.

Retention of the suppressing effect of punishment is also attenuated by electroconvulsive shock (ECS) following punishment (e.g., Weissman, 1963), with degree of attenuation diminishing as the interval between punishment and ECS increases (Chorover &

Schiller, 1965, 1966; Hudspeth, McGaugh, & Thomson, 1964; Quartermain, Paolino, & Miller, 1965; Weissman, 1964). Results of research on the permanence of this effect are conflicting (Luttges & McGaugh, 1967; Zinkin & Miller, 1967). Various explanations of the ECS influence on punishment are discussed in the articles cited.

The Role of Punishment in Personality Development and Therapy

Reward and punishment of specific types of response are important events in the social development of the child. Sears, Maccoby, and Levin (1957) described the results of an extensive correlational study between patterns of child rearing and social behavior. Bandura and Walters (1963) presented a detailed consideration of various effects of punishment in the development of the major forms of social behavior.

Psychoanalytic (Freudian) theories of personality development and modification can be related to the basic principles of learning (Dollard & Miller, 1950). Most applications of the principles of learning to therapy, however, are unrelated to psychoanalysis, and various basic approaches are described in a book edited by Krasner and Ullman (1965). The behavior therapies are designed (1) to train new adaptive instrumental responses in subjects who have not learned appropriate methods of adjustment (e.g., some psychotic and mentally retarded individuals), and (2) to eliminate maladaptive instrumental acts (e.g., neurotic compulsions) and maladaptive emotional responses (e.g., phobias). Systematic desensitization, and other special procedures for the reduction of anxiety, have received considerable attention (Wolpe, 1958). Of particular relevance to this book, however, is the use of punishment to suppress maladaptive instrumental acts. This procedure has been used to suppress stuttering, writer's cramp, alcoholism, sexual fetishes, transvestism, homosexuality, and so on. A critical review of various aversion therapies for sexual deviations has been provided by Feldman (1966). Case studies of the successful application of punishment procedures to suppression of maladaptive responses can be found in Eysenck (1960, 1964), Ullman and Krasner (1965), and in various articles in the journal, *Behavior Research and Therapy*.

References

Adler, N., & Hogan, J. A. (1963) Classical conditioning and punishment of an instinctive response in *Betta splendens*. *Animal Behavior, 11,* 351–354.

Akhtar, M. (1963) The role of counterconditioning in intermittent reinforcement. *Dissertation Abstracts, 23,* 4428–4429.

Anderson, N. H. (1962) On the quantification of Miller's conflict theory. *Psychological Review, 69,* 400–414.

Appel, J. B., & Peterson, N. J. (1965) Punishment: Effects of shock intensity on response suppression. *Psychological Reports, 16,* 721–730.

Azrin, N. H. (1956) Some effects of two intermittent schedules of immediate and non-immediate punishment. *Journal of Psychology, 42,* 3–21.

Azrin, N. H. (1958) Some effects of noise on human behavior. *Journal of the Experimental Analysis of Behavior, 1,* 183–200.

Azrin, N. H. (1959) A technique for delivering shock to pigeons. *Journal of the Experimental Analysis of Behavior, 2,* 161–163.

Azrin, N. H. (1960a) Effects of punishment intensity during variable-interval reinforcement. *Journal of the Experimental Analysis of Behavior, 3,* 123–142.

Azrin, N. H. (1960b) Sequential effects of punishment. *Science, 131,* 605–606.

Azrin, N. H., & Holz, W. C. (1966) Punishment. In W. K. Honig (Ed.), *Operant behavior: areas of research and application.* New York: Appleton-Century-Crofts. Pp. 380–447.

Azrin, N. H., Holz, W. C., & Hake, D. F. (1963) Fixed-ratio punishment. *Journal of the Experimental Analysis of Behavior, 6,* 141–148.

Bandura, A., & Walters, R. H. (1963) *Social learning and personality development.* New York: Holt, Rinehart, and Winston.

Banks, R. K. (1966) Persistence to continuous punishment following intermittent punishment training. *Journal of Experimental Psychology, 71,* 373–377.

Barlow, M. C. (1933) The influence of electric shock in mirror tracing. *American Journal of Psychology, 45,* 478–487.

Benedict, R. (1938) Continuities and discontinuities in cultural conditioning. *Psychiatry, 1,* 161–167.

Bernard, J. (1941) A note on non-informative shock. *Journal of Experimental Psychology*, 29, 407–412.

Bernard, J., & Gilbert, R. W. (1941) The specificity of the effect of shock for error in maze learning with human subjects. *Journal of Experimental Psychology*, 28, 178–186.

Boe, E. E. (1964) Extinction as a function of intensity of punishment, amount of training, and reinforcement of a competing response. *Canadian Journal of Psychology*, 18, 328–342.

⁓Boe, E. E. (1969) Bibliography on punishment. In B. A. Campbell & R. M. Church (Eds.), *Punishment and aversive behavior*. New York: Appleton-Century-Crofts, in press.

Boe, E. E., & Church, R. M. (1967) Permanent effects of punishment during extinction. *Journal of Comparative and Physiological Psychology*, 63, 486–492.

Bolles, R. C., & Seelback, S. E. (1964) Punishing and reinforcing effects of noise onset and termination for different responses. *Journal of Comparative and Physiological Psychology*, 58, 127–131.

Boroczi, G., Storms, L. H., & Broen, W. E., Jr. (1964) Response suppression and recovery of responding at different deprivation levels as a function of intensity and duration of punishment. *Journal of Comparative and Physiological Psychology*, 58, 456–459.

Bower, G. H., Fowler, H., & Trapold, M. A. (1959) Escape learning as a function of amount of shock reduction. *Journal of Experimental Psychology*, 58, 482–484.

Bower, G. H., & Miller, N. E. (1960) Effect of amount of reward on strength of approach in an approach-avoidance conflict. *Journal of Comparative and Physiological Psychology*, 53, 59–62.

Brady, J. V. (1959) A comparative approach to the study of drug effects on the behavior of higher animals. In A. D. Bass (Ed.), *Evolution of nervous control from primitive organisms to man*. Washington, D. C.: American Association for the Advancement of Science. Pp. 115–133.

Brady, J. V., & Hunt, H. F. (1950) An exploratory study of some effects of electroconvulsive shock on a conditioned emotional response. *American Psychologist*, 5, 256. (Abstract)

Brady, J. V., & Hunt, H. F. (1951) A further demonstration of the effects of electroconvulsive shock on a conditioned emotional response. *Journal of Comparative and Physiological Psychology*, 44, 204–209.

Brogden, W. J., Lipman, E. A., & Culler, E. (1938) The role of incentive in conditioning and extinction. *American Journal of Psychology*, 51, 109–117.

Brookshire, K. H., Littman, R. A., & Stewart, C. N. (1961) Residue of shock-trauma in the white rat: A three factor theory. *Psychological Monographs*, 75(10, Whole No. 514).

Brown, J. S. (1948) Gradients of approach and avoidance responses and their relation to level of motivation. *Journal of Comparative and Physiological Psychology, 41,* 450–465.

Brown, J. S. (1969) Factors influencing self-punitive behavior. In B. A. Campbell & R. M. Church (Eds.), *Punishment and aversive behavior.* New York: Appleton-Century-Crofts, in press.

Brown, J. S., Martin, R. C., & Morrow, M. W. (1964) Self-punitive behavior in the rat: Facilitative effects of punishment on resistance to extinction. *Journal of Comparative and Physiological Psychology, 57,* 127–133.

Brown, W. (1937) Punishment does work: A note on the paper by Tolman and Honzik in this journal. *Journal of Comparative Psychology, 24,* 145–146.

Brown, W. (1939) The positive effect of punishment. *Journal of Comparative Psychology, 28,* 17–22.

Brown, W. P. (1965) The Yerkes-Dodson law repealed. *Psychological Reports, 17,* 663–666.

Brush, F. R., Brush, E. S., & Solomon, R. L. (1955) Traumatic avoidance learning: The effects of CS-US interval with a delayed-conditioning procedure. *Journal of Comparative and Physiological Psychology, 48,* 285–293.

Bugelski, R., & Miller, N. E. (1938) A spatial gradient in the strength of avoidance responses. *Journal of Experimental Psychology, 23,* 494–505.

Bunch, M. E. (1928) The effect of electric shock as punishment for errors in human maze-learning. *Journal of Comparative Psychology, 8,* 343–359.

Bunch, M. E. (1935) Certain effects of electric shock in learning a stylus maze. *Journal of Comparative Psychology, 20,* 211–242.

Bunch, M. E., & Hagman, E. P. (1937) The influence of electric shocks for errors in rational learning. *Journal of Experimental Psychology, 21,* 330–341.

Bunch, M. E., & McTeer, F. D. (1932) The influence of punishment during learning upon retroactive inhibition. *Journal of Experimental Psychology, 15,* 473–495.

Camp, D. S., Raymond, G. A., & Church, R. M. (1967) The temporal relationship between response and punishment. *Journal of Experimental Psychology, 74,* 114–123.

Campbell, B. A., & Masterson, F. A. (1969) Psycophysics of punishment. In B. A. Campbell & R. M. Church (Eds.), *Punishment and aversive behavior.* New York: Appleton-Century-Crofts, in press.

Campbell, B. A., & Teghtsoonian, R. (1958) Electrical and behavioral effects of different types of shock stimuli on the rat. *Journal of Comparative and Physiological Phychology, 51,* 185–192.

Chorover, S. L., & Schiller, P. H. (1965) Short-term retrograde amnesia in rats. *Journal of Comparative and Physiological Psychology, 59,* 73–78.

Chorover, S. L., & Schiller, P. H. (1966) Reexamination of prolonged retrograde amnesia in one-trial learning. *Journal of Comparative and Physiological Psychology, 61,* 34–41.

Church, R. M. (1963) The varied effects of punishment on behavior. *Psychological Review, 70,* 369–402.

Church, R. M. (1969) Response suppression. In B. A. Campbell & R. M. Church (Eds.), *Punishment and aversive behavior.* New York: Appleton-Century-Crofts, in press.

Church, R. M., Brush, F. R., & Solomon, R. L. (1956) Traumatic avoidance learning: The effects of CS-US interval with a delayed-conditioning procedure in a free-responding situation. *Journal of Comparative and Physiological Psychology, 49,* 301–308.

Church, R. M., Raymond, G. A., & Beauchamp, R. D. (1967) Response suppression as a function of intensity and duration of a punishment. *Journal of Comparative and Physiological Psychology, 63,* 39–44.

Cole, L. W. (1911) The relation of strength of stimulus to rate of learning in the chick. *Journal of Animal Behavior, 1,* 111–124.

Conger, J. J. (1951) The effects of alcohol on conflict behavior in the albino rat. *Quarterly Journal of Studies in Alcohol, 12,* 1–29.

Crafts, L. W., & Gilbert, R. W. (1934) The effect of punishment during learning upon retention. *Journal of Experimental Psychology, 17,* 73–84.

Crespi, L. P. (1942) Quantitative variation of incentive and performance in the white rat. *American Journal of Psychology, 55,* 467–517.

Delgado, J. M. R., Roberts, W. W., & Miller, N. E. (1954) Learning motivated by electrical stimulation of the brain. *American Journal of Physiology, 179,* 587–593.

Dinsmoor, J. A. (1952) A discrimination based on punishment. *Quarterly Journal of Experimental Psychology, 4,* 27–45.

Dinsmoor, J. A. (1954) Punishment: I. The avoidance hypothesis. *Psychological Review, 61,* 34–46.

Dinsmoor, J. A. (1955) Punishment: II. An interpretation of empirical findings. *Psychological Review, 62,* 96–105.

Diserens, C. M., & Vaughn, J. (1931) The experimental psychology of motivation. *Psychological Bulletin, 28,* 15–65.

Dodson, J. D. (1915) The relation of strength of stimulus to rapidity of habit-formation in the kitten. *Journal of Animal Behavior, 5,* 330–336.

Dodson, J. D. (1932) The relative values of satisfying and annoying situations as motives in the learning process. *Journal of Comparative Psychology, 14,* 147–164.

Dollard, J., & Miller, N. E. (1950) *Personality and psychotherapy.* New York: McGraw-Hill.

Estes, W. K. (1944) An experimental study of punishment. *Psychological Monographs, 57*(3, Whole No. 263).

➤Estes, W. K. (1969) Outline of a theory of punishment. In B. A. Campbell & R. M. Church (Eds.), *Punishment and aversive behavior.* New York: Appleton-Century-Crofts, in press.

Estes, W. K., & Skinner, B. F. (1941) Some quantitative properties of anxiety. *Journal of Experimental Psychology, 29,* 390–400.

Eysenck, H. J. (Ed.) (1960) *Behavior therapy and the neuroses.* New York: Macmillan.

Eysenck, H. J. (Ed.) (1964) *Experiments in behavior therapy.* New York: Macmillan.

Feirstein, A. R., & Miller, N. E. (1963) Learning to resist pain and fear: Effects of electric shock before versus after reaching goal. *Journal of Comparative and Physiological Psychology, 56,* 797–800.

Feldman, M. P. (1966) Aversion therapy for sexual deviations: A critical review. *Psychological Bulletin, 65,* 65-79.

Feldman, S. M. (1961) Differential effects of shock in human maze learning. *Journal of Experimental Psychology, 62,* 171–178.

Ferster, C. B. (1953) The use of the free operant in the analysis of behavior. *Psychological Bulletin, 50,* 263–274.

Ferster, C. B., & Appel, J. B. (1961) Punishment of S$^\Delta$ responding in matching to sample by time out from positive reinforcement. *Journal of the Experimental Analysis of Behavior, 4,* 45–56.

Finney, D. J. (1948) The Fisher-Yates test of significance in 2 x 2 contingency tables. *Biometrika, 35,* 145–156.

Fisher, A. E. (1955) The effects of differential early treatment on the social and exploratory behavior of puppies. Unpublished doctoral dissertation, Pennsylvania State University.

Fowler, H. (1963) Facilitation and inhibition of performance by punishment: The effects of shock intensity and distribution of trials. *Journal of Comparative and Physiological Psychology, 56,* 531–538.

Fowler, H., & Miller, N. E. (1963) Facilitation and inhibition of runway performance by hind- and forepaw shock of various intensities. *Journal of Comparative and Physiological Psychology, 56,* 801–805.

Fowler, H., & Wischner, G. J. (1965) Discrimination performance as affected by problem difficulty and shock for either the correct or incorrect response. *Journal of Experimental Psychology, 69,* 413–418.

Fowler, H., & Wischner, G. J. (1969) The varied functions of punishment in discrimination learning. In B. A. Campbell & R. M. Church (Eds.), *Punishment and aversive behavior*. New York: Appleton-Century-Crofts, in press.

Fox, S. S., Kimble, D. P., & Lickey, M. E. (1964) Comparison of caudate nucleus and septal-area lesions on two types of avoidance behavior. *Journal of Comparative and Physiological Psychology, 58*, 380–386.

Freeburne, C. M., & Taylor, J. E. (1952) Discrimination learning with shock for right and wrong responses in the same subject. *Journal of Comparative and Physiological Psychology, 45*, 264–268.

French, T. (1937) Reality testing in dreams. *Psychoanalytic Quarterly, 6*, 62–77.

Freud, S. (1937) Metapsychological supplement to the theory of dreams. In S. Freud, *Collected Papers*. Vol. 4. London: Hogarth. Pp. 137–151.

Geller, I., & Seifter, J. (1960) The effects of meprobamate barbituates, d-amphetamine and promazine on experimentally induced conflict in the rat. *Psychopharmacologia, 1*, 482–492.

Grossman, S. P. (1961) Effects of chlorpromazine and perphenazine on bar-pressing performance in an approach-avoidance conflict. *Journal of Comparative and Physiological Psychology, 54*, 517–521.

Guthrie, E. R. (1934) Reward and punishment. *Psychological Review, 41*, 450–460.

Guthrie, E. R. (1935) *The psychology of learning*. New York: Harper.

Gwinn, G. T. (1949) The effects of punishment on acts motivated by fear. *Journal of Experimental Psychology, 39*, 260–269.

Hake, D. F., & Azrin, N. H. (1965) Conditioned punishment. *Journal of the Experimental Analysis of Behavior, 8*, 279–293.

Hamilton, J. A., & Krechevsky, I. (1933) Studies in the effect of shock upon behavior plasticity in the rat. *Journal of Comparative Psychology, 16*, 237–253.

Harvey, J. A., Lints, C. E., Jacobson, L. E. & Hunt, H. F. (1965) Effects of lesions in the septal area on conditioned fear and discriminated instrumental punishment in the albino rat. *Journal of Comparative and Physiological Psychology, 59*, 37–48.

Heron, W. T., & Skinner, B. F. (1939) An apparatus for the study of animal behavior. *Psychological Record, 3*, 166–176.

Hilgard, E. R. (1948) *Theories of learning*. New York: Appleton-Century-Crofts.

Hilgard, E. R., & Bower, G. H. (1966) *Theories of learning* (3rd ed.). New York: Appleton-Century-Crofts.

Hilgard, E. R., & Marquis, D. G. (1940) *Conditioning and learning*. New York: D. Appleton-Century.

Hoffman, H. S., Flesher, M., & Jensen, P. K. (1962) Aversive training: Long term effects. *Science, 138,* 1269–1270.

Hoge, M. A., & Stocking, R. J. (1912) A note on the relative value of punishment and reward as motives. *Journal of Animal Behavior, 2,* 43–50.

Holt, E. B. (1931) *Animal drive and the learning process.* New York: Holt.

Holz, W. C., & Azrin, N. H. (1961) Discriminative properties of punishment. *Journal of the Experimental Analysis of Behavior, 4,* 225–232.

Holz, W. C., & Azrin, N. H. (1962) Interactions between the discriminative and aversive properties of punishment. *Journal of the Experimental Analysis of Behavior, 5,* 229–234.

Horney, K. (1937) *The neurotic personality of our time.* New York: Norton.

Hudspeth, W. J., McGaugh, J. L., & Thompson, C. W. (1964) Aversive and amnesic effects of electroconvulsive shock. *Journal of Comparative and Physiological Psychology, 57,* 61–64.

Hull, C. L. (1929) A functional interpretation of the conditioned reflex. *Psychological Review, 36,* 498–511.

Hull, C. L. (1934a) The concept of habit-family hierarchy and maze learning, I. *Psychological Review, 41,* 33–54.

Hull, C. L. (1934b) The concept of habit-family hierarchy and maze learning, II. *Psychological Review, 41,* 134–152.

Hull, C. L. (1937) Mind, mechanism, and adaptive behavior. *Psychological Review, 44,* 1–32.

Hull, C. L. (1943) *Principles of behavior.* New York: D. Appleton-Century.

Hunt, H. F., & Brady, J. V. (1951a) Some effects of electroconvulsive shock on a conditioned emotional response ("anxiety"). *Journal of Comparative and Physiological Psychology, 44,* 88–98.

Hunt, H. F., & Brady, J. V. (1951b) Some quantitative and qualitative differences between "anxiety" and "punishment" conditioning. *American Psychologist, 6,* 276–277. (Abstract)

Hunt, H. F., & Brady, J. V. (1955) Some effects of punishment and intercurrent "anxiety" on a simple operant. *Journal of Comparative and Physiological Psychology, 48,* 305–310.

Hunt, H. F., Jernberg, P., & Brady, J. V. (1952) The effect of electroconvulsive shock on a conditioned emotional response: The effect of post-ECS extinction on the reappearance of the response. *Journal of Comparative and Physiological Psychology, 45,* 589–599.

Hunt, H. F., & Otis, L. S. (1953) Conditioned and unconditioned emotional defecation in the rat. *Journal of Comparative and Physiological Psychology, 46,* 378–382.

Hunt, W. A., & Landis, C. (1936) The overt behavior pattern in startle. *Journal of Experimental Psychology, 19,* 309–315.

Imada, H. (1959) The effects of punishment on avoidance behavior. *Japanese Psychological Research, 52,* 27–28.

Isaacson, R. L., & Wickelgren, W. O. (1962) Hippocampal ablation and passive avoidance. *Science, 138,* 1104–1106.

Jenkins, T. N., Warner, L. H., & Warden, C. J. (1926) Standard apparatus for the study of animal motivation. *Journal of Comparative Psychology, 6,* 361–382.

Jensen, M. B. (1934) Punishment by electric shock as affecting performance on a raised finger maze. *Journal of Experimental Psychology, 17,* 65–72.

Kaada, B. R., Rasmussen, E. W., & Kveim, O. (1962) Impaired acquisition of passive avoidance behavior by subcallosal, septal, hypothalamic, and insular lesions in rats. *Journal of Comparative and Physiological Psychology, 55,* 661–670.

Kalikow, D. N. (1966) The effects of innervation density on the psychophysical function for electro-cutaneous stimulation. Unpublished master's thesis, Brown University.

Kamin, L. J. (1954) Traumatic avoidance learning: The effects of CS-US interval with a trace-conditioning procedure. *Journal of Comparative and Physiological Psychology, 47,* 65–72.

Kamin, L. J. (1957) The gradient of delay of secondary reward in avoidance learning tested on avoidance trials only. *Journal of Comparative and Physiological Psychology, 50,* 450–460.

Kamin, L. J. (1959) The delay of punishment gradient. *Journal of Comparative and Physiological Psychology, 52,* 434–437.

Karsh, E. B. (1959) The effect of intensity of punishment and number of rewarded and punished trials on running speed in a conflict situation. Unpublished doctoral dissertation, Yale University.

Karsh, E. B. (1962) Effects of number of rewarded trials and intensity of punishment on running speed. *Journal of Comparative and Physiological Psychology, 55,* 44–51.

Karsh, E. B. (1963) Changes in intensity of punishment: Effect on running behavior of rats. *Science, 140,* 1084–1085.

Karsh, E. B. (1966) Resistance to punishment resulting from training with delayed, partial, and increasing shock. *Proceedings of the 74th annual convention of the American Psychological Association 1966,* 51–52.

Katz, L. (1964) Effects of differential monetary gain and loss on sequential two-choice behavior. *Journal of Experimental Psychology, 68,* 245–249.

Kimble, D. P. (1963) The effects of bilateral hippocampal lesions in rats. *Journal of Comparative and Physiological Psychology, 56,* 273–283.

Kimble, D. P., Kirkby, R. J., & Stein, D. G. (1966) Response perseveration interpretation of passive avoidance deficits in hippocampectomized rats. *Journal of Comparative and Physiological Psychology, 61,* 141–143.

Kleemeier, R. W. (1942) Fixation and regression in the rat. *Psychological Monographs, 54*(4, Whole No. 246).

Krasner, L., & Ullman, L. P. (Eds.) (1965) *Research in behavior modifications: New developments and implications.* New York: Holt, Rinehart, & Winston.

Kurtz, K. H., & Pearl, J. (1960) The effects of prior fear experiences on acquired-drive learning. *Journal of Comparative and Physiological Psychology, 53,* 201–206.

Kurtz, K. H., & Walters, G. C. (1962) The effects of prior fear experiences on an approach-avoidance conflict. *Journal of Comparative and Physiological Psychology, 55,* 1075–1078.

Leitenberg, H. (1965) Is time-out from positive reinforcement an aversive event? A review of the experimental evidence. *Psychological Bulletin, 64,* 428–441.

Lichtenstein, P. E. (1950) Studies of anxiety: I. The production of a feeding inhibition in dogs. *Journal of Comparative and Physiological Psychology, 43,* 16–29.

Lindquist, E. F. (1940) *Statistical analysis in educational research.* Boston: Houghton Mifflin.

Linton, R. (1942) Age and sex categories. *American Sociological Review, 7,* 589–603.

Logan, F. A. (1960) *Incentive.* New Haven: Yale University Press.

Lorge, I. (1933a) An approximation to the value of rewards and of punishment in learning. *Psychological Bulletin, 30,* 540–541. (Abstract)

Lorge, I. (1933b) The efficacy of intensified reward and of intensified punishment. *Journal of Experimental Psychology, 16,* 177–207.

Lorge, I., & Thorndike, E. L. (1933) The comparative strengthening of a connection by one or more occurrences of it in cases where the connection was punished and was neither punished nor rewarded. *Journal of Experimental Psychology, 16,* 374–382.

Lubar, J. F. (1964) Effect of medial cortical lesions on the avoidance behavior of the cat. *Journal of Comparative and Physiological Psychology, 58,* 38–46.

Luttges, M. W., & McGaugh, J. L. (1967) Permanence of retrograde amnesia produced by electroconvulsive shock. *Science, 156,* 408–410.

Martin, E. G. (1908a) A quantitative study of faradic stimulation: The variable factors involved. *American Journal of Physiology, 22,* 61–74.

Martin, E. G. (1908b) A quantitative study of faradic stimulation: The calibration of the inductorium for break shocks. *American Journal of Physiology, 22,* 116–132.

Martin, R. C. (1962) Resistance to extinction of an escape response as a function of number of reinforcements. Unpublished master's thesis, University of Florida.

Martin, R. F. (1940) 'Native' traits and regression in rats. *Journal of Comparative Psychology, 30,* 1–16.

Masserman, J. H. (1943) *Behavior and neurosis.* Chicago: University of Chicago Press.

Masserman, J. H. (1946) *Principles of dynamic psychiatry.* Philadelphia: Saunders.

Masserman, J. H., & Yum, K. S. (1946) The effects of alcohol on experimental neuroses in cats. *Psychosomatic Medicine, 8,* 36–52.

Matsumiya, Y. (1960) The effects of US intensity and CS-US pattern on conditioned emotional response. *Japanese Psychological Research, 2,* 35–42.

McCleary, R. A. (1961) Response specificity in the behavioral effects of limbic system lesions in the cat. *Journal of Comparative and Physiological Psychology, 54,* 605–613.

McGeoch, J. A. (1946) *The psychology of human learning.* New York: Longmans, Green.

McNemar, Q. (1947) Note on the sampling error of the difference between correlated proportions or percentages. *Psychometrika, 12,* 153–157.

McTeer, W. (1931) A study of certain features of punishment in serial learning. *Journal of Experimental Psychology, 14,* 453–476.

Mead, M. (1930) *Growing up in New Guinea.* New York: Morrow.

Meryman, J. J. (1952) Magnitude of startle response as a function of hunger and fear. Unpublished master's thesis, State University of Iowa.

Miller, N. E. (1951) Learnable drives and rewards. In S. S. Stevens (Ed.), *Handbook of experimental psychology.* New York: Wiley. Pp. 435–472.

Miller, N. E. (1954) Fear. In R. H. Williams (Ed.), *Human factors in military operations.* Chevy Chase, Md.: Johns Hopkins.

Miller, N. E. (1959) Liberalization of basic S-R concepts: Extensions to conflict behavior, motivation, and social learning. In S. Koch (Ed.), *Psychology: A study of a science.* Vol. II. *General systematic formulations, learning, and special processes.* New York: McGraw-Hill. Pp. 196–292.

Miller, N. E. (1960) Learning resistance to pain and fear: Effects of overlearning, exposure, and rewarded exposure in context. *Journal of Experimental Psychology, 60,* 137–145.

Miller, N. E., & Barry, H., III. (1960) Motivational effects of drugs: Methods which illustrate some general problems in psychopharmacology. *Psychopharmacologia, 1,* 169–199.

Miller, N. E., & Dollard, J. (1941) *Social learning and imitation.* New Haven: Yale.

Morgan, C. T. (1943) *Physiological psychology.* New York: McGraw-Hill.

Mowrer, O. H. (1938) Preparatory set (expectancy)—A determinant in motivation and learning. *Psychological Review, 45,* 62–91.

Mowrer, O. H. (1940) An experimental analogue of 'regression' with incidental observations on 'reaction-formation.' *Journal of Abnormal and Social Psychology, 35,* 56–87.

Mowrer, O. H. (1947) On the dual nature of learning—A reinterpretation of "conditioning" and "problem solving." *Harvard Educational Review, 17,* 102–148.

Mowrer, O. H. (1950) *Learning theory and personality dynamics.* New York: Ronald.

Mowrer, O. H. (1960) *Learning theory and behavior.* New York: Wiley.

Mowrer, O. H., & Aiken, E. G. (1954) Contiguity vs. drive-reduction in conditioned fear: Temporal variations in conditioned and unconditioned stimulus. *American Journal of Psychology, 67,* 26–38.

Mowrer, O. H., & Jones, H. M. (1943) Extinction and behavior variability as functions of effortfulness of task. *Journal of Experimental Psychology, 33,* 369–386.

Mowrer, O. H., & Kluckhohn, C. (1944) Dynamic theory of personality. In J. McV. Hunt (Ed.), *Personality and the behavior disorders.* Vol. 1. New York: Ronald. Pp. 69–138.

Mowrer, O. H., & Lamoreaux, R. R. (1942) Avoidance conditioning and signal duration—A study of secondary motivation and reward. *Psychological Monographs, 54*(5, Whole No. 247).

Mowrer, O. H., & Solomon, L. N. (1954) Contiguity vs. drive-reduction in conditioned fear: The proximity and abruptness of drive-reduction. *American Journal of Psychology, 67,* 15–25.

Mowrer, O. H., & Ullman, A. D. (1945) Time as a determinant in integrative learning. *Psychological Review, 52,* 61–90.

Moyer, K. E. (1955) A study of some of the variables of which fixation is a function. *Journal of Genetic Psychology, 86,* 3–31.

Moyer, K. E. (1957) The effects of shock on anxiety-motivated behavior in the rat. *Journal of Genetic Psychology, 91,* 197–203.

Muenzinger, K. F. (1934) Motivation in learning: I. Electric shock for correct response in the visual discrimination habit. *Journal of Comparative Psychology, 17,* 267–277.

Muenzinger, K. F., & Baxter, L. F. (1957) The effects of training to approach vs. training to escape from electric shock upon subsequent discrimination learning. *Journal of Comparative and Physiological Psychology, 50,* 252–257.

Muenzinger, K. F., Bernstone, A. H., & Richards, L. (1938) Motivation in learning: VIII. Equivalent amounts of electric shock for right and wrong responses in a visual discrimination habit. *Journal of Comparative Psychology, 26,* 177–186.

Muenzinger, K. F., Brown, W. C., Crow, W. J., & Powloski, R. F. (1952) Motivation in learning: XI. An analysis of electric shock for correct responses into its avoidance and accelerating components. *Journal of Experimental Psychology, 43,* 115–119.

Muenzinger, K. F., & Mize, R. H. (1933) The sensitivity of the white rat to electric shock: Threshold and skin resistance. *Journal of Comparative Psychology, 15,* 139–148.

Muenzinger, K. F., & Newcomb, H. (1936) Motivation in learning: V. The relative effectiveness of jumping a gap and crossing an electric grid in a visual discrimination habit. *Journal of Comparative Psychology, 21,* 95–104.

Muenzinger, K. F., & Powloski, R. F. (1951) Motivation in learning: X. Comparison of electric shock for correct turns in a corrective and noncorrective situation. *Journal of Experimental Psychology, 42,* 118–124.

Muenzinger, K. F., & Walz, F. C. (1934) An examination of electrical current stabilizing devices for psychological experiments. *Journal of General Psychology, 10,* 477–482.

Muenzinger, K. F., & Wood, A. (1935) Motivation in learning. IV. The function of punishment as determined by its temporal relation to the act of choice in the visual discrimination habit. *Journal of Comparative Psychology, 20,* 95–106.

Ni, C. F. (1934) The influence of punishment for errors during the learning of the first maze upon the mastery of the second maze. *Journal of Comparative Psychology, 18,* 23–28.

O'Kelly, L. I. (1940a) An experimental study of regression. I. Behavioral characteristics of the regressive response. *Journal of Comparative Psychology, 30,* 41–53.

O'Kelly, L. I. (1940b) An experimental study of regression. II. Some motivational determinants of regression and perseveration. *Journal of Comparative Psychology, 30,* 55–95.

Olds, J., & Milner, P. (1954) Positive reinforcement produced by electrical stimulation of the septal area and other regions of rat brain. *Journal of Comparative and Physiological Psychology, 47,* 419–427.

Olds, J. A. (1956) A preliminary mapping of electrical reinforcing effects in the rat brain. *Journal of Comparative and Physiological Psychology, 49,* 281–285.

Parsons, T. (1942) Age and sex in the social structure of the United States. *American Sociological Review, 7,* 604–620.

Pavlov, I. P. (1927) *Conditioned reflexes.* Trans. by G. V. Anrep. London: Oxford University Press.

Pearl, J. (1961) The effect of prior experiences of electric shock on the punishment value of loud noises. Unpublished master's thesis, University of Buffalo.

Pearl, J. (1963) Effects of preshock and additional punishment on general activity. *Psychological Reports, 12,* 155–161.

Pearl, J., Walters, G. C., & Anderson, D. C. (1964) Suppressing effects of aversive stimulation on subsequently punished behavior. *Canadian Journal of Psychology, 18,* 343–355.

Porter, E. H., & Biel, W. C. (1943) Alleged regressive behavior in a two-unit maze. *Journal of Comparative Psychology, 35,* 187–195.

Postman, L. (1947) The history and present status of the law of effect. *Psychological Bulletin, 44,* 489–563.

Postman, L. (1962) Rewards and punishments in human learning. In L. Postman (Ed.), *Psychology in the making.* New York: Knopf. Pp. 331–401.

Prince, A. I., Jr. (1956) Effect of punishment on visual discrimination learning. *Journal of Experimental Psychology, 52,* 381–385.

Quartermain, D., Paolino, R. M., & Miller, N. E. (1965) A brief temporal gradient of retrograde amnesia independent of situational change. *Science, 149,* 1116–1118.

Renner, K. E. (1964) Conflict resolution and the process of temporal integration. *Psychological Reports, 15,* 423–438.

Renner, K. E. (1966) Temporal integration: Relative value of rewards and punishments as a function of their temporal distance from the response. *Journal of Experimental Psychology, 71,* 902–907.

Sanders, M. J. (1937) An experimental demonstration of regression in the rat. *Journal of Experimental Psychology, 21,* 493–510.

Schoenfeld, W. N. (1950) An experimental approach to anxiety, escape, and avoidance behavior. In P. H. Hoch and J. Zubin (Eds.), *Anxiety.* New York: Grune & Stratton.

Sears, R. R., Maccoby, E. E., & Levin, H. (1957) *Patterns of childrearing.* Evanston, Ill.: Row, Peterson.

Seward, J. P., King, R. M., Chow, T., & Shiflett, S. C. (1965) Persistence of punished escape responses. *Journal of Comparative and Physiological Psychology, 60,* 265–268.

Seward, J. P., & Raskin, D. C. (1960) The role of fear in aversive behavior. *Journal of Comparative and Physiological Psychology, 53,* 328–335.

Sheffield, F. D. (1948) Avoidance training and the contiguity principle. *Journal of Comparative and Physiological Psychology, 41,* 165–177.

Sheffield, F. D. (1949) Hilgard's critique of Guthrie. *Psychological Review, 56,* 284–291.

Sheffield, F. D., & Temmer, H. W. (1950) Relative resistance to extinction of escape training and avoidance training. *Journal of Experimental Psychology, 40,* 287–298.

Sidman, M. (1953) Two temporal parameters of the maintenance of avoidance behavior by the white rat. *Journal of Comparative and Physiological Psychology, 46,* 253–261.

Siegel, S. (1956) *Nonparametric statistics for the behavioral sciences.* New York: McGraw-Hill.

Skinner, B. F. (1938) *The behavior of organisms.* New York: D. Appleton-Century.

Skinner, B. F. (1953) *Science and human behavior.* New York: Macmillan.

Smart, R. G. (1965) Effects of alcohol on conflict and avoidance behavior. *Quarterly Journal of Studies in Alcohol, 26,* 187–205.

Solomon, R. L. (1964) Punishment. *American Psychologist, 19,* 237–253.

Solomon, R. L., Kamin, L. J., & Wynne, L. C. (1953) Traumatic avoidance learning: The outcome of several extinction procedures with dogs. *Journal of Abnormal and Social Psychology, 48,* 291–302.

Spiegel, S. (1957) The effect of consistent and inconsistent punishment on the exploratory behavior of the white rat. *Dissertation Abstracts, 17,* 2060–2061.

Steckle, L. C., & O'Kelly, L. I. (1940) The effect of electrical shock upon later learning and regression in the rat. *Journal of Psychology, 9,* 365–370.

Stephens, J. M. (1934) The influence of punishment on learning. *Journal of Experimental Psychology, 17,* 536–555.

Stephens, J. M. (1940) Some anomalous results of punishment in learning. *School and Society, 52,* 703–704.

Sternbach, R. A., & Tursky, B. (1964) On the psychophysical power function in electric shock. *Psychonomic Science, 1,* 217–218.

Stevens, S. S., Carton, A. S., & Shickman, G. M. (1958) A scale of apparent intensity of electric shock. *Journal of Experimental Psychology, 56,* 328–334.

Stone, G. R. (1950) The effect of negative incentives in serial learning. II. Incentive intensity and response variability. *Journal of General Psychology, 42,* 179–224.

Thorndike, E. L. (1913) *Educational psychology.* Vol. 2. *The psychology of learning.* New York: Teacher's College, Columbia University.

Thorndike, E. L. (1932a) *The fundamentals of learning.* New York: Teacher's College, Columbia University.

Thorndike, E. L. (1932b) Reward and punishment in animal learning. *Comparative Psychology Monographs, 8,* No. 39.

Thorndike, E. L. (1935) *The psychology of wants, interests, and attitudes.* New York: D. Appleton-Century.

Tolman, C. W., & Mueller, M. R. (1964) Laboratory control of toe-sucking in a young rhesus monkey by two kinds of punishment. *Journal of the Experimental Analysis of Behavior, 7,* 323–325.

Tolman, E. C. (1933) Sign-gestalt or conditioned reflex? *Psychological Review, 40,* 246–255.

Tolman, E. C., Hall, C. S., & Bretnall, E. P. (1932) A disproof of the law of effect and a substitution of the laws of emphasis, motivation, and disruption. *Journal of Experimental Psychology, 15,* 601–614.

Ullman, L. P., & Krasner, L. (Eds.) (1965) *Case studies in behavior modification.* New York: Holt, Rhinehart, & Winston.

Valentine, R. (1930) The effects of punishment for errors on the maze learning of rats. *Journal of Comparative Psychology, 10,* 35–54.

Vaughn, J., & Diserens, C. M. (1930) The relative effects of various intensities of punishment on learning and efficiency. *Journal of Comparative Psychology, 10,* 55–66.

Walters, G. C. (1963) Frequency and intensity of pre-shock experiences as determinants of fearfulness in an approach-avoidance conflict. *Canadian Journal of Psychology, 17,* 412–419.

Walters, G. C., & Rogers, J. V. (1963) Aversive stimulation of the rat: Long-term effects on subsequent behavior. *Science, 142,* 70–71.

Warden, C. J. (1926) A comparison of different norms of mastery in animal maze learning. *Journal of Comparative Psychology, 6,* 159–179.

Warden, C. J., & Aylesworth, M. (1927) The relative value of reward and punishment in the formation of a visual discrimination habit in the white rat. *Journal of Comparative Psychology, 7,* 117–127.

Warden, C. J., & Diamond, S. (1931) A preliminary study of the effect of delayed punishment on learning in the white rat. *Journal of Genetic Psychology, 39,* 455–461.

Warner, L. H. (1928) A study of hunger behavior in the white rat by means of the obstruction method. *Journal of Comparative Psychology, 8,* 273–299.

Warner, L. H. (1932) An experimental search for the "conditioned response." *Journal of Genetic Psychology, 41,* 91–115.

Weiner, H. (1964) Response cost and fixed-ratio performance. *Journal of the Experimental Analysis of Behavior, 7,* 79–81.

Weissman, A. (1963) Effect of electroconvulsive shock intensity and seizure pattern on retrograde amnesia in rats. *Journal of Comparative and Physiological Psychology, 56,* 806–810.

Weissman, A. (1964) Retrograde amnesic effect of supramaximal electroconvulsive shock on one-trial acquisition in rats. A replication. *Journal of Comparative and Physiological Psychology, 57,* 248–250.

Wheeler, R. H. (1940) *The science of psychology.* New York: Crowell.

Whiteis, U. E. (1956) Punishment's influence on fear and avoidance. *Harvard Educational Review, 26,* 360–373.

Whiting, J. W. M. (1941) *Becoming a Kwoma.* New Haven: Yale.

Whiting, J. W. M., & Mowrer, O. H. (1943) Habit progression and regression—A laboratory study of some factors relevant to human socialization. *Journal of Comparative Psychology, 36,* 229–253.

Williams, D. R., & Barry, H., III. (1966) Counter conditioning in an operant conflict situation. *Journal of Comparative and Physiological Psychology, 61,* 154–156.

Wischner, G. J. (1947) The effect of punishment on discrimination learning in a non-correction situation. *Journal of Experimental Psychology, 37,* 271–284.

Wischner, G. J., Fowler, H., & Kushnik, S. A. (1963) The effect of strength of punishment for "correct" or "incorrect" responses on visual discrimination performance. *Journal of Experimental Psychology, 65,* 131–138.

Wischner, G. J., Hall, R. C., & Fowler, H. (1964) Discrimination learning under various combinations of food and shock for "correct" and "incorrect" responses. *Journal of Experimental Psychology, 67,* 48–51.

Wolpe, J. (1958) *Psychotherapy by reciprocal inhibition.* Stanford: Stanford University Press.

Wood, T. W. (1934) The effect of approbation and reproof on the mastery of nonsense syllables. *Journal of Applied Psychology, 18,* 657–664.

Woodworth, R. S., & Schlosberg, H. (1954) *Experimental psychology.* (Rev. ed.) New York: Holt.

Yerkes, R. M. (1907) *The dancing mouse.* New York: Macmillan.

Yerkes, R. M., & Dodson, J. D. (1908) The relation of strength of stimulus to rapidity of habit formation. *Journal of Comparative Neurology and Psychology, 18,* 459–482.

Yerkes, R. M., & Watson, J. B. (1911) Methods for studying vision in animals. *Behavior Monographs, 1* (Whole No. 2).

Yoshioka, J. G. (1929) Weber's law in the discrimination of maze distance by the white rat. *University of California Publications in Psychology, 4,* 155–184.

Young, P. T. (1961) *Motivation and emotion: A survey of the determinants of human and animal activity.* New York: Wiley.

Zeaman, D. (1949) Response latency as a function of the amount of reinforcement. *Journal of Experimental Psychology, 39,* 466–483.

Zimmerman, J., & Ferster, C. B. (1963) Intermittent punishment of S^Δ responding in matching to sample. *Journal of the Experimental Analysis of Behavior, 6,* 349–356.

Zinkin, S., & Miller, A. J. (1967) Recovery of memory after amnesia induced by electroconvulsive shock. *Science, 155,* 102–103.

Zucker, I. (1965) Effect of lesions of the septal limbic area on the behavior of cats. *Journal of Comparative and Physiological Psychology, 60,* 344–352.

Author Index

Subject Index

DATE DUE		
~~NOV 0 1 1990~~	~~AUG 2 0 2001~~	
~~DEC~~		
~~3/ /85~~		
~~M S MAR 3 1~~		
~~D JUL 1 3 198/~~		
~~AUG 4 1987~~		
JAN 9 1989		
~~AUG 1 1991~~ ~~MAY 0 1 1994~~		
~~MAY 0 1 1994~~		
~~MAY 0 7 1998~~		
		MP 728